THE INFINITE BOUNDARY

ALSO BY D. SCOTT ROGO

BOOKS

NAD, a study of some unusual other-world experiences
A Psychic Study of the "Music of the Spheres"
Methods and Models for Education in Parapsychology
The Welcoming Silence
An Experience of Phantoms
Parapsychology: A Century of Inquiry
In Search of the Unknown
Exploring Psychic Phenomena
The Haunted Universe
Minds and Motion
The Haunted House Handbook
The Poltergeist Experience
Miracles
ESP and Your Pet
Leaving the Body
Our Psychic Potentials
The Search for Yesterday
Life after Death
On the Track of the Poltergeist
Mind over Matter
Psychic Breakthroughs Today

CO-AUTHOR

Phone Calls from the Dead (with Raymond Bayless)
Earth's Secret Inhabitants (with Jerome Clark)
The Tujunga Canyon Contacts (with Ann Druffel)

ANTHOLOGIES

Mind Beyond the Body
UFO Abductions

THE INFINITE BOUNDARY

A Psychic Look at
Spirit Possession, Madness,
and Multiple Personality

D. Scott Rogo

Dodd, Mead & Company • *New York*

No part of this book may be reproduced in any form
without permission in writing from the publisher.
Published by Dodd, Mead & Company, Inc.
71 Fifth Avenue, New York, New York 10003.
Manufactured in the United States of America.
Designed by Nick Scelsi

First Edition

1 2 3 4 5 6 7 8 9 10

Library of Congress Cataloging-in-Publication Data
Rogo, D. Scott.
The infinite boundary.
Bibliography: p.
Includes index.
1. Spirit possession. 2. Spiritualism. 3. Multiple
personality. I. Title.
BL482.R64   1987   133.4'2   87-15692
ISBN 0-396-08968-2

TO CHRIS GLASER

*In appreciation of his past
and future ministry*

CONTENTS

Acknowledgments   xi

Preface   xiii

  1. Cured by an Exorcism?   1

PART I
The Psychic Odyssey of James H. Hyslop

  2. The Strange Case of Frederic Thompson   13

  3. R. Swain Gifford Returns   29

  4. A Case of Incipient Obsession?   53

  5. The Possession of Etta De Camp   71

  6. The Search for Evidence   95

  7. The Many Faces of Doris Fischer—Part 1   117

  8. The Many Faces of Doris Fischer—Part 2   137

PART II
Successors in the Work

 9. The Work of Dr. Titus Bull   159
10. From Clergyman to Exorcist   183
11. The Ministry of Dr. Elwood Worcester   201

PART III
Rescue Work Today

12. Rescuing the Dark Spirits   219
13. The Spiritual Side of Multiple Personality   243
14. Obsession and the Case for Survival   267
Epilogue   297
References   301
About the Author   309
Index   311

ACKNOWLEDGMENTS

The original draft of this book dates back to 1970. I would therefore like to extend some belated thanks to several people who helped me so many years ago: to Raymond Bayless for providing me with several sources of information; to Dr. Jule Eisenbud for sharing his thoughts on this project and the cases therein with me; to the late Grace Gause, who spent an afternoon—bound to her wheelchair—reminiscing about her work with Dr. Titus Bull; and to Mrs. Lois West, for making the introduction. I am also indebted to the late Winifred Hyslop for sharing her memories of her father with me and for providing some scarce material from the James H. Hyslop Foundation. Added insights were given by Mary Crowell. Thomas Tietze also shared some of his unpublished work on the life of W. Franklin Prince and the Doris Fischer case.

When I returned to this project in 1986, I became indebted to some further individuals. First, to J. Fraser Nicol, who answered some of my historical questions and directed me to some much-appreciated and valuable reference materials. The New York Historical Society helped me ferret out more information on the Thompson case, and Wayne Norman provided source material from the library of the Parapsychology Foundation. Special thanks, too, to Donna McCormick of the American Society for Psychical Research for Xeroxing material from their library and getting it to me so promptly. James Matlock was also especially gracious in looking up obscure information in the ASPR's archives and helped in securing photographs for this book. The ASPR kindly granted permission to reproduce photographs and sketches from its files. Dr. Stanley Krippner provided some of the information concerning Brazilian depossession work.

Every writer is deeply indebted to those rare individuals willing to share their personal experiences. For helping me understand the sheer complexity of the multiple personality syndrome, I wish to thank Dr. Ralph Allison and Dr. Donald Schafer and his group at the University of California, Irvine. I am also grateful to Matthew Bronson for the time he gave me, which helped me understand the personal side of rescue work.

Finally (and perhaps provisionally), I'd like to thank the surviving spirits (?) of Dr. Titus Bull and Dr. Elwood Worcester for guiding me through the complex streets of Los Angeles so that I could find their books and publications.

Of course, the opinions and contents—as well as any possible errors—of this book are solely the author's.

Portions of Chapters 1 and 13 originally appeared in different form in *Fate* magazine and are reprinted with the permission of the editors. Portions of chapters 2 and 5 originally appeared in *Metapsychology-the Journal of Discarnate Intelligence*. Extracts from M. Scott Peck's *People of the Lie* (© 1983 by M. Scott Peck, M.D.) are published with the permission of Simon and Schuster, while extracts from George G. Ritchie's *Return from Tomorrow* (© 1978 by George G. Ritchie, M.D.) are reprinted with the permission of Chosen Books Publishing Co. The original Thompson sketches reproduced in this book are used by courtesy of the American Society for Psychical Research, Inc.

PREFACE

Can mental illness be complicated by purely psychic or paranormal factors? For years, many psychiatrists and parapsychologists have felt that within the bizarre hallucinations and delusions of the mentally disturbed there might lurk some level of paranormal perception—some way of apprehending reality that goes far beyond the normal perception of the five senses. For instance, what if a mental patient's delusions that he is being persecuted by the spirit of a dead person contained verifiable information about that individual? Can "insanity" result in some cases because these patients really are being victimized by the dead?

This is the topic of *The Infinite Boundary*. This book will include cases of several people who have been seemingly influenced by the dead to develop remarkable skills or artistic talents. These talents corresponded to the skills and talents possessed by the donor personalities during their terrestrial lives. But these people also exhibited pathological behavior as a result of these interactions. This book also describes remarkable experiments in which psychics were brought in to help diagnose such patients and even cure them!

The Infinite Boundary is essentially a history book. The story begins in the early 1900s, when well-known philosopher and psychic investigator Prof. James H. Hyslop confronted the strange case of Frederic Thompson of New Bedford, Massachussets. Thompson was a craftsman who suddenly began painting oils and drawing sketches in the style of a recently deceased artist, even though he claimed he had no formal artistic training. Hyslop gradually came across similar cases while still fighting belief in the obsession hypothesis. Finally, shortly before his death in 1920, he realized that obsession by the dead could indeed pass for insanity and that it constituted a hitherto unrecognized factor in mental illness. After his death, his views were elaborated and researched by the eminent New York neurologist Dr. Titus Bull; by the famous psychical investigator Dr. W. Franklin Prince; by noted clergyman Dr. Elwood Worcester (who founded the Emmanuel Movement in Boston); and by the highly unorthodox Dr. Carl Wickland. All their work is chronologized for the first time in this volume.

To bring the information up to date, reports from other researchers engaged in similar work today are included, such as the work of Dr. Ralph Allison, one of this country's leading authorities on the strange phenomenon of multiple personality. Dr. Allison believes that many cases of this rare disorder are actually genuine cases of spirit obsession. The current status of this continuing search for evidence will keep the historical chapters relevant to the interests of the contemporary reader. Although no responsible psychologist or parapsychologist would suggest that all—or even many—cases of insanity are cases of "psychic control," the evidence suggests that sometimes what is diagnosed as mental illness is really possession—some sort of invasion from without, not from within.

It makes little difference just how you approach this book. It can be read as a study in parapsychology, as a report on the evidence for life after death, or simply as a curious chapter in the history of American psychiatry. My goal in writing this book has been solely to remind today's public of the essentials of a forgotten search—a search undertaken by some genuinely brilliant minds who implicitly believed in the important work they were doing. It is more than revealing that several explorers of the unknown are still engaged in this work today. It seems that the spiritistic theory of mental illness is a concept that will not die; and perhaps in these confused times it is time to look at the lives and work of those researchers who championed it and those who still support it.

D. Scott Rogo

CHAPTER 1

CURED BY AN EXORCISM?

Western society radically changed the way it viewed deviant behavior shortly after the turn of the century. This was primarily due to the Freudian revolution that swept Europe, and later the United States. Before Sigmund Freud explored the nature of the unconscious mind, psychiatrists had attributed abnormal behavior to unknown emotional factors coupled with constitutional (i.e., biological) predispositions. Freud's great achievement was to show that deviant psychological behavior was *meaningful* behavior, since it symbolized and expressed messages buried deep within the unconscious mind. For once it really did seem as though the mysteries of the unconscious had finally been successfully probed and deciphered.

Despite these gains, the clinical success of the early psychoanalysts was limited. Often their theoretical understanding of deviant behavior wasn't borne out when patients were actually treated. Although these pioneers made considerable strides in the study and treatment of neurosis (and especially hysteria), most of the early therapists still found treating psychotics—those unfortunate patients totally out of touch with reality—a nearly impossible task. Nor could they cure some patients who *should* have responded to conventional treatment. For this reason the psychoanalytic movement eventually schismatized into diverging factions, each with its own self-proclaimed solution and insight into the nature of the psyche. By even the most conservative estimates, there exist today over one hundred different schools of psychotherapy. They all claim limited success, and they all try to prove their claims by publishing reports of remarkable cures. Despite these self-indulgent kudos,

1

though, people continue to become mentally ill, and some stubbornly refuse to respond to treatment of any kind.

The fact remains that today's psychology and psychiatry do not possess complete answers about the various mysteries of human behavior. Despite the knowledge they are accumulating, these disciplines cannot yet explain why some people behave, by all social standards, in a pathological way.

In fact, there is a growing belief among some critics of the psychological establishment that psychoanalysis and contemporary psychology have failed. In his book *The Psychological Society*, for example, Martin L. Gross—one of psychology's most acerbic critics—complains that "the psychological revolution has damaged the psychic fiber of individual man and woman" and has brainwashed us into thinking that we are sick and deluded. He posits that psychoanalysis is a religion more than a science. Gross came to this conclusion after making a detailed study of whether psychiatry and psychology have really helped improve the quality of our daily lives. He is far from alone in his views and was interviewed sympathetically in *Human Behavior* magazine after his book came out.

The following case is an example of the failure of psychiatry, a failure later corrected in a totally bizarre manner.

Dr. David H. Barlow and Dr. Gene G. Abel first met the patient whom they identify only as "John" in 1969. John was a clear case of lifelong gender dysphoria, even by the most conservative criteria. They were counseling him for sexual reassignment surgery at the time of his strange cure.

Gender dysphoria is the psychiatric term for what is commonly called transsexualism, the obsession that one has been born as the wrong sex. This behavioral disorder often leads to conduct that isn't too socially acceptable, such as cross-dressing (transvestism) and seeking change-of-sex surgery. Surgery is, however, the only treatment that seems to resolve the conflicts that plague transsexuals. But even this treatment is not always successful; for some transsexuals are so confused about their identities that they will go back to role-playing their original gender, even though their surgery is irreversible. Psychotherapeutic forms of treatment seem useless, and there is only a single case in the literature that reports the cure of a transsexual. That cure consisted of months of work with the patient using behavior modification.

What causes gender dysphoria isn't known, and theoretical explanations for the condition range from psychological causes to possible biological reasons. Extreme gender confusion in early childhood has been suggested as a cause, but an unidentified hormonal disorder could conceivably be a contributing factor also. (For example, girls born with congenital adrenal hyperplasm—a disorder in the adrenal glands—will grow up exhibiting masculine behavior.) Whatever the case, transsexualism is a long-lived problem that is resistent to change. For this reason the two psychiatrists at the University of Tennessee Medical School were stunned when John suddenly showed up one day completely cured—not by psychiatry or medicine but as the result of an exorcism!

The strange story began in 1952 when the patient was born. From early childhood John considered himself to be a girl. His gender confusion was probably the result of family problems. His mother and father, who raised their family in Tennessee, were thirty-two and forty-five years old respectively, and they didn't get along very well. They finally separated when the boy was eight, by which time John's transsexualism was already fairly ingrained. The couple were already the parents of two other children (a boy and a girl) before John came along, so he was the baby of the family. He was a pampered child, too, for his mother was very protective and wouldn't let him engage in any rough-and-tumble boys' play. She instead kept him at home, where he occupied his time—with his mother's encouragement—cleaning and performing other household work.

When he was four years old, John began to imitate his mother openly by putting on makeup and dressing in his sister's clothes. This behavior continued even after he started school, and he often made excuses to stay home to indulge his feminine fantasies. The only physical trauma John suffered during these early years came when he broke his leg when he was six. The broken leg didn't bother him very much, but the cast he was forced to wear prevented him from cross-dressing, which he found a constant source of frustration.

John's feminine traits and identification soon pervaded his entire life. He refused to participate in gym while at grammar school, while his growing effeminacy caused the other boys at school to make life miserable for him. His older brother often had to come to his defense. John's greatest personal satisfaction came when his mother took a job and he took over full responsibility as family housekeeper, a role he enjoyed immensely.

The next phase in John's ever-increasing gender dysphoria came during adolescence. By this time he was going to high school, but was doing only passably well. His main preoccupation was still his family's home, where he could engage in his favorite pastime, domestic work.

But when he was fifteen, something happened that permanently changed his life. He read a magazine article about transsexualism, learned about sexual reassignment surgery, and began corresponding with experts at Johns Hopkins Hospital in Baltimore. Surgery seemed to be the obvious course of action for him, so he began to prepare for it. To achieve this goal, the teenager dropped out of school and began studying the literature on transsexualism. He became so versed on the subject that he successfully conned a physician into giving him estrogen by claiming that he needed it to treat a previously diagnosed endocrine disorder. His real purpose, of course, was to prepare himself physically for the change-of-sex surgery.

Soon the oral doses and injections took effect, and his body hair began to thin while his breasts enlarged. The estrogen also affected him psychologically, and he later reported that it made him feel more tranquil than he had ever felt before.

It is impossible to determine how far the young man would have gone with this self-therapy were it not for an automobile accident that disrupted his life in 1969. He was then sixteen. His use of estrogen was discovered by the doctors who treated him after the accident, and they informed his family about the situation. They were shocked by the revelation, as might be expected.

The disruption these revelations caused within John's family can't be overestimated, and seemed to exacerbate his previously disturbed relationship with his mother. She resolutely insisted that he seek psychiatric treatment, and she even threatened suicide should he refuse. John eventually gave in to his mother's histrionics and committed himself to a state hospital, but there was nothing the therapists could do for him. Since he was well in touch with reality and was not psychotic, he was merely formally diagnosed as a transsexual and discharged. This conveniently allowed John to go to work at a fast-food restaurant and once again plan for change-of-sex surgery. The hospital psychiatrists felt, however, that their patient could benefit from psychotherapy, and they encouraged him to see Dr. David H. Barlow at the University of Tennessee Medical School. (Dr. Barlow would later help bring the case to public attention. He is a renowned pioneer in the use of behavior modification techniques for the treatment of sexual disturbances.) This course of action didn't strike John as unreasonable. He began taking estrogen again, but this time under the supervision of a private psychiatrist. He also went back to cross-dressing.

While personally satisfied with the way his life was going, the only real problem still facing him was his mother's possessiveness. He complained that she continually tried to smother him while at the same time she fiercely rejected his transsexualism. To escape the situation, the young man—with his psychiatrist's blessing—joined the Navy in 1972, but he was rejected for psychiatric reasons. His mother tried to take advantage of the circumstances and even tried to move into his apartment with him, much to his annoyance. The situation between John and his mother became so intolerable that finally he tried to commit suicide by overdosing on his medication.

This unsuccessful suicide attempt brought him back to the hospital and back to the attention of Dr. Barlow and his colleague Dr. Gene G. Abel, who had also previously worked extensively with transsexuals. They counseled the patient, agreed with him that surgery would probably resolve his gender dysphoria and began preparing him. This entailed giving him full therapeutic dosages of estrogen and electrolysis and subjecting him to a complete psychiatric examination for gender identity, gender role behavior, and sexual arousal patterns. These standard objective psychological tests, which are always given before change-of-sex surgery is seriously considered, were conducted by Drs. Barlow and Abel.

The results of every one of the tests were consistent with a diagnosis of transsexualism. Even the way John moved and walked was typically feminine, according to a test that the researchers used to check for masculine and feminine motor behavior. For all practical purposes, John was really a woman trapped in a man's body. For this reason the therapists did not hesitate to continue recommending a change-of-sex operation.

The process leading up to this radical surgery is very slow, however. For two years the researchers kept continual tabs on John, repeatedly giving him tests for gender identity and masculine versus feminine motor behavior. The results consistently came up feminine, which constituted further evidence that change-of-sex surgery was warranted in his case.

By this time John was living openly as a woman and was going by the name Judy. He successfully adapted to his new lifestyle, and no one who casually knew him realized he was a pre-op transsexual. His therapists even stated when they wrote up the case that he "was successfully wearing a bikini having progressed to bra size 38B."

By the summer of 1973, John was ready for his change-of-sex operation, to which he was looking forward eagerly. Both of his therapists agreed that his adjustment would probably be successful and that he wouldn't suffer later conflicts over his decision. They suggested that he have the surgery at a medical center in a nearby state, and he duly checked in.

Then came the shock. The therapists never received word back about the surgery, and several silent months passed before they heard from John again. When he resurfaced the following fall, he had been remarkably transformed.

"One day in late fall," report Drs. Barlow and Abel, "a research assistant who had worked with the case came back from a half-finished lunch of fried chicken and shouted, 'Judy is back at the restaurant, but she's not Judy anymore, she's John!' Other reports quickly confirmed the report, and John was invited back to our offices for a session which occurred in early January of 1974. He entered the office in a three-piece business suit with polished shoes, neatly cut short hair, clipped fingernails, and consistently masculine motor behaviors. Even to trained eyes, the only sign of his former feminine role was the almost complete absence of facial hair, which in view of his light complexion and in the context of his total masculinity would normally go unnoticed."

The story he told was as remarkable as his transformation. While he was working at the fast-food restaurant, he had grown very attached to his employer, who was a Christian fundamentalist. She refused to be judgmental about her employee's transsexualism, but she did ask that he consult with a physician she knew in town before undergoing the final surgery. This physician was also a fundamentalist. Although John considered himself a Southern Baptist, neither he nor anyone else in his family was religious. But he went to see the doctor anyway as a favor to his boss. The doctor examined him and spoke with him for some time and even agreed that his change-of-sex adjustment would probably be good. He then told John that his real problem was possession by evil spirits! John was astounded by this announcement, even more when the physician asked if he could perform an exorcism. For some reason John agreed.

The exorcism lasted from two to three hours, and it involved prayer, the laying-on-of-hands, and exhortations against the evil spirits possessing the patient. John later explained to his therapists that he fainted several times during the ritual, but when the ordeal was over, the physician assured him that twenty-two spirits had been driven from his body.

(The physician later explained to Dr. Barlow that one of these entities had been female and was the cause of John's problem.)

The result of the exorcism was nothing short of amazing. When the ritual was over, John announced that it had worked! Now, for the first time in twenty years, he perceived himself as a man. His desire to cross-dress ceased instantly and he immediately went to a barbershop to have his hair cut short. This conversion to a totally masculine identity lasted for two weeks, during which time he lived back with his mother. But then he began to feel his old tendencies returning, so he and his employer visited a fundamentalist faith healer at a public meeting in town. They were able to talk with her and she agreed to pray over John. Once again he fainted dead away. He fainted again after regaining consciousness for a few moments, which ended the treatment. It was at this point that John realized that another miracle had transpired. While leaving the public platform where he had been treated, he saw that his breasts—fully formed from the estrogen treatment—had returned to normal. He had now fully returned to his male gender, although the effects of estrogen are long-lasting and his claim medically impossible. (While checking into the story, Dr. Barlow received confirmation of the "miracle" from the young man's employer.)

Even though they could plainly see that their former patient's feminine characteristics had completely and mysteriously disappeared, Dr. Barlow and his colleagues were incredulous about their patient's story and spent considerable effort in verifying it. The story consistently checked out. But to be sure of their personal observations, the therapists asked John to retake the same battery of psychological tests that they had used to diagnose him a transsexual. This time the test results all came out consistent with a masculine identity . . . which was a total reversal of the prior results he had given while being monitored over the previous two years. Even his gait and body movements were now firmly masculine, possibly for the first time in his life.

The two therapists followed John's life for the next two and a half years to see if the cure would be permanent. It certainly seemed to be, for John's transsexual tendencies never returned. By 1975 he was dating women but had not engaged in premarital sex because of his new-found religious beliefs. They learned that he still occasionally felt fleeting homosexual urges, but their former patient assured them that he was perfectly capable of banishing these from his mind when they arose. His adjustment to his masculine life seemed as perfect as it was inexplicable.

What is a psychiatrist to make of such a bizarre case? Does it prove the existence of spirit possession, or could the exorcism have produced some sort of psychological miracle akin to hypnotic suggestion?

It is clear from their report that neither Dr. Barlow nor Dr. Abel feels competent to explain why and how this unexpected cure came about. Writing in the *Archives of Sexual Behavior* in 1977, they noted that "what is important in this case is that no psychotherapeutic procedure of any kind with whatever element of suggestion or persuasion, has been effective for transsexualism, with the possible exception of behavior modification in one case. But even the most facile operant conditioner would be hard pressed to explain the sudden and massive behavioral change observed and objectively measured in this case." They add that the one reported case of a patient cured through behavior modification responded only after months of treatment. That patient only learned to behave "masculinely" by practicing new behavioral strategies for walking and acting. The patient had to be carefully taught these strategies, while John's cure had been instantaneous.

"What cannot be denied," the two researchers conclude, ". . . is that a patient who was very clearly a transsexual, by the most conservative criteria, assumed a long-lasting masculine gender identity in a remarkably short time following an apparent exorcism."

Dr. Barlow was in a position to know, too, since he has personally specialized in the "cure" of gender dysphoria. He had invariably found that the process takes an extremely long time to complete.

No matter how one chooses to interpret this case, the fact remains that conventional psychiatry cannot explain why John grew up with the internal feelings that he was a woman and not a man, why counseling and therapy accomplished nothing by way of a cure, or how the young man accomplished a 100 percent change in behavior almost instantaneously.

But let's go back in time a bit, to an era before the contemporary development of the behavioral sciences. During the Middle Ages, it was widely believed that some people who acted strangely were possessed either by evil spirits or by spirits of the dead. This belief was most eloquently promoted by Michael Psellus, a church scholar of the eleventh century. The belief has withstood the test of time, for it is still taught in many technologically unsophisticated societies, where the mentally ill are treated by shamans instead of physicians. The cosmology of primitive shamans teaches that madness occurs when the soul has been torn away from the body, thereby allowing spirit possession or psychological dysfunction to occur. The shaman—like the psychiatrist—heals through the use of special rituals and by virtue of his "special" knowledge concerning the workings of the body and the soul. His success rate easily rivals that of even the best Park Avenue psychiatrist, as psychiatrist E. Fuller Torrey was forced to admit after he studied shamanism around the world. (He published his findings in his celebrated book *The Mind Game* before returning to conventional psychiatry to work with schizophrenics at St. Elizabeth's Hospital in Washington, D.C.)

So it seems to me that there is plenty of reason to consider all sorts of seemingly bizarre theories about the nature of human behavior. The rest of this book will consider the possibility that some cases of deviant behavior are not due simply to the dysfunction of the brain or mind, but that certain unseen influences might be a complicating factor. Since John's cure by exorcism was psychiatrically inexplicable, would it be too outrageous to suggest that perhaps some sort of foreign influence had been responsible for the youth's feminine behavior? We can at least explain his cure by adopting this provisional view.

For several years, some enlightened psychiatrists and psychologists have believed that within the bizarre hallucinations and delusions of the mentally disturbed, there might lurk some level of paranormal perception. For instance, take a patient who believes he is being persecuted by spirits of the dead. What if that patient started coming up with obscure and verifiable information about real people whom he never knew and who died years before—the very people he claimed were persecuting him? Such a case would suggest that the patient's delusions were based on some glimmer of reality. In fact, there are several such cases buried within the literature on the paranormal. During the course of the next several chapters, we will take a detailed look at these cases—and at what they have to teach us about the nature of the mind and life itself.

PART I

THE PSYCHIC ODYSSEY OF JAMES H. HYSLOP

CHAPTER 2

THE STRANGE CASE
OF FREDERIC THOMPSON

The critical date was a cold evening in January 1907, when a rather
upset gentleman showed up at the offices of the American Institute for
Scientific Research in New York. Section B of this organization constituted the American Society for Psychical Research (ASPR), and the
gentleman asked to speak with Prof. James H. Hyslop. Hyslop had recently resigned his faculty position at Columbia University to run the
ASPR. He had no idea what the visitor wanted, but he invited the man
in and asked how he could help.

The gentleman introduced himself as Frederic Thompson. He was
thirty-nine years old, and he explained that a friend had suggested they
meet. He then explained that he was experiencing vivid hallucinations
depicting landscapes. He felt compelled to paint them and he believed
that he was being possessed or at least influenced by a deceased artist
who had once lived in his home town of New Bedford, Massachusetts.

At the turn of the century, New Bedford represented New England
at its best and loveliest, especially in the fall. Situated on the east bank
of the Acushnet River near its mouth at Buzzards Bay, the city is only
fifty-five miles south of Boston. Because it is located so near the coast,
its climate is milder than the more inland areas in the summer and
winter. It had been an historic whaling port, and one of its local land-
marks was made famous by Herman Melville in his epic *Moby Dick*.
Since the 1880s the city had been an important textile center and boasted

13

a population of about seventeen thousand residents. At the turn of the century its major commerces were farming, dairying, and fishing. The coastal areas outside New Bedford were especially distinctive. They were rich with vegetation that served as a scenic border to the broad expanses of the outlying ocean. The flora were not to be outdone by the local fauna, and these coastal areas attracted both artists (professionals and Sunday dabblers alike) and hunters.

It was here, too, that Frederic Thompson first met Robert Swain Gifford, a prominent local artist with an international reputation. Thompson liked to hunt along the coast, while Gifford would often set up his easel to sketch or paint scenes suggested by the landscape. Gifford was a native of the area and had first studied art in New Bedford under Benjamin Russell. He was considerably older than Thompson and was well into his fifties when they first met accidentally sometime before 1898. After lengthy travels and a protracted stay in New York, where he had gained some fame (both in the United States and in Europe) for his sketches and paintings, Gifford had by this time returned to New Bedford. His accessible style combined elements from the Hudson River School of landscape painting and from the newer Impressionism. Prints of his work were commonly sold in New England, and his paintings had been shown at the National Academy of Design in New York.

Frederic Thompson was about thirty years old when he chanced upon the artist while hunting and rambling along the coast. He was employed as a metal worker but was also an aspiring artist of sorts. He would later recall of his meetings with the celebrated artist,

> During this time I became familiar with the country around New Bedford, as I was fond of gunning and often made trips along the shores of the ocean, especially in the Autumn. Occasionally on the rambles I met the late R. Swain Gifford (artist) sketching an old tree or bit of shore scenery. In this way I became slightly acquainted with him and I made a few attempts at art work. When I attempted anything beyond the copying of prints, my efforts were so crude and laborious I soon gave it up. . . . Mr. Gifford also did not encourage painting as a profession and was interested in my work at the factory and spoke of the artistic possibilities of metal work.

It is fairly clear from this account that Thompson and Gifford didn't know each other very well. In fact, apart from these impromptu run-ins, Thompson had only one other significant encounter with the painter.

It was this encounter that probably set the stage for the psychic adventure in which he would soon become engulfed.

The Pairpont Manufacturing Company, which employed Thompson, folded in 1898, leaving the young man in a financially precarious situation. This led him to think back to his acquaintance with Gifford, and he decided to call upon the older man in hope of getting a letter of introduction for employment with the Tiffany Glass Company in New York. A letter from the esteemed painter, he felt, would at least secure him an interview.

Thompson described their meeting at Gifford's New Bedford home in some autobiographical notes he wrote in 1907.

> Mr. Gifford did not recognize me at first and probably thought I was an artist for he told me that it was very difficult for an artist to succeed in New York, but on my explanation that I was interested in glass and metal work and wished to find employment with the Tiffany Glass Company, Mr. Gifford then gave me his New York address and asked me to call on him when I came to New York. He then said that there were great possibilities in the combination of glass and metal work.

This autobiographical fragment gives a fairly accurate indication of Thompson's personal relationship with Gifford. While it was cordial, it was certainly not a friendship in any sense of the word. It is more than revealing that Gifford didn't even recognize his acquaintance when he showed up at his door.

Despite the painter's offer, Thompson didn't make it to New York that year. He decided to remain in Massachusetts and found employment in Boston with the Low Art Tile Company, where he was hired to make tile molds. He only moved to New York in 1900 where he first worked with a silversmith firm and then with a jewelry concern, where he manufactured silver trinkets. In 1901 he decided on a course of self-employment. He visited Gifford once in 1904 to show him some of his jewelry, but he gave up the business after a few unsuccessful years. He then joined another jewelry firm. By then it was the fall of 1905, and he had no idea—nor apparent concern—that Gifford had died on January 15, after succumbing to a long-standing heart condition. He was sixty-four at the time of his death.

Despite the fact that Thompson had lost interest in Gifford, he began having the urge to sketch and, finally, paint all during the summer and fall of 1905. Although he had previously been interested in painting, these sudden impulses struck him as bizarre and alien. Not only were they overpowering, they were accompanied by visual hallucinations and mental images of trees and landscapes. These mental scenes soon became the subjects of his paintings—paintings that seemed to literally paint themselves. Thompson later recorded,

> Sometime during the Summer of 1905 I seemed to have constantly in my mind a group of trees near the sea that I did not remember having seen in nature, and my desire to paint them became so great that I got some art materials and worked evenings on the picture and I was surprised at the result. The picture seemed to paint itself. In the Fall I was possessed by such a great desire to paint from nature that for several Sundays I went into the country near the sound in Westchester sketching, and was greatly surprised at the ease with which I could paint the most delicate effects.

Despite the ego-alien nature of these urges, there was little evidence that there was anything truly extraordinary about them. Thompson had long been intrigued by painting, and he even had taken some sketching lessons years earlier while attending public school. He must have had some incipient but undeveloped talent, for during one of his periods of self-employment he tried to capitalize on his ability by going into partnership with another artist. Their idea had been to take photographs and turn them into oil paintings. Thompson did the rough work, while his partner did the more demanding finishing and detailing. The whole venture, unfortunately, had been a failure.

Only after submitting to these preliminary impulses did Thompson begin to intuitively link Robert Swain Gifford to his experiences. While walking along the Long Island marshes near New York, he would sometimes see in his mind's eye a painting that Gifford had once executed of a marsh. The marsh was located near New Bedford, and Thompson had seen it twenty-five years before. It was the only painting of Gifford's that he had seen. It was also the mental picture that first made Thompson feel, in his own words, "that I was actually Mr. Gifford himself." This bizarre and seemingly pathological identification with Gifford (whom he thought was still alive) became even greater as he painted. "The subjects I selected around the marshes of Westchester were so much like a picture by Mr. Gifford," he later wrote, "that during the time I was sketching I remembered having the impression that I was Gifford himself." He would even tell his wife that "Mr. Gifford" wanted to go sketching when these urges became overpowering.

These accounts did not merely rely solely on Thompson's word. Carrie Thompson, the jeweler's ailing wife, later confirmed for Professor Hyslop that her husband's first urges to paint and sketch nature scenes began in the fall of 1905. She recollected that these urges usually came on Sundays and that he referred to his alter ego as "Mr. Gifford." She told the researcher that, "I could not understand what he meant as his acquaintance with Mr. Gifford was very slight."

There were no noticeable developments in the case during the next few months, although it was becoming more and more obvious to both Thompson and his wife that something unusual was happening. Then, one day in January 1906, something finally happened that forced him to place his experiences in a new perspective. He was taking his usual lunch break from work, but for some reason, he didn't go to the restaurant where he usually ate. He instead walked down Fifth Avenue and turned on Twenty-Third Street.

Looking up I saw a notice at the American Art Galleries of a sale of paintings by the late R. Swain Gifford. I was surprised to see this notice as this was my first knowledge of his death and his face came to mind as I had seen him two years previous and then he looked the picture of health. I went to the galleries and was much interested in the collection as they were the first finished pictures I had ever seen of his. They were for the most part painted around New Bedford and I was familiar with many scenes. A large coast picture impressed me very much and after looking at it a short time I fancied myself out of doors and could hear sounds of insects and birds. I could feel the breeze on my face. Then suddenly all was still and I heard the words very clearly, "You see what I have done. Go on with the work."

Thompson blacked out after he heard these words and suffered a fugue (a short-term amnesia) for the next hour. He later found himself back at work with no memory of returning.

During the spring and summer months that followed, Thompson continued sketching and painting. His mind was so plagued by various visions and mental landscapes that he felt he could no longer continue with his normal employment. So in November 1906 he and his wife left for Connecticut to stay with relatives. Thompson was not indifferent to the precariousness of his position, even though he didn't have the strength to resist his impulses. The situation must have been grossly unpleasant for him, for he soon found himself on the verge of financial ruin because of his inability to ward off his strange impulses to paint. Even his wife was becoming increasingly alarmed. Both he and his wife began to realize, in fact, that perhaps some sort of force was working behind the scenes and influencing him. It was also at this time that he fully acknowledged that Gifford was somehow invading his life.

Even though he couldn't resist his urges to paint, Frederic Thompson was fully cognizant of the disintegrative effects the compulsions were having on his life. He talked to several friends about the situation, and one of them suggested that he seek out James Hyslop, who was famous in New York because of his work as a psychic investigator. It was also well known that Hyslop was interested both in psychical research and in abnormal psychology, and Thompson sought him out in hopes of learning how to deal with his hallucinations. During their first meeting, which took place on January 16, 1907, he told Hyslop that he was afraid that he was going insane, and he emphasized that the problem started when he saw the exhibition of Gifford's paintings the previous year. He particularly complained about a scene of a gnarled oak tree that ceaselessly haunted him. The sheer unrelentless nature of these images, he explained, had convinced him that he needed professional guidance.

It would appear that Hyslop was not impressed by the story, and he certainly didn't think that there was anything psychic about Thompson's complaint. He was reluctant to spend much time pursuing it since he was already overburdened with other responsibilities. He was then in sole charge of the American Society for Psychical Research, which he had just completed reincorporating as Section B of his American Institute for Scientific Research. (The original ASPR had been founded in 1885 as part of a British parent organization, the SPR, but it had floundered after the death of the SPR's hand-picked administrator in 1905.) Reorganizing the ASPR had occupied Hyslop's attention throughout 1906 and the newly structured and independent society had just opened its doors. Hyslop was primarily interested in researching trance mediumship; so the subject of abnormal psychology was somewhat alien to his immediate interests. (Section A of the American Institute for Scientific Research was supposed to devote itself to the study of abnormal psychology, but it never became active; it existed only on paper.)

Despite his understandable reluctance to get involved in the Thompson case, Hyslop questioned him for about two hours during their first visit. His chief impression was both logical and inevitable: he felt that Thompson was undergoing a personality disintegration, probably due to some sort of mental illness. He felt that his client was probably suffering from an organic condition, the nature of which could only be determined by an eventual autopsy. His only advice to the disturbed man was that he should give up painting, go back to his jewelry work, and try to forget about the whole thing.

Luckily, though, Hyslop was not willing to let the matter drop completely, for he was interested in conducting at least one special experiment. *If* there were any truth to Thompson's claim that R. Swain Gifford was influencing him, Hyslop felt that the matter could be resolved by taking him to a gifted trance medium. Perhaps, he thought, an entity might communicate that would shed light on the possible paranormal reality of Thompson's experiences.

The suggestion struck Thompson's fancy. So on the morning of Friday, January 18, 1907, Hyslop took him anonymously to the home of a gifted professional psychic he had discovered in New York. Thompson was introduced to Margaret Gaule (who was identified as "Mrs. Rathbun" in all Hyslop's reports) only as a "Mr. Smith." But even before the séance began, Miss Gaule sensed the presence of an artist in the room. She particularly focused on his striking nose, his tapering fingers, and his fondness for painting. She also sensed that her anonymous sitter had done automatic writing—which was perhaps (in light of his art work) a near-miss. She felt that the spirit presence might have committed suicide but then picked up something about rheumatism. Thompson and Hyslop were impressed by these preliminary perceptions since they represented a fairly accurate description of some of Gifford's idiosyncrasies. The artist had not committed suicide, but his sudden death had been caused by rheumatism of the heart.

Of course, it is certainly possible that the psychic was reading either Thompson's or Hyslop's mind, and the latter was sensitive to this problem. During his earlier career, Hyslop had been particularly interested in whether some mediums, in fact, were only gifted mind-readers. But he had long since rejected the telepathic hypothesis and gave it little credence during his later work on trance mediumship.

The sitting progressed as Miss Gaule's psychic sense continued to focus on the phantom intruder. She began to lock into the dynamics binding her sitter to the unidentified artist; then she suddenly began describing landscape scenes. Her descriptions were similar to some of the scenes that were haunting her sitter.

Miss Gaule: I see foliage of American autumn. One tree is fallen over.
 Thompson: Yes.
Miss Gaule: Covered with leaves. Trees are down. One is broken. It is a knotty
              sort of tree.
 Thompson: Yes.
Miss Gaule: Two are standing, one is falling. Leaves are brown and yellow.
 Thompson: What is the color of the sea?
Miss Gaule: Bluish rather than green. Looks as if the leaves are blown into it.
              A vista looks through brown beautiful tints.
 Thompson: Where?
Miss Gaule: No, I don't see. Looks as if it took a steamer. It is far, very far.
              Mild temperature.
 Thompson: It is a place where people seldom go?
Miss Gaule: Seems so there never was and never will be another picture from
              that. The water looks black now. It is not populated thickly. The
              tree was knotty, was it not?
 Thompson: Yes.
Miss Gaule: There was not a green leaf on it.

What was so astounding was that this scene, so concisely described by
the psychic, exactly matched one that Thompson had been recently
envisioning. In fact, he had described it to Hyslop in some detail only
two nights before! This development immediately alerted Hyslop to the
possibility that there was more to the Thompson case than met the eye.

   The obvious success of their first sitting was so encouraging that
Hyslop decided to pursue this line of experimentation further. So on
March 16 he took Thompson to Boston to sit with Minnie Soule, who
was one of the best and most successfully tested mediums of the day.
Hyslop and Thompson made the trip on a Saturday, and Mrs. Soule
was given no information about the case she was to work on. (It should
be noted that Mrs. Soule was not a professional psychic, and her identity was always concealed under the name "Mrs. Chenoweth" in the
many reports Hyslop published about her.) Mrs. Soule practiced her
trance work in accordance with the Spiritualist customs of her day. She
would enter a trance, during which her spirit guide, or control, would
control her and offer messages to the sitter. Mrs. Soule's control was a
cute little entity who rather unconvincingly called herself "Sunbeam."

   The sitting got off to a fairly good start. The psychic was able to
make contact with an unnamed entity who claimed that he was trying
to influence the sitter. This remark immediately alerted Hyslop and
Thompson to the possibility that the psychic was onto something.

Mrs. Soule went on to describe several of R. Swain Gifford's idio-syncrasies—idiosyncrasies that Thompson had noted when talking to him near the New Bedford shore. She also described some of Gifford's cloth-ing and a rug in his home, but neither of the sitters were in a position to evaluate the accuracy of these impressions. But the precision of Mrs. Soule's earlier remarks convinced Thompson that Gifford was indeed trying to reach and use him, and he grew more and more excited as the sitting progressed. He was hopeful that perhaps the entity communicat-ing through the psychic could direct him to the actual locations where he could find the scenes of his visionary experiences.

By the time of this séance, Thompson was being particularly haunted by a vision of a group of trees, so he asked the psychic about it. He believed that Gifford must have painted the scene, so he was sure that the communicator could help him find it.

He didn't give the psychic very much to go on, though. "There is a picture of an old group of trees near the ocean," he said. "I would like to get to it. Can you see it?"

Mrs. Soule's control, speaking for the communicator, responded with a remarkable description of the scene that Thompson had in mind:

> I want to tell you little boy, I think he [the communicator] has seen the trees and I think he is giving you the picture of it. I think you will see them too. I don't know the place, but it looks like that to me—when you go up here on this hill, as I told you about, and ocean in front of you it will be on your left and you will go down a little incline, almost a gully, and then up a little bit and a jut out. That is just the way it seems. Now you have this so that you can follow, can't you. They look like gnarled trees. There is one that stands up quite straight and some that you can see, not dead, but part dead. Some are roots and gnarled and then the rest. They are nice.

This was the final evidence Thompson needed to prove to himself that he wasn't insane after all. The accuracy of the communication was as-tonishing, and it really was beginning to look as though a spirit agency were trying to manipulate his thoughts. Not for a minute did he doubt that his communicator was R. Swain Gifford.

Because of these impressive developments in the case, Thompson decided that he had to locate the scenes of his hallucinations to further prove the reality of his experiences. So on July 2, 1907, he placed sev-eral of his sketches in Hyslop's custodianship and left for New Bedford.

These sketches dated back to the summer and fall of 1905 when his urges to paint first commenced. Hyslop locked them in his files at the ASPR along with an affidavit to that effect. Hyslop could not have fully realized the importance of these sketches, nor how critical they would be in solving the case.

Thompson's psychic odyssey took him to several locations around the New Bedford area and out to Cuttyhunk, the southernmost of the Elizabeth Islands, during early August. These islands constitute the eastern border of Buzzards Bay and extend down from the Barnstable Peninsula. He spent considerable time inspecting and sketching on Cuttyhunk and during this trip he experienced many more psychic impressions. He kept hearing phantom music while wandering about the island, and he began dipping into altered states of consciousness.

For example, while sketching at Cuttyhunk he had the following unusual experience.

> As I sketched I suddenly heard sounds of music. I thought at first that some persons were behind some of the hills with guitars, but I looked around and there was no one in sight. As I again resumed my work, I heard the music again, this time it seemed to be in the air around me and as I listened intently the sounds changed and were like distant chimes of bells, then they were guitars or banjos, then like harps, the sounds varied in intensity and always in chords and rather quick in March time. I tried to catch some theme but could not, the music was always in changing chords, and seemed to combine a great number of notes but always in harmony. After a while it died away and I did not hear it again for several days.

This bizarre "psychic music" did not seem to be a simple hallucination. It did not occur at random but only became noticeable when Thompson was working on his paintings with deep concentration. The jeweler himself stated that "I was always entirely absorbed in sketching when I heard sounds of music, as I sketched they would continue but died away as I stopped to listen and stopped painting and tried to catch the melody or analyze the music."

In fact, this strange music seemed to occur specifically at those times when the *soi-disant* Gifford was most actively trying to communicate or influence him. These strange experiences reached their climax a week or so later, when Thompson was invited by a party of friends to visit Naushon Island, a privately owned island north of Cuttyhunk. (Visits to the island could only be made by permit.) As soon as he arrived on the island, Thompson felt as if the deceased Gifford were guiding him from place to place. He subsequently recorded his experiences in his diary.

> I was actually led from place to place where the best views could be obtained as if I had reached the home of the spirit of Mr. Gifford and he was delighted in showing me its beauties and I know his spirit must take great delight in hovering around the spot that must have filled him with grand inspiration. When in life he wandered over these grey hills and filled himself with the beauty of the rock and sky, trees, and the distant sea over the moorlands.
>
> After looking at the old trees and picturesque bits, I was led up a rough hillside and there from the top I saw before me the exact spot where the picture that first impressed me at the exhibition in New York was painted, altho I did not know the picture was taken from one of the Elizabeth Islands, its title was "The Shore of the Vineyard Sound." As I looked at the scene the same sensations came to me that I felt at the exhibition in New York, except the sounds of insects or songs of birds I heard then, now seemed like grand chords of music at first like distant harps, then like chimes of bells, then softly like guitars; the music always in chords the same as I heard at Cuttyhunk, like a march and music quite lively, although always soft and harmonious, and the same voice I heard at the exhibition said—"See how beautiful, you must paint them better than I. This is to be your life work. . . . You must come back when the leaves are red and work; then I will help you."

The bewildered artist seemed to be closing in on R. Swain Gifford's roots.

Frederic Thompson spent several months that summer and fall exploring the Elizabeth Islands. The most dramatic event of the sojourn came during his second visit to Naushon Island. There he found a number of scenes that had been continually haunting his mind over the previous three years, including one that he had sketched previously and left with Hyslop in New York.

It was also during this excursion that another strange incident took place. While back exploring Naushon Island, he stumbled across a peculiar and striking group of trees that he had seen in some of his visions.

While sketching them, he heard a voice—the same one that he had heard several times before—instructing him to look on the other side of the trees. They were about sixty feet away, and when he followed the voice's instructions, Thompson found the initials R.S.G. 1902 carved into the bark.

This psychic odyssey also took Thompson to Nonquitt, where Gifford and his wife had lived during the summer months. The landscape there also struck a chord in Thompson's mind, and on August 24 he took the initiative of visiting Gifford's widow. This was a visit he had long been planning.

It was a bold move to take, but Mrs. Gifford greeted him cordially, invited him in, and offered to show him some portfolios of her late husband's work. She also invited him to visit Gifford's studio, located in a separate structure behind the cottage. It was an old and very artistic-looking place, and it was there that Thompson had the shock of his life.

> Mrs. Gifford left me there and said I could probably look things over better alone.
>
> The first thing I noticed was a picture on an easel that made me hold my breath. It was a group of old trees on a hillside at twilight, and was one of the identical group of trees I had in my mind since I first received my inspiration and felt I must finish it.
>
> I left a sketch of this group with Prof. Hyslop in New York. . . . (Mrs. Gifford told me afterwards that the subject for the picture was taken from the Island of Nashawena.)

Thompson took a photograph of the easel and the unfinished painting and later, back in New York, showed it to Hyslop, who had to agree that the match was almost perfect. He eventually published both the sketch and the photograph of the painting, and it takes no art expert to see the obvious correspondence. Thompson had also looked around the studio and found the rug that Minnie Soule had described during their sitting six months before. Several other sketches in Gifford's portfolios also matched some of Thompson's own most recently executed sketches. These seemed to match locations on Cuttyhunk; Thompson had previously felt a sense of déjà vu while drawing them. As he recorded in his diary,

> I also saw sketches of many groups of trees on one of the Elizabeth Islands that I recognized having been led to on my visit to that place, also

a group of trees that impressed me on my visit to that place on my second visit and the group in which I found "R.S.G. 1902" on the trunk. So Mr. Gifford had also stood in the same place that I was and felt those strange sensations and that I was told to look on the back of the tree where I found his initials.

I found amongst his sketches a great many pictures of oriental scenes, as he spent considerable time in the Orient. Also many pictures of the polar regions, but it is apparent that in his last days his thoughts turned to the old trees of these islands and shores, as he shows by his last sketch of the old trees on Nashawena and he wants me to be sure that of all the countries he has visited and sketched these scenes are the most beautiful and most worthy of study.

The fact that Thompson was not experiencing pathological or organically caused hallucinations now seemed evident.

It wasn't until the following October, when he was again exploring the Elizabeth Islands, that the jeweler accidentally found a key group of old and gnarled oak trees on Naushon Island—the same ones that had been haunting his visions and which had been previously described clairvoyantly by Margaret Gaule and Minnie Soule. A sketch of these oaks was among those placed in Hyslop's safekeeping earlier that year. These oaks would soon become critical to the case.

But now it is time for Prof. Hyslop to reenter the case.

He was, of course, tremendously excited when he learned about these new developments. The only problem was that many of the truly impressive features of the story rested solely on Thompson's word. It was clear to Hyslop that he would have to verify everything Thompson was reporting to him. His first step was to make sure that Thompson could not have seen the painting that was displayed in Gifford's studio before the summer of 1907. (This was when the original sketch that matched it had been placed in his custody.) But by the time Hyslop made Mrs. Gifford's acquaintance, the unfinished oil painting had been sent to the Boston Museum, where it was still on display.

Mrs. Gifford assured the researcher that the painting had never been offered for sale and that she had placed it on the easel in her late husband's studio well after his death. Nor had it ever been previously exhibited. Hyslop borrowed the painting from the Boston Museum anyway and turned it over to an art dealer, asking him to examine it to see if it had ever been placed on sale. This was unlikely since the painting was unfinished, but Hyslop asked the art dealer to check it for a stencil mark commonly affixed to commercially available paintings. The psychic nature of the case was cinched in Hyslop's mind when the art dealer reported that he could find no stencil mark on the painting.

It was now obvious that something very extraordinary was going on. But Dr. Hyslop was hardly through with Frederic Thompson, for there was still more work he wanted to do on the case. He had to find out if Thompson could ever have previously visited the Elizabeth Islands, and he also wanted to get some expert opinions on the art itself. He also realized that he had to personally visit the islands to verify that the sketches placed in his custody genuinely matched real locations there.

With this goal in mind Hyslop made an important trip to the Elizabeth Islands. He was keenly interested in finding the old gnarled oaks that had served as the source of some of the critical sketches executed by Thompson and placed in his hands the previous July. Hyslop ultimately made three trips to Naushon Island to search for the oaks. The first trip was unsuccessful. He went alone to the island and found plenty of trees grouped in suggestive configurations but nothing that exactly matched Thompson's sketch. "I photographed a few trees," reported Hyslop in his lengthy report on the case, "thinking that perhaps Mr. Thompson had put trees from various localities together and had made an idealized picture." He showed these various photographs to Thompson upon his return to the mainland, but Thompson denied that any of them represented the crucial scene. A second trip to the island was similarly unfruitful.

Not until the third trip to Naushon did the professor hit pay dirt. According to his report,

> On the second trip when he failed to find the trees, I remarked to Mr. Thompson that he must have painted the picture from an hallucination, but his reply was that this was impossible because he had carved his initials on one of the trees. He conjectured that he might have painted it on the north shore of the island, as the day was stormy and foggy when he painted it. The third trip was made to investigate this north shore with the hope of finding our quest.
>
> We investigated this shore for two or three miles and examined every tree to find what we wanted, but there was no trace of any single tree or group of trees that had any specific resemblance to the desired scene. Nor was the shore itself sufficiently like the one needed to make a technical resemblance. There were gnarled oaks in plenty, but nothing that suggested the picture. We then resolved to sail around the island into Vineyard Sound and examine a small group of trees that we had not investigated on the second trip. . . .

But after we had examined the north shore of the island we sailed into Hadley Bay and anchored there, taking a row boat with the purpose of going into Vineyard Sound, and in trying to row under a bridge found the tide coming in so strong that we could not go through. Mr. Thompson threw his coat upon the bridge and helped us to carry the boat around and into the water. He went back for his coat, but instead of getting it took his stand on the bridge, facing east, and ignoring three separate calls to get his coat and come on, he seemed to go into a sort of trance. Soon he ran down the bridge leaving his coat there for someone else to get, and ran with all his might around the shore to a small promontory and shouted back that he had found the trees. He threw the old grocery box into the air which he said before leaving New York that we would find on the spot where the trees were. Mr. Thompson's initials were on one of the trees.

Hyslop thereby proved the physical existence of the trees that had played a critical part in the case. By this discovery the professor showed that Thompson had genuinely tread that slim but infinite boundary between the living and the dead.

Prof. Hyslop's subsequent investigation provided sufficient evidence that Thompson had never visited the Elizabeth Islands, other than Cuttyhunk, before 1905. His visit to Cuttyhunk had lasted only for a few days some twenty years before.

The next stage in the case was about to begin.

CHAPTER 3

R. Swain Gifford Returns

With the success of the Elizabeth Islands expedition behind him, Hyslop decided to step up his investigation of the Thompson/Gifford case. He had two goals in mind: first, to prove that Thompson had genuinely taken over R. Swain Gifford's skills; second, to establish psychic contact with the deceased painter. But why was the professor so concerned about the skill exhibited in Frederic Thompson's art? Wasn't proving its relationship to scenes existing on the Elizabeth Islands enough? It takes a little background in turn-of-the-century psychical research to fully appreciate Hyslop's concern with this side of the case.

So far we have been concentrating on the story behind Thompson's obsession with painting, which resulted in several uncanny resemblances between his work and scenes undoubtedly familiar to the late R. Swain Gifford. However, this is irrelevant to the issue of the artistic merit of the psychically inspired paintings. Did they genuinely exhibit any artistic merit? Was the deceased artist's skill being exhibited by the New Bedford jeweler along with his memories? This issue remains crucial even today, and its significance was not lost on Hyslop. Even at the turn of the century, psychical researchers realized that proving the reality of life after death was no easy matter. The issue came down to what the Hyslop called the "spirit vs. telepathy" controversy. The existence of telepathy demonstrates that we are capable of gathering information through extrasensory channels. Because of this fact, the first psychical researchers sometimes rejected the evidence for survival provided by trance mediums such as Margaret Gaule and Minnie Soule, whose sittings for Frederic Thompson were discussed in Chapter 2. The researchers realized that perhaps these psychics could pick up information concerning a deceased person telepathically—i.e., from their still-living relatives. This information could then be passed off in the form of communications from the dead, probably by way of secondary personalities produced by splits within the psychic's own psyche.

But the development of a skill represents a totally different matter. There is simply no evidence that extrasensory perception can be used to help a psychic develop a skill. Skills result from more than simple information gathering; their development is contingent on practice, trial and error, and correction. For this reason, parapsychologists today believe that cases in which a psychic exhibits a specific skill possessed by a specific deceased person represents the best evidence for life after death. Speaking in a language that the psychic has never formally studied would also represent such evidence.

Hyslop probably fully understood this fact. He probably also realized that the Thompson case rested to some extent on whether the jeweler possessed both Gifford's skill and his memories. This concern opened a new chapter in the professor's study of the case.

But before studying this phase, perhaps we should discuss James Hyslop and his background. Just who was he? Why was he insightful enough to realize that Thompson might be suffering from something infinitely more complex than simple delusions? Knowing a bit about his background will set the stage for his subsequent research into the Thompson/Gifford case.

James Hyslop was born on August 18, 1854, on a small farm near the town of Xenia, Ohio. Both his parents were devout Presbyterians who expected their son to enter the ministry, but young Hyslop never shared his parents' dream. Being by nature extremely inquisitive, he began reading copiously in the natural sciences. It was this reading, coupled with his personal doubt about the Bible's literal meaning, that led him to a crisis in faith. The subjects of philosophy and psychology had long appealed to him, so he enrolled in Wooster College where he took his B.A. in 1877. Sometime after his graduation, he traveled to Germany to the University of Leipzig, where he studied with Wilhelm Wundt, who opened the first formal psychology laboratory in 1879. Hyslop remained in Germany for seventeen months before returning to the United States to teach philosophy at Lake Forest University in Lake Forest, Illinois, where he taught previously. He stayed there but a year before he relocated to Massachusetts, where he taught psychology and

ethics at Smith College. By relocating to the east coast, Hyslop was able
to continue with his own formal education. He enrolled at Johns Hopkins University where he took his doctorate under G. Stanley Hall. (This
was ironic, since later in life G. Stanley Hall became an outspoken
critic of belief in psychic phenomena.) Hyslop eventually joined the
faculty of Columbia University in 1889, where he rose from tutor to
instructor between 1889 and 1891. He became a full professor of ethics
and logic in 1895. During those crucial years he wrote several texts,
including his *Elements of Logic* (published in 1892) and his *Elements
of Ethics* (published in 1895).

Hyslop was in many respects a typical fin-de-siècle scholar and
intellectual. His studies were far-reaching and eclectic, since his interests ranged from philosophy to psychology to geology and biology. He
made his mark not in the field of philosophy and ethics, however, but
in the field of education.*

With such a wide and scholarly background, it wasn't odd that
Hyslop should eventually become attracted to the young science of
psychical research. The origins of this science date back to the rise of
Spiritualism in the United States and England during the late 1840s
and 1850s. Spiritualism taught that contact between the living and the
dead could be reliably established. Table-tilting and psychic (i.e., automatic) writing were two such methods, but the most reliable method
was through the use of a psychic. These special people could enter into
a trance and directly bring through spirits of the dead. The Spiritualist
movement also gave rise to scientific interest in psychic phenomena in
general. Belief in such phenomena as apparitions, thought transference,
precognition, and telekinesis became respectable for the first time. The
culmination of the Spiritualist movement came in 1882, when several
British intellectuals educated at Cambridge University banded together
to form the Society for Psychical Research (SPR). These founders included Prof. Henry Sidwick of Cambridge, his brilliant student F.W.H.
Myers, and Edmund Gurney, who had been a medical student and
scholar. Their organization was devoted to the scientific study of psychic
phenomena, and Prof. Sidgwick et.al. eschewed purely religious approaches to such incidents. The founding of the SPR also sparked the

---

*Rodger Anderson, a recent biographer of the professor, has written that as a
philosopher, Hyslop "was considered competent but not inspired. His numerous books
and articles on ethics, logic, and psychology made for a solid reputation, but however
voluminous his output, Hyslop's work was never regarded by his peers as either particularly original or important."

interest of several intellectuals in the United States, and in 1885 an American Society for Psychical Research was formed in Boston. Its first president was Prof. Simon Newcomb of Harvard, but its leading light soon became Dr. Richard Hodgson, who was sent over from England to supervise the work of the fledgling society. He became the society's chief investigator and secretary, and extended this position when the ASPR became a branch of the British organization in 1889.

The early work of the SPR was devoted primarily to the study of crisis and post-mortem apparitions—i.e., "ghosts", to use common parlance. The society's founders were keenly interested in the possibility that we survive death, so their concern with the subject was certainly understandable. The tide changed, however, toward the end of the society's first decade. The reason for this reorientation stemmed from the discovery in Boston of the society's first reliable trance medium. Leonore Piper was a young housewife who lived in the fashionable suburb of Arlington Heights. She first developed her psychic talents while consulting a blind clairvoyant/healer in her home city. She suddenly slipped into a trance during one of his healing circles and became a medium in spite of herself. It wasn't long before she was conducting private sittings. She was never a professional Spiritualist and would probably never have come to prominence within psychical research circles but for a single fortuitous event. In 1885 she was visited by the mother-in-law of William James, the eminent Harvard philosopher and psychologist. The elderly woman was so impressed by Mrs. Piper's performance that she reported back to the psychologist about her discovery. He in turn was intrigued by the report, and a few days later he and his wife visited Mrs. Piper. Several of Prof. James's own deceased relatives purported to communicate during this séance, often giving their proper names and concise information concerning their former lives. To say that the Harvard professor was impressed would be an understatement. His final conclusion was that either Mrs. Piper knew his family history intimately (though they had never met), or that she possessed some sort of paranormal faculties. "My later knowledge of her sittings and personal acquaintance with her," he later wrote in his report, "has led me to absolutely reject the former explanation, and to believe that she has supernormal powers."

This "personal acquaintance" was firmly established over a period of eighteen months, during which time the psychologist personally supervised Mrs. Piper's mediumship. He made the arrangements for prospective clients to sit with her, but even under these strict conditions, Mrs. Piper's spirit communicators successfully convinced her sitters that they were speaking with the dead.

William James eventually contacted the SPR in England about Leonore Piper, and they brought her to Europe in 1889 for even more stringent tests. She performed brilliantly as usual, and some of the SPR founders became personally convinced of life after death through their sittings with her. Even the most skeptical SPR leaders came to believe that she was at least a gifted thought-reader. They decided to employ her services for more extended research, so when she returned to Boston, Richard Hodgson took up the continuing investigation of her powers. He spent the next several years supervising her sittings, wrote two reports on his findings, and continued his research until he died in 1905.

The subject of psychical research first came to James Hyslop's attention in 1886, when he read an article in *The Nation* magazine. The report dealt with a crisis apparition case—i.e., a case in which a phantom is seen at the exact time the person projecting it dies. Hyslop was skeptical, but he made some inquiries into the case and ended up being impressed by it. Despite this brief foray into the world of the paranormal, Hyslop dropped the study of psychical research for two years. His interest was reignited, however, in 1889 when he attended a lecture given by Richard Hodgson in New York. This talk concerned his research into the strange case of Ansel Bourne, an evangelist from Coventry, Rhode Island, who suddenly lost his memory in 1887. The poor man was subsequently controlled by a secondary personality who moved to Pennsylvania where the "original" Bourne regained his primary personality two months later. (Richard Hodgson and William James had both studied the case, finding that Bourne could trace his travels when hypnotized.) After hearing this lecture, Hyslop joined the SPR, became directly involved with the U.S. branch, and began seriously studying the society's publications. He also started discussing the subject with his Columbia students—to the predictable annoyance of his colleagues, who relieved him of his psychology classes! Soon Hyslop found himself confined to teaching epistemology and metaphysics.

Despite his enthusiasm for psychical research, Hyslop's interest in the field remained primarily intellectual. But this state of affairs changed radically in 1898. During the previous several years, the professor had read many reports concerning Leonore Piper, and he was simultaneously becoming less sure how the case could be explained except by believing in some form of life after death. His curiosity was so piqued that in 1898/9 he undertook a series of sittings with the psychic in Boston. These sittings changed his life forever.

Since he wanted to be totally in control of the sittings, Hyslop booked the experiments through Richard Hodgson. Mrs. Piper was specifically left in the dark concerning who her future client would be. Since he and Mrs. Piper had once met, Hyslop drove by carriage to the Piper home wearing a mask. He only removed the disguise when the sittings were in progress and the psychic was entranced. He replaced it before she regained consciousness. *

Despite the fact that the professor tried to conceal his identity, the sittings—which extended into a protracted series—were relatively productive. He was placed in contact with four of his deceased relatives, including his father, and their personations were entirely convincing. Often the communicators would discuss very private incidents from their lives or they simply reminisced. His father particularly liked to discuss his strong religious beliefs, which was totally characteristic of him. But even more astonishing was the way each of the communicators often mentioned specific people they and the professor had both known. Since the professor's relatives had been private people living far away in Ohio, it is unlikely that Mrs. Piper had come by this information normally.

Hyslop realized, of course, that there were two possible explanations for these communications. Either they emanated from genuine discarnate entities, or the psychic had successfully extracted the information from his own mind. The researcher grappled with this issue for months, but when he finally produced his lengthy report on Leonore Piper in 1901, he favored the spiritistic theory.

"I am satisfied," he stated in that report, "that the evidence forces us in our rational minds to tolerate the spiritistic theory as rationally possible and respectable." But his personal predilection was to endorse the spiritistic theory completely.

"Whatever supernormal power we may be pleased to attribute to Mrs. Piper's secondary personalities," he stated, "it would be difficult to make me believe that these secondary personalities could have completely reconstituted the mental personality of my dead relatives. To admit this would involve me in too many improbabilities. I prefer to

---

*This all struck Mrs. Piper rather comically. She was upstairs when her visitor's cab arrived, looked out a window, and immediately recognized the sitter. She played the charade with good humor, though. But she had no way of knowing Hyslop was scheduled for the sitting until she first saw him leave the carriage.

believe that I have been talking to my dead relatives in person; it is simpler."

By the turn of the century, Hyslop—encouraged by his work with Mrs. Piper—was devoting considerable time to psychical research. Since the ASPR was merely a branch of the British organization, he began thinking in terms of a society free from European constraints. But these plans were bound to be forestalled by some traumatic events that befell the energetic scholar. The first blow came when his wife died in October 1900. They had been married for only nine years, and the tragedy left Hyslop a widower with three children to care for. His own health faltered the next year, resulting in a breakdown from overwork complicated by emerging tuberculosis. These drastic occurrences prompted him to leave Columbia University. He was bound never to permanently return to teaching. He traveled to Vermont to take up gold mining, but later settled back in New York for a career in writing. It was a productive career, and by 1905 he produced his book *Problems of Philosophy*, which is probably his most important contribution to the field. This signal year was conspicuous in another way, too, for Richard Hodgson suddenly collapsed during a handball game on December 20. Even though he had been a vigorous sportsman, the collapse proved fatal. The fate of the American Society for Psychical Research now seemed in jeopardy.

No one felt the sting of Hodgson's death more intensely than Hyslop, who was nearly thrown into despair by his colleague's death. Not only did it signal the possible cessation of the ASPR's operations, but even future research with Leonore Piper also suddenly seemed questionable.

It was, no doubt, fortuitous that Prof. Hyslop had by this time managed to collect a $25,000 fund for the formation of a new psychical research society. He and some of his fellow enthusiasts had incorporated the organization, but the society still existed solely on paper. Several lines of communication were opened with the SPR in Great Britain, and in 1906 the ASPR temporarily closed its doors for a total reorganization. The new ASPR was established in New York and commenced operations in 1907, the same year that Hyslop began work on the Thompson case. Hyslop's original plan was to make the newly structured and independent ASPR part of a more wide-ranging society, but his proposed American Institute for Scientific Research never existed except for the society.

This brief history of psychical research's early years sets the stage for the Thompson/Gifford case. By 1907, Hyslop was not the only psychical researcher who believed in the reality of spirit communication. But neither he nor any of his British colleagues had even encountered anything resembling spirit obsession before. They knew that the Spiritualists believed in this curious phenomenon, but they had never come by any scientific evidence that established its existence. So when Frederic Thompson first met Hyslop in January 1907, it makes sense that the professor wasn't keen on spending much effort on the case. The offices of the ASPR were cluttered with boxes of reports and records that the perplexed professor was still sorting through, and the infant organization badly needed more funds. It was probably for these reasons that Hyslop let Frederic Thompson conduct his own fieldwork in the New Bedford area, while he agreed to take the sketches into custody. The case also probably didn't strike the professor as promising enough for protracted study. The following six months proved him wrong, as should be obvious from Chapter 2. So after the psychic elements of the case became irrefutable, Hyslop threw himself into the Thompson/Gifford investigation with a vengeance.

Although it was clear that Thompson's bizarre experiences were not pathological, proving that the jeweler was in contact with the dead was a different issue. By the beginning of 1908, Hyslop fully realized the importance of the case. Not only did it promise to demonstrate the irrefutable existence of psychic phenomena, but it also documented a hitherto unrecognized form of mediumship—the involuntary influence of the dead over the living. The foundations for the study of spirit obsession had been laid, and it was time for Hyslop to follow the clues. For this reason his interest began focusing on the skill displayed in Frederic Thompson's paintings. The psychic researcher had to discover, not whether his subject was being influenced by the deceased R. Swain Gifford, but to what extent this influence was clouding Thompson's life.

By 1908, Frederic Thompson had gone beyond simple sketching and was copiously producing full-scale, well-executed oil paintings. Not only was he producing them regularly, he was even selling them for profit. Since the jeweler claimed relatively little training in art, this fact was in itself phenomenal. But even more uncanny was his apparent ability to catch the precise technique and style of Gifford's previous work.

The first full-scale painting Thompson produced was sold in New York to James B. Townsend, who was then the prominent editor of the

American Art News. This was certainly impressive, especially for somebody whose previous work had been rough-painting photographs. When
Hyslop learned of the sale, he personally contacted the critic and asked
him to evaluate the painting. Sometime after meeting together, Townsend sent the following statement, dated May 29, 1908, to the professor:

> I would say that when he [Thompson] first brought the same [painting]
> to me some months ago, I said at once "this has all the characteristics of
> the late Swain Gifford." I was amazed to have Mr. Thompson tell me
> that he had never seen any of Gifford's pictures when he painted this
> canvas.* I was so pleased with the picture, as it recalls so strongly the
> work of Gifford, which I have always admired, that I purchased it from
> Mr. Thompson, and it now hangs over my desk in the office as I write.
> There is surely something of the spirit of Swain Gifford in Mr. Thomp-
> son's work, but I fear that art lovers who do not know Mr. Thompson
> and therefore who might question his veracity would say that he is an
> imitator of Gifford's work and must have long studied it to produce can-
> vases so like the originals in subject and treatment.

This report confirmed Hyslop's own impression that Gifford's presence
and style were coming through Frederic Thompson in no uncertain
terms. He felt that the craftsman was tapping into more than merely the
deceased's memories.

Hyslop's feelings were corroborated further when he consulted with
a colleague from Columbia about the paintings. Prof. Arthur Dow was
then a professor of fine arts at Teachers College, a component college
of Columbia University. Dow was enlisted in March 1908 to examine
the subject's paintings, although he was told nothing concerning their
history or connection to the late Swain Gifford. Hyslop only explained
that he wanted his colleague to examine the paintings to see if, to his
mind, they resembled the work of any other artist he knew. With this
simple goal in mind, Hyslop visited his colleague's office on March 15,
laid out several of the sketches and asked his colleague's opinion. Professor Dow's first reactions were not recorded, but later that day, the
researcher took Dow to Thompson's residence in New York. He was
impressed by what he saw, for he later wrote back to Hyslop;

---

*This was the painting Frederic Thompson produced during the summer of 1905,
before learning of Gifford's death. R. Swain Gifford had only been sketching when
Thompson met with him, and the jeweler had still not seen any of the painter's finished
oils.

The first pictures shown were marines; one of which had a vague resemblance to Winslow Homer's work. Another landscape had a suggestion of Innes. Soon appeared pictures of marshes and dunes, of moraines and storm-blown trees. Some of the compositions were very bold and unusual schemes both in mass and in color. He painted the great rolling hills with the sea beyond—the wild scenery of [Naushon]—the violence of storms—a great variety of subjects all with a dash and force that were most surprising. Nevertheless, there was always the lack of those qualities that would make them pictures of power.

Dow was surprised to learn that this promising artist had been painting for only a short while. (Remember that at this time Dow knew nothing of the bizarre story behind the paintings.) He opined that the artist was obviously familiar "with all the methods of handling oil paint" and that his brushwork "was that of a man who had a long experience in painting."

It was only after viewing several more of the paintings that Dow spontaneously noted that

I then clearly recognized the style of R. Swain Gifford. This was more marked as he went on showing his work. The composition and technique resembled Gifford's but always fell short of his finer qualities of tone and color.

Dow was also impressed by Thompson's ability to depict fine relationships between sunlight and shadow. The correspondence between the style of the paintings and Gifford's style was so strong that Dow was embarrassed to point it out, fearing that he might insult Thompson by implying that he was copying the celebrated artist.

Whatever the nature of the paintings, Frederic Thompson's career seemed to be taking off. His work was being appreciated by several patrons in the city, and his sales were picking up. Thompson was even approached by a dealer who suggested that he forge Giffords.

Luckily, in retrospect we have more than the opinions of the two New York critics to go by. Throughout the early part of 1908, Hyslop gathered the opinions of other artists in New York who were familiar with Thompson's paintings. He sought the opinions of three professional painters—Henry W. Ranger, James Carroll Beckwith, and Ben Foster—in May 1908. These artists knew nothing of the strange story behind their production, and Hyslop was curious as to whether they would spontaneously see the resemblance between these paintings and Gifford's.

The results of this project were diverse. Each of them studied several of the paintings, although it is not clear under what conditions they were first seen. Two of the painters were unimpressed with the work. Carroll Beckwith reported back to the researcher that "they show more feeling than knowledge and I am inclined to think show more influence of other pictures than of study of nature." Beckwith continued by saying that "the resemblance to R. Swain Gifford's work is remote and in his method I do not trace any resemblance."

Hyslop took pains in his report to emphasize that Beckwith saw only some of the paintings, but this doesn't weaken the fact that Ben Foster's reactions were similar. He apparently spent considerable time examining the paintings and wrote to Hyslop that "the resemblance to Swain Gifford's work is slight and due largely to the similarity of themes." The exception to these critiques came from Henry Ranger, who didn't dismiss the paintings but found their resemblance to Gifford's work superficial.*

Despite these developments, Hyslop still harbored suspicions that Thompson's experiences were partly pathological. So early in 1908 he decided to get some medical opinions. He extended his "blind" evaluations of the case from painters to physicians. For if the true source of the subject's obsession lay beyond the grave, believed Hyslop, his case would not fit the pattern of any recognized pathology.

In order to implement this plan, Hyslop persuaded a friend to help. Dr. Titus Bull was a prominent neurologist in New York who lived close to Hyslop's own residence on the Upper West Side. He was casually interested in psychical research and would later become involved with the American Society for Psychical Research. (He was not a member in 1908.) While studying the stylistic elements of the case, Hyslop asked Dr. Bull to have his subject evaluated by a fellow clinician. Bull, in turn, sent Thompson to the chief neurologist of a local hospital, who turned the case over to a colleague. Dr. Charles C. At-

---

*According to Hyslop's report, Thompson met with Henry Ranger on May 25, 1906. This is probably a misprint for May 25, 1908. Carroll Beckwith, Henry Ranger, and Ben Foster were well known in their day, although no biographical data for them is given by Hyslop. Carroll Beckwith (b. 1852) won numerous awards for his paintings, and his work hung in the National Museum in Washington, D.C. Ben Foster (b. 1852) won the Carnegie prize of the National Academy of Design in 1906, and Henry Ranger's (b. 1858) work hangs (or once hung) in the Metropolitan Museum of Art.

wood (whose credentials are not cited by Hyslop) interviewed Frederic Thompson sometime in March and reported back to the ASPR on April 5. Dr. Atwood's reaction was that Thompson probably suffered from incipient paranoia, but he was surprised by the fact that the subject realized his experiences were extraordinary. Since the physician could find no toxic causative factor for the subject's experiences (such as evidence of a brain lesion), he couldn't fully explain the case.

The results of all these various evaluations were mixed, but as the months went by, Hyslop became progressively convinced that the deceased R. Swain Gifford really was behind his subject's problems. There was only one line of investigation left: Hyslop realized that he should make direct contact with the deceased artist. Since he was sure that Thompson wasn't going insane, he wanted to open more direct lines of communication with Gifford. The professor wasted no time. He began making plans to establish contact with Gifford while Dr. Atwood was making his final evaluations.

Hyslop scheduled the first séance for the evening of April 3. The scene was the home of Margaret Gaule, the same psychic who had sat for Frederic Thompson the previous year. Miss Gaule, who did not go into trance, psychically picked up the presence of a discarnate entity guiding her client, but little else of significance was communicated. A subsequent sitting was held the next evening, but the same problem arose.

The meager results of these sessions caused Hyslop to change the focus of the experiments by taking Thompson to Boston, where they began to work with Minnie Soule. She conducted what was to be the first of several trance sessions for the two psychic explorers on April 10 and 11, and these sittings seemed to bear fruit. Several pieces of information directly pertinent to the life and death of R. Swain Gifford were picked up by Mrs. Soule or delivered via her "spirit" guides during these preliminary sittings. Since the first real intimations that Gifford was trying to get through to the researchers were now finally coming to light, Hyslop brought Mrs. Soule to New York on the first of June and installed her in a hotel where he could schedule daily séances. Mrs. Soule's usual spirit guide communicated copiously during the first sitting and insisted several times that a painter was influencing the client. These descriptions became more pertinent to the life of R. Swain Gifford as the sittings progressed on June 2 and 3. Some communications directly relating to the deceased artist were received again on June 4, 1908, when the two researchers returned to Mrs. Soule's hotel for a fourth séance.

It must be remembered that during the course of these experiments, Minnie Soule never knew her client's identity. Hyslop insisted that Frederic Thompson enter and leave the room while she was entranced. This plan worked well, since her trance proceeded in specific stages. So before continuing with a description of these experiments, the procedure she used to conduct her sittings should be explained.

Minnie Soule would sit at a desk or table at the beginning of a session, with her client positioned in front of or beside her. Her eyes closed when she entered trance, and she would first enter a subliminal phase of consciousness in which she became clairvoyant. She would deliver her information vocally but would not subsequently recall what she said. (Sometimes, however, she would be directly controlled by her spirit guide during the subliminal state, who would speak through her.) This primary stage of the trance could continue for a considerable period of time, sometimes for more than an hour. When the trance deepened still further, Mrs. Soule would stop speaking and her hand would begin making scrawling movements. This signaled her sitter or experimenter to place a pencil in her hand, and the psychic—or the personality using her body—would write through it. When the séance drew to a close, the phases would reverse themselves, and she would vocalize her communications. She would then gradually awaken to the external world.

During the séance of June 4, R. Swain Gifford first tried to communicate with Hyslop and Thompson more directly. The sitting commenced at four o'clock that afternoon. Hyslop employed his usual procedure of keeping the jeweler out of the room until the psychic entered trance. Several deceased friends of the professor purported to communicate during the subliminal phase of Mrs. Soule's trance, but the psychic eventually focused her powers on the alleged presence of R. Swain Gifford. It soon became apparent to the sitters that she sensed the presence of a communicator who had died painfully and who wished to establish contact with the sitter. (This was true enough, since Gifford had died from rheumatism of the heart.) She also correctly sensed that the communicator had taken a journey right before his death. (Gifford and his wife had gone to Weehawken, New Jersey, to walk the docks a week before his death). Then she began to pick up the painter's presence directly.

"He is . . . he seems . . . I think he smokes, you know," she stated while still deeply entranced. "It is something that he holds in his mouth. He doesn't seem to be always smoking but it seems as though he holds something in his mouth, you know, quite a lot; really, like a . . . like a . . . I think it is like a little cigarette."

Although the late R. Swain Gifford didn't smoke, Hyslop learned that he did have a peculiar habit to which this impression obviously referred. While he worked, Gifford was in the habit of placing a twig in his mouth. This was certainly an evidential communication, and as far as Hyslop was concerned, it finally seemed as if the deceased artist were ready to communicate with them. The sitting continued as Mrs. Soule correctly described a painting that the deceased painter had executed, his home, and the fact that he worked in two different locations. (This was true, since Gifford worked both from his studio in Nonquitt and from another in town.) Several other possible allusions to the artist were offered as the sitting proceeded. But the best was yet to come, for as the session came to its close, Mrs. Soule sensed Swain Gifford's presence even more forcefully.

"He is so elated over his power to return and finish his work," she stated, "that it is a joy to see him."

Since the sittings were finally bearing psychic fruit, Thompson and Hyslop naturally asked the communicator just what he was trying to accomplish. Mrs. Soule replied (while still in trance) by describing a scene the communicator was trying to impress on her client.

"It is a misty day . . ." she described clairvoyantly, "on the old road or a misty day in the marshes. I do not know which. It has come out friend a number of times that a misty day that is . . . a soft day would be a good subject."

This rather confused communication made sense to the sitters, for in his own work R. Swain Gifford had been partial to such scenes—scenes that had plagued Frederic Thompson's mind continually since 1905.

"As I told you," the psychic continued while speaking for the deceased communicator, "the grays were the hardest but they came along all right, when yellow showed up more. That was early in the work."

This message contained deep personal meaning for Thompson, since it referred to a problem concerning his painting with which he was currently grappling. But after that bit of evidence, the sitting came to a speedy end and Mrs. Soule gradually emerged from trance.

The next sitting to contact Gifford was held that night. Hyslop and Thompson must have been extremely excited by Mrs. Soule's revelations, since they drove immediately from the hotel to Margaret Gaule's residence. It's probable that Hyslop was hoping that she would pick up on the same information communicated earlier that day, thus producing "cross-reference" between the two psychics. Prof. Hyslop's plan was a good one, but he miscalculated his timing. By this time, news of the case was being reported in the press, and when he and Thompson arrived at Miss Gaule's home, she immediately realized who her client was. She gave a reading anyway, the sitting was successful, and the psychic picked up some highly detailed information concerning the deceased artist. But, in retrospect, it is difficult to determine what role her own inferences or extrasensory perception played in this session.

It is probably because of this problem that Hyslop phased out research with Miss Gaule for the remainder of the case. It would now be up to Minnie Soule to provide the next clues in establishing Gifford's identity.

The eighth sitting to contact the elusive R. Swain Gifford was held at Minnie Soule's hotel room the next day. During this session the psychic successfully described some of the late artist's furniture and his paintbrushes. It was only after these preliminaries, though, that the sitting really began to progress.

By now it was clear that the communicator was an artist and that he was somehow linked to Frederic Thompson. The problem was that, even considering the evidential information the communicator and Mrs. Soule were delivering, the entity was still refusing to properly identify himself. This trend continued during the June 5 sitting even though the communicator's identity was obvious. Even before beginning the writing stage of her trance, Mrs. Soule was focusing on the "unknown" painter. So Hyslop turned the subject to the communicator's earthly work.

> *Hyslop:* What particular kind of objects was he especially fascinated with in painting pictures?
> *Mrs. Soule:* Well, I suppose you mean whether it is boats or trees or things like that, don't you?
> *Hyslop:* Yes.
> *Mrs. Soule:* When you first spoke to me, I looked at boats, you know, but I don't think that is it. . . . Do you know yourself?

> *Hyslop:* Yes.
> *Mrs. Soule:* I really don't see, yet. Now, wait a moment and I will see if I can. You know, yesterday everything I saw was so still, so quiet, so beautiful, you know, those little dreamy things. Today I am getting all activity. I think it was bits of industry, bits of activity, one thing after another, you know, that seems to come before him. More water; oh, so much more water than I saw yesterday! And—there is some living thing you know, but I don't see.
> *Hyslop:* All right.

Shortly after these communications were received, Mrs. Soule described a scene depicting an overhang with a boat underneath. She also saw gnarled oaks. This vision confused her since the location she was seeing was generally devoid of trees.

Unfortunately, the sitting began to deteriorate at this point and was apparently coming to a close. But to the surprise of both Hyslop and Thompson, Mrs. Soule's communicator suddenly began directly controlling her!

> *Mrs. Soule's "communicator":* I have been to him as in dreams at times.
> *Hyslop:* Yes, I understand.
> *Mrs. Soule's "communicator":* And will do so again.
> *Hyslop:* Thank you.
> *Mrs. Soule's "communicator":* Ask him if he remembers an incident when standing on a bridge and looking down he saw . . . pictures in the water like reflections and a great desire came over him to paint.
> *Hyslop:* Yes, he says he remembers that well. Thank you.
> *Mrs. Soule's "communicator":* I was there and followed him for some time. Sometimes, in the old days, he was so disheartened and blue as if he had not found the right path but now he is far happier and life seems more complete.

When the séance was over, Thompson explained to Hyslop that this event had occurred during his first visit to the Elizabeth Islands some months previously. While standing on a bridge, his focus had become fixed on the play of the reflections in the water below. The slight dissociation caused by the experience caused him to become ecstatic, and he found himself compelled to paint. He further claimed that the event helped him conquer an overwhelming depression.

This sitting was so impressive that Hyslop couldn't contain himself. He immediately left for Nonquitt to consult with Gifford's widow and hopefully to find the scene previously described by Mrs. Soule.

This trip was a turning point in the investigation. The researcher learned from Mrs. Gifford that the psychic's description perfectly matched a sketch her husband had once drawn. The model for the sketch was a cliff near their home. Gnarled oaks and brush highlighted the scene, while a boat was penciled in in the distance. This was all very impressive information, so Hyslop remained in the New Bedford area and spent considerable time searching in vain for the exact location of the scene. This setback was perhaps inevitable, though, for Mrs. Gifford had previously warned him that her husband used the location to suggest the scene. He did not exactly reproduce it in his sketch.

Even though the case was finally progressing to Hyslop's satisfaction, Mrs. Soule's employment in New York had ended. She had returned home to Boston so Hyslop visited her there on July 15 for a further séance. The session was productive and the ostensible Gifford communicated easily, though still without giving his name. The entity seemed cognizant of Hyslop's trip to Nonquitt and even began the sitting by asking about it! The professor was enormously pleased by this incident, since the psychic had been told nothing about his week's activities. Since Hyslop still hoped to find the scene that had served as Gifford's model for the cliff sketch, he took the opportunity to ask the communicator to describe it. The communicator was not cooperative, though. The entity began instead to describe a misty marsh scene with a red sunset. (Hyslop later learned from Mrs. Gifford that her husband had painted just such a scene, too.)

The congenial visitor from the beyond didn't focus on the scene for long. He inquired about Frederic Thompson (whom Hyslop had left in New York) and explained that he was still trying to influence him. When Mrs. Soule entered the writing stage of her trance, the communicator added that he had sent a personification of death to the jeweler, complete with a beckoning angel.

"It is for him," explained the communicator through psychic writing. "He has seen it in a sort of dream. It will come. The angel to be the bright future. Death is the angel between the past and future."

It must have been extremely important for the communicator to deliver this message. Mrs. Soule's subliminal trance had been brief during this sitting, her writing beginning within only fifteen minutes. But the spirit presence of Swain Gifford didn't remain long after this message was delivered either, but departed within a few moments. The rest of the short séance was devoted to some messages purporting to come from the deceased Richard Hodgson, whom Hyslop was also trying to reach during this phase of his research.

Despite the urgency of this message, the communication made no sense to Hyslop until he returned to New York. While working either at the ASPR or at his home on June 17, he was visited by Frederic Thompson's wife. She was extremely upset over her husband's mental state. It seems that three days before—the day before the sitting in Boston with Soule—Thompson had experienced a startling vision representing death. He had sketched it, and Mrs. Thompson now wanted Hyslop to examine it. She produced two sketches, both somewhat resembling the scene described in Boston.

It now looked as if Hyslop were close to establishing two-way contact with the celebrated Swain Gifford. But despite these gains, he was becoming impatient with the sittings. While Mrs. Soule had successfully communicated hundreds of bits of evidence concerning Gifford's identity, never once had the communicator forthrightly identified himself. The sittings in New York and Boston had reached their climax with the communicator's description of his own paintings. But the denouement of the case had not yet been realized, and Hyslop was eager to resolve it. This final resolution of the Thompson/Gifford case had to wait several months, though, for the June 15 sitting in Boston was the last séance he conducted with Mrs. Soule. Hyslop discontinued work on the case for six months and only returned to it the following December. He never explained in his report why he suddenly withdrew from the case, but only stated that by December 1908, "circumstances made it desirable to implicate [sic] further mediumistic experiments in an attempt to solve the problem before me." What these circumstances constituted will never be known, although they possibly referred to some further distress on Frederic Thompson's part.

Whatever the cause of Hyslop's concern, he recruited another psychic to help unravel the Gifford case in December. Mrs. Willis M. Cleaveland lived in Virginia where she was the wife of a prominent clergyman. She had played with planchette writing throughout childhood, but began systematically working with the procedure in 1895. At first she received rather wild communications concerning life on other planets. These, no doubt, emanated from her own psyche, since they were received shortly after she read an article by Percival Lowell (the famous astronomer) in *The Atlantic Monthly.* (The piece concerned the canals of Mars.) Mrs. Cleaveland also received communications from some of her own deceased relatives, but then her mediumship went into a latent phase that lasted five years. When her "psychic powers" returned in September 1900, these fanciful communications returned as well, complete with drawings and an extraterrestrial alphabet! These nonsensical messages finally dwindled and she began receiving more conventional spiritistic messages.

Reverend and Mrs. Cleaveland contacted Hyslop in December 1901, but the (then) Columbia University professor hadn't been impressed by their story. He felt that the case was of some psychological interest, however, so he kept tabs on it for the next several years. He even brought Mrs. Cleaveland to New York to personally supervise some of her sittings. Slowly and gradually—and perhaps prompted by Hyslop's caring tutelage—the psychic finally started channeling evidential communications from the spirit world. Hyslop thereupon began publishing reports on this new psychic, although he concealed her identity by calling her "Mrs. Smead" in his books and papers.

"The case of Mrs. Smead began," he wrote in 1906 for the *Annals of Psychical Science,* ". . . in the most naive secondary personality and ended in the production of phenomena much like those of Mrs. Piper, showing a gradual development from purely secondary consciousness to what might possibly be complicated with occasionally spiritistic messages."

By the end of 1907, Hyslop's faith in Mrs. Cleaveland's mediumship was complete. He stated in his book *Psychical Research and the Resurrection,* published that year, that the case for her psychic sense was "beyond any question whatever."

Hyslop recruited Mrs. Cleaveland for a series of five sessions to contact Swain Gifford. He brought her to New York from Virginia especially for that purpose, and each of the sittings took place in her hotel room. Mrs. Cleaveland knew nothing concerning the case she was working on, and Hyslop kept her in the dark concerning it throughout the series. He even made sure that none of the newspapers in Virginia had reported on the Thompson/Gifford case. He also employed the same protocol he previously used with Mrs. Soule—i.e., by not letting Frederic Thompson enter the séance room until the psychic was entranced.

Hyslop and Frederic Thompson first sat with Mrs. Cleaveland on the mornings of December 1 and 2, but the sittings were relatively disappointing. Despite the meager results, the psychic did manage to determine and state through her trance writing that a painter wished to speak with the sitters.

The third session on December 7 represented a radical improvement. By this time Prof. Hyslop had procured some of the late Gifford's paintbrushes from his widow, and since the psychic had previously identified her primary communicator as a painter, the researcher allowed her to see and hold them. He was hoping that this contact with some of Gifford's possessions would help focus the sittings. The researcher's hunch was correct, and the evidential value of the sittings improved instantly. This new development in the case prompted Hyslop and Thompson to visit Mrs. Cleaveland the next morning for a fourth experiment.

The séance that constituted the climax to the Thompson case, and to the months Hyslop had devoted to unraveling it, commenced the next day. The sitting began promptly at ten o'clock that morning. Mrs. Cleaveland sat before a table, grabbed a pencil and some paper, cleared her mind, and proceeded to enter trance. Soon her hand began swaying, and her head fell to the side. "While the pencil point was resting on the paper, and before the writing began," commented Hyslop, "there was a sort of helpless swaying of the hand and pencil without any movement across the paper, as if trying to begin writing. This occurred several times, and when the writing did begin, it was unusually rapid for the first attempts."

Then the formal writings began.

"Coming. Yes, we are coming. Wait for us," wrote the entranced psychic.

It wasn't long before Mrs. Cleaveland was deeply entranced. It was only then that Prof. Hyslop got up from the table, opened the door, and let Frederic Thompson enter the room. He was determined to get Gifford to identify himself, and he reminded the communicator of his wish. He then gave the psychic the brushes to hold. The persona communicating through the psychic began to grow confused and asked Hyslop to leave the room, for he obviously wanted to be alone with Thompson.

"Have you a message for me this morning?" asked Thompson. It was the first time he had ever been left alone with the psychic, so he was probably nervous.

The spirit communicator responded immediately to the sitter's presence. "You asked this—them to give my work to you," the discarnate entity scribbled. "Did you ask them to give my work to you? Yes. Do not neglect it."

Thompson replied that he wouldn't.

"I want you to have it," continued the communicator.

Then slowly but steadily, the ostensible R. Swain Gifford tried to communicate his initials. These trials were partially successful, but then the communicator began drawing sketches through Mrs. Cleaveland's hand—sketches that precisely matched visions and drawings that Thompson had recently produced in private! The communicator next reminisced about his life on the Elizabeth Islands, and talked of his joy in sketching there.

Mrs. Cleaveland's communicator:	It was not far away . . . and . . .
Thompson:	Was it there you sketched?
Mrs. Cleaveland's communicator:	I told you it was sketched there. . . . yes . . . and I did other landscapes there too . . . when I was small. Yes.
Thompson:	Did the island have any other charm for you?
Mrs. Cleaveland's communicator:	Swimming was a sport of which I was very fond. Yes.
Thompson:	Yes, good.
Mrs. Cleaveland's communicator:	There on this island shore in . . . [illegible]
Thompson:	I do not understand the middle word.
Mrs. Cleaveland's communicator:	Island shore . . . yes . . . on it.
Thompson:	Yes, I understand. Do you remember anything else you loved there?
Mrs. Cleaveland's communicator:	Cottage. Yes . . . mother too. Yes, was there, yes . . . and we used to worry her for fear . . . we would get drowned. Yes.

Shortly after this exchange Mrs. Cleaveland's hand began to sketch again. The drawing depicted a gnarled old tree. This type of scene seemed to be a special signal from Gifford, since he had often focused on gnarled trees while sketching. (Remember, too, that similar scenes had haunted Thompson's mind since 1905). The communicator continued by trying to write the name of the specific island where he once lived.

"Will come again," wrote Mrs. Cleaveland under the communicator's influence. "Do not forget my paintings. Do not forget the work I asked you to do."

"You want me to keep on?" asked Thompson.

"Yes. And finish mine also. Thank you." The reply was clear. "I must go. Do not want to."

Before departing the communicator finally managed to sign his messages, and the psychic's hand scrawled out the initials "R.S.G." The communicator began reminiscing again, but then his scribbled chatter began to dissipate. Gradually the spirit presence faded back into the cloudy unknown that had originally given him birth, and the séance ended shortly after. The messages were complete and obvious, and as far as Hyslop was concerned, the case had reached its conclusion. The researcher undertook no additional experiments to contact R. Swain Gifford and withdrew from further involvement in the case. He was convinced he had proved the reality of life after death and that Frederic Thompson had been the recipient of Gifford's influence and talents. There was simply nothing more to accomplish or research. It was all reminiscent of Henry James's *The Turn of the Screw*, in which the ghostly Peter Quince banishes himself by revealing his true identity.

Hyslop apparently learned nothing new concerning the Thompson/Gifford case after 1910. He included a chapter on the investigation in his book *Contact with the Other World* (which was published in 1919), but this was merely a summary of his previous report.

Whatever became of Frederic Thompson is something of a mystery. He told Hyslop in 1909 that he was still fixated on painting and sketching, and he never went back to the jewelry business. While researching his later life, I was able to discover the following pertinent information:

Frederic Thompson pursued his artistic career in New York and eventually became a member of the prestigious Salmagundi Club, whose members were all professional painters, in 1912. By this time he worked out of a studio at 126 West 23rd Street and lived just four blocks south. Later he relocated and took residence for several months on the island of Martha's Vineyard, across from the Elizabeth Islands near the New Bedford coast. Even at this time he hadn't abandoned his painting. During the summer of 1922, for instance, an exhibition of psychically inspired paintings and sketches was shown at the Anderson Galleries in New York City. Several of his paintings were featured, along with the work of four other painters who claimed inspiration from the world beyond. This show was reviewed in the June 10, 1922, issue of *The New York Times*. The reviewer reported sanguinely that "none of the paintings and drawings is a great work of art, but many are striking."

The restless painter didn't exile himself from New York for long, and by 1926 he was still engaged in painting and sculpting while living on East 75th Street, a more fashionable neighborhood than the lower west side. It is tempting to wonder just how successful Thompson became; but by the 1920s his transformation from artisan to artist was obviously complete, and we can only conjecture to what extent R. Swain Gifford's personality continued to influence him. The latest I have been able to trace the painter is 1927, by which time he was living in Miami, Florida. He was still keeping up his membership in the Salmagundi Club and from what I can determine, he probably died sometime between 1927 and 1935.

CHAPTER 4

A Case of Incipient Obsession?

Toward the end of his life, James Hyslop would describe his research with Frederic Thompson as "the case which first suggested obsession to me." Obviously the case significantly influenced his subsequent work in psychical research, and the possible existence of spirit obsession would be central to his research for the rest of his life.

The strange case of Frederic Thompson proved to Hyslop that contacting the dead was a risky business. He knew, of course, that some psychics—such as Mrs. Piper—could enter into this contact and suffer no ill effects from the practice. But the ex-Columbia University professor was beginning to wonder whether a person could sometimes be involuntarily influenced by the dead. Can the dead force themselves on us?

The Thompson/Gifford research was not the only case that suggested they could. During the gradual unfolding of that research and its climax, Hyslop had been keeping his eye on a related case. This report, too, suggested that seemingly pathological symptoms could be the result of the paranormal influences of the dead.

Hyslop probably didn't consider this second case very evidential, since he didn't publish it until shortly before his death—i.e., after he had proved the reality of spirit obsession to his personal satisfaction. The crux of this case concerned some striking out-of-body experiences that his witness was undergoing—experiences that neither he nor Hyslop ever fully appreciated. He investigated the case primarily through correspondence, and only met the witness several months after learning of his plight.

S. Henry first contacted Hyslop after reading the professor's book *Science and a Future Life,* which had been published in the summer of 1905. He introduced himself in his first letter, dated April 24, 1906, as a thirty-six-year-old German immigrant. He explained that he was Lutheran by religion and a gymnast by profession. He had retired from the entertainment business five years previously and was currently living in upstate New Jersey, where he was employed by a wealthy woman as a gardener and coachman. The reason for his retirement, he proceeded to explain, was the devastating shock he had suffered because of his wife's serious illness and subsequent death the previous November. Since he never considered himself a religious man, he didn't believe in life after death. This was the principal cause of his current problems, for the prospect of never seeing or hearing from his wife again had thrown him into a profound depression.

This shock presaged a series of bizarre events in his life.

Two days after his wife's death, the ex-performer began to experience drastic changes in his personality. For one thing, he suddenly became sensitive to psychic presences in the barn where he lived. He wrote to Hyslop,

> On the 22nd (day after burial) when doing my chores in barn between 8 and 9 o'clock forenoon, I felt something a few feet away from me, and a little above my height. Somehow I did not turn around at once, and when I did, I saw, for a moment, what I may describe as a revolving circle of sparks and small flashes, and heard a fluttering as—well, a bird perhaps, would make. A great sweet feeling of comfort, delight, content, I cannot describe it, ran all over me. Now I have been reasoning with myself for nearly four months, that I never saw or heard any such thing, and after such reasoning, I am the more sure that I heard it.

Whatever the cause of this bizarre experience (which sounds like the result of a temporal lobe seizure in the brain), the incident profoundly disturbed the coachman.*

"Gradually a change came over me," he wrote to the professor. "I lost all interest in fiction and newspapers. Books, which I would never have cared for before became of the greatest interest to me, and I am

---

*Such neural firings in the brain tend to result in bizarre sensory experiences, such as strange sights, smells, and sounds. Sometimes these sensory experiences will be coupled with feelings of elation and religiosity, though bodily seizures rarely complicate the syndrome.

(in a fair and commonsense way) to be a convinced believer that our bodily death does not end all. I know now, after what I experienced, that something in me or out of me will meet my Sofia some time."

Henry was sure that in some way his experience related to the surviving soul of his wife.

Just why he decided to write to Hyslop is not clear from his letter, since he ended by writing that "I do not expect an answer from you, Prof. Hyslop, and I wish you to consider this letter a private matter between us." But the coachman underestimated the researcher, who found the letter somewhat provocative.

Hyslop wrote back to his correspondent right after receiving his letter. His common sense and skepticism were ripe, and he didn't know what to make of the letter. His first impression was that, with a bit of probing, he could discover a reasonable explanation for his correspondent's experience. So he asked him several specific questions concerning the incident, searching for just such a cause. The coachman answered immediately but still insisted that the experience had been a visitation from his deceased wife.

During the course of the subsequent months, Hyslop heard relatively little from his correspondent. The eager researcher had no way of knowing that his involvement with this problematic case would last two more years. It wasn't until sometime later that further psychic influences began to play a precarious role in Henry's life. These encounters prompted him to reestablish contact with Hyslop in 1907. It seems that during the previous summer, Henry had started to notice poltergeist like "raps" in the barn, where he was still living. He reported to Hyslop by mail that the sounds often occurred simultaneously with bizarre sensations and noises in his ears, which he described as "persistent singing" sounds. These sounds usually announced the arrival of visitors, his mail, or other daily events.

Fortunately, Henry fully realized that something extraordinary was occurring, so he decided to prove that the rappings were real. He wrote of the success of his experiments to Hyslop the following May.

> I investigated the knocks and got sure that dry wood, worms, wind, would not explain entirely. When I waited for knocks they would not come, but they put in an appearance unexpected, generally evenings. Finally I came to believe that my wife made her presence known to me and I was glad and thankful. Took neighboring coachman in my confidence and in my cottage one evening, to find out really if I only imagine these noises. I

sat on chair, he was reclining on couch, both of us talking about the resp. [respective] value of our horses, etc. No knocks. Friend waited an hour and told me laughingly that he would come again some other evening. Very suddenly came two loud knocks on the wall near my friend's head. Friend ran away and I could not induce him to come again to me after dark. But it convinced me that I heard right.

What had first been a suspicion was fast becoming a conviction, for the coachman was becoming increasingly convinced that his deceased wife was behind the poltergeist.

But things were soon to become even wilder.

One afternoon in June, about five o'clock, or so, I felt an irresistible impulse to go in my room and sit down. I did so. After a while I saw the air 4 or 5 feet away from me beginning to boil, get thick, look as smoke, then form itself to a small cloud, come to me and settle on my head. This happened again in the same way a few weeks later. I felt certain that it was my wife's spirit, and I was happy. When it made the 3rd appearance, again in the same way, I waited until it had settled on my head, then I put very gently my hands up to caress it and received a feeling as if my face and hands were covered with very fine, moist silk. As it was a very disagreeable and sickly feeling, I began having doubts as to what it was.

The coachman was now beginning to realize that something dreadful was happening to him. The paranormal events disrupting his life didn't end with these uncanny experiences either. Psychological changes were also disturbing his sleep. Upon awakening, he wrote to Hyslop, he would see wonderful scenery cascading before his eyes—usually projected against the wall opposite from his bed.

Despite these incidents, there was at first little evidence that Henry's personality was being influenced by the dead. But this all changed dramatically the following October, when he began to sense an evil presence entering his room at night.

I never forgot one night in October I woke up, wide awake but unable to move, resisting with all my strength a powerful, shapeless body of light which either was trying to get into me or else wanted to take me with it,

I do not know, I cannot explain it any better. I felt for days the effect of the battle in my limbs.*

Last winter the knocks changed; they came not so often and electric; they kept away from table and boxes, but went to walls and floor of room, they were louder and resembled the putting down a cane.

One evening during January, 1907, when I was undressing myself to go to bed, I heard behind me a very sharp, part whistle, part bad laugh, followed by the noise of a splash of water on the floor. I was frightened, it took me so unaware and there was no mistake about its reality. Then I got angry and spoke out loud something as: "This is not my wife; she would never frighten me so." I put on my clothes and spent the night sitting near the stove (with my gun near me). It has not come back again and I hope it never will.

The next morning I gave notice to my former employer that I would like to leave as soon as someone else would take my place.

By this time the coachman suspected that he was the object of some form of psychic attack. So he wrote once again to Hyslop on May 13, explaining how he was planning to handle the situation. Since the possible presence of his deceased wife was of consolation to him he wanted to determine whether he could receive written messages from her. He explained to Hyslop that if he could establish contact with his wife through automatic writing, she could help him understand what was happening in the barn and to him personally. This reasonable plan turned into a self-fulfilling prophecy, for Henry soon discovered that he could easily produce or receive writing by entering into a self-induced trance.

Unfortunately, this phase of his psychic development had a distressing side-effect. While engaged in the trance writing, he would suddenly find himself separated from his physical form, while electrical currents would simultaneously sizzle through his body. These sensa-

---

*The contemporary student of psychology could probably posit a perfectly reasonable explanation for some of these experiences. During our dreaming (REM, or rapid-eye-movement) sleep, the body becomes totally paralyzed. This paralysis is a biochemical reaction produced by the brain so that we don't thrash about in response to our dreams. When we awaken prematurely, sometimes the body fails to adjust instantly from the REM state back to normal. The result is a short period of post-sleep catalepsy, during which we sometimes see residual dream images. Since the sleeper is awake but still technically dreaming, he or she will experience these images and figures as objectively real—especially if they represent humanlike forms. These experiences can be extremely frightening, and some people interpret them as visitations from the beyond. (For more information on this interesting phenomenon, see David J. Hufford's excellent *The Terror that Comes in the Night*.)

tions were intensely unpleasant, and the frightened man could only conclude that he was being forced out of his body.

For example, on June 1 he wrote a brief letter to Hyslop in which he described his most recent experiment in contacting his wife through the writing. He had undertaken the experiment the night before, and the writing had come easily. During the session, however, he suddenly found himself out-of-the-body and—to his complete shock—he felt another being enter his body. Because of this incident, the coachman became firmly convinced that he was being possessed by a spirit of the dead. This fixation would slowly but surely drive him into the depth of insanity.

These curious but disturbing sensations led Henry to write a frantic letter to Hyslop a few days later. He was so frightened that he didn't dare go into trance again, and explained that several discarnates were currently fighting to control him! The experiences were so disorienting that, for the first time in his correspondence, the coachman beseeched Hyslop to personally meet with him in New Jersey.

It was at this point in the case that Hyslop became personally involved with Mr. Henry and his strange life. It was clear that the coachman desperately needed his help, so Hyslop lost little time acting on the request. He left for Englewood (a small city across the Hudson River north of New York City) the same day he received the summons. It isn't clear what Hyslop hoped to accomplish by making the trip, but it is doubtful that he felt that there were any paranormal dimensions to the case. Since he was well trained in the psychology of his era, he probably felt that Henry was undergoing some sort of psychotic episode. He was interested in the possibility that the raps his informant was reporting were genuine, but his primary goal in undertaking the trip was to personally observe Henry producing his trance writing. He most likely felt he could offer the coachman some guidance and help clear the case of its pathological elements.

During his interview with the professor that evening, Henry recounted the strange out-of-body experiences that he had been undergoing for some time. Hyslop probably didn't know what to make of the stories, since in 1907 virtually nothing was known about the phenomenology of out-of-body travel. (Popular interest in this subject would not burgeon until the 1920s, when a few chronic experiencers began publishing their records.) Hyslop merely listened to the reports and placed them in his extensive notes on the case.

He told me spontaneously in connection with his earlier experiences that he recalls an incident two or three days, or there-abouts, before his wife's death. She was in the hospital dying slowly. He went to visit her one day and saw her in such a state that he could not talk and did not feel like saying anything. All at once he said, "I felt myself out of my body above her for the first time in my life and yet she was with me. Her eyes had a strange light in them."

In the course of questioning him regarding his last experience received in his letter today I learned that, during the experiment and as he was going into trance, he felt as if an opening had been made in the back of his head and that he went out of this opening. He had a severe headache afterward. He also said that when the man who tried to write entered his body, he seemed to thrust his arm down his (Mr. H—'s) body beginning at the shoulder, and Mr. H.— also felt him all over his body.

This simple report is so strikingly significant that it is a shame Hyslop couldn't recognize its value. So I would like to examine these brief paragraphs in some detail before continuing with the description of this case and Hyslop's report on it. I think they provide an important clue concerning the nature of Henry's experiences that Hyslop totally missed.

Parapsychologists today know a great deal about the out-of-body experience—i.e., the sensation that the psyche can occasionally function outside the perimeters of the physical body. While the fact was hardly known when Hyslop was conducting his research, we now know that this phenomenon is very common. We also know that the sensation of "being pulled through the head" is a fairly widespread symptom of the experience. This curious feature of the out-of-body experience (OBE) first came to light in 1920, when a young British writer began publishing reports on his personal experiences. Hugh Callaway (who wrote under the pseudonym of Oliver Fox) was one of those rare people who could induce the experience either from the sleep state or purely at will. His first writings appeared in the *Occult Review*, which was a rather uncritical monthly magazine published in London, but later expanded them to produce a fascinating book on the subject. One notable feature of Callaway's youthful exploits was the strange phenomenology that accompanied his experiences. He often felt that he could leave the body through his head, and he wrote extensively about this sensation. He even dubbed this procedure the pineal "doorway," since the pineal gland is the legendary seat within the brain of mankind's psychic capacity. It is also extremely significant that Callaway (like Henry) found this method of leaving the body extremely unpleasant. In fact, Callaway eventually dropped this method completely in favor of other less stressful procedures, such as inducing the OBE from the pre- or post-sleep stage.

Looking back at Callaway's reports from a contemporary perspective, his experiences do not seem unique, since several parallels can be found in more current accounts.

Some four decades after Callaway began recording his personal experiences, the first critical studies of the OBE were undertaken by Dr. Robert Crookall in Great Britain. During the late 1950s he began collecting dozens of cases, although his primary interest was in collecting reports from people who had undergone spontaneous OBEs. (Such OBEs sometimes occur when a person is falling asleep or resting, or they can also result from an illness. They also often occur when a person has had a close brush with death.) Dr. Crookall's plan was to carefully map out the characteristics of the experience, hoping to determine whether the content of these reports conformed to specific patterns. It was during the course of this content analysis that he made a significant discovery. He found that the sensation of leaving the body through the head was not unusual. Dr. Crookall finished his research by publishing several hundred OBE cases, of which 7 percent included this specific phenomenology.

The importance of these cases can't be emphasized enough, for they bear critically on the experiences Henry was reporting in 1907. The skeptical reader might suggest that the coachman was simply going insane, possibly due to the stress of his wife's death. Earlier, I even suggested that Henry's strange experiences suspiciously resembled the reports of people suffering from temporal lobe seizures. But in retrospect, it seems difficult to explain the coachman's experiences solely by positing either of these possibilities. The parallels between his experiences and the well-established phenomenology of the OBE are simply too consistent.

But couldn't the OBE itself result from some form of brain seizure or from stress? This would be a natural possibility to consider, but it is unlikely for several reasons. For one thing, recent surveys indicate that 10 to 20 percent of the general public commonly report out-of-body experiences. This is a stunning number of people, and it demonstrates that the OBE is not generally pathological in nature. (By contrast, temporal lobe epilepsy is a relatively rare disorder.) Out-of-body experiences also occur primarily when the percipient is extremely relaxed, such as when he or she is beginning to fall asleep or in deep meditation. This would indicate that stress isn't usually a significant factor in their occurrence.

Recently, too, several researchers have slowly been collecting evidence that the OBE really might well entail a physical separation of the consciousness from the body. During a lengthy series of experiments conducted at the Durham, North Carolina–based Psychical Research Foundation in 1973, for example, one psychic proved that he could project to a distant location and make a kitten respond to his presence.

It therefore seems possible that Henry was probably undergoing genuine out-of-body experiences. Whether or nor it is possible that some evil entity was taking advantage of the situation by possessing the coachman's body is, of course, purely conjectural. Each reader of this book will have to evaluate this possibility for himself or herself.

Please keep this information and these possibilities in mind as we return to Hyslop and his peculiar case.

When Hyslop first met with Henry that critical day in June, he primarily wanted to witness his subject's production of psychic writing. Henry was willing to comply, and that evening the two men conducted an informal sitting at the coachman's home—the same barn where the raps had previously manifested. However, the experiment didn't amount to much, since the self-proclaimed psychic simply couldn't produce any scripts during the session. He instead reported by voice several of his impressions, mainly concerning several presences he sensed in the room. Hyslop didn't know what to think of the session, but he felt that his subject's self-induced trance was probably genuine. He was especially impressed by the disorientation Henry suffered after he emerged from the trance state.

The sitting did include a rather unexpected surprise, though. The professor recorded,

> We had hardly sat down when he remarked that he had a sensation in his hand and arm like an electrical current. He also said he felt the chair tremble and heard some raps in the back of it. I heard none there. But at 8.20, I heard what seemed a distinct rap in the corner of the room to my right ten feet away. I sat between Mr. H [enry] and this corner. He did not seem to hear it. But I have no evidence that the rap was anything more than some casual noise anywhere in the room not accurately localized. Mr. H.— had told me that he often heard raps in that corner where the trunk sat, the raps appearing to him to be in the trunk.

What transpired during the rest of the meeting is not known, but Hyslop was intrigued enough by the sitting to suggest that he would return to New Jersey sometime in the future. But Henry was diffident about conducting further experiments and wrote to Hyslop the next day that such a trip wouldn't be necessary. He explained that he could best handle his current situation by giving up his trance writing entirely or by calling upon friendly discarnates when he felt threatened by the unwanted entities possessing him.

Despite the coachman's self-confidence, it was obvious to Hyslop that Henry's mental state was getting worse. This was clear from the disturbed letters he kept posting to the ASPR over the next several weeks. Henry obviously didn't think much of his own plan, for by the end of the month he was once again going into trance. He still fervently hoped to establish direct contact with his deceased wife, still felt he was being possessed, and was becoming increasingly unhinged.

During this period, Henry wrote a second series of fascinating descriptions of his subjective experiences. These remarks were included in a letter he sent to Hyslop on June 26 in which he explained that he had found the solution to his symptoms of possession. He recorded in that letter that "all the trouble is with a certain fluid which resides in my left side, stomach region, and which I do not know how to handle right." It was this fluid, he emphasized, that was causing his personality to fall apart and that was at the root of his psychic experiences. He didn't elaborate on this point, and Hyslop probably didn't know what to make of the claim. He probably considered it little more than a symptom of his subject's psychotic disintegration.

But were these rantings really the ravings of a psychotic? This is a debatable point.

Students of religion and the paranormal will easily recognize the close parallels between Henry's "fluid" and the doctrine of the kundalini, which is commonly taught in yoga and in some schools of Buddhism. The kundalini is supposed to be an energy or fluid that resides at the base of the spine that, when stimulated, grants a person psychic and spiritual powers. The discovery of the kundalini (or something like it) by Henry opened a new, surprising, and unrecognized dynamic in the case. But like his descriptions of the out-of-body experience, few researchers of that day could have appreciated the discovery since knowledge concerning esoteric yogic thought was not widespread in the United States at the turn of the century.

Of course, the information Henry included in this letter to Hyslop was extremely sketchy. But as the case progressed, the coachman became fixated and obsessed with this "fluid." Talk of this mysterious substance would occupy several of his subsequent letters, in which he unknowingly expounded on the doctrine of the kundalini in precise and extraordinary detail.

By the end of that June, James Hyslop had been keeping track of this problematic case for over a year. He was keeping his eye on it despite the fact that the coachman's letters were becoming more and more incoherent. The letters kept ranting about the forces trying to possess his body, the raps he was hearing daily, and other problems besetting him. Despite these problems, however, the coachman was still somewhat in touch with reality and was still working as a gardener and coachman for his employer in New Jersey.

Not only was the German-born immigrant's condition deteriorating badly, but the fact was becoming increasingly obvious to those who knew him. So during the rest of the summer, Hyslop gently withdrew from the case. His reasons for taking this course of action are not clear from his report. He simply turned the correspondence over to his assistant at the ASPR, who counseled Henry several times by letter to stop experimenting with psychic phenomena. Hyslop actually had little personal contact with the stricken man until the following winter, when he began receiving letters from him again. (It seems that Henry had become dissatisfied with the professor's assistant.) During the course of these renewed communications, Henry claimed that he was still hearing raps in his room and was being forced to leave the body. He also now insisted that psychokinesis was breaking out in his presence! Things were getting so bad, in fact, that Hyslop was forced to take charge of the case again on November 7, when he received an urgent telegram from Henry's employer stating that there was an emergency concerning her coachman. Hyslop's first fear when he read the telegram was that Henry had finally gone stark raving mad, so he immediately visited the woman at her residence in Englewood, New Jersey. The professor's goal was to meet with her privately, but his plan misfired badly when he ran into Henry who was working at her house raking the lawn.

> He was in a somewhat agitated state of mind and in the course of his statements about his trouble, which was not clearly defined, I found much emotional disturbance, but mainly of the type of fear whose object was only incoherently indicated. But there was not to me any clear evidence of a dangerous condition. He seemed to be no more abnormal than he

has seemed every time I have seen him. He showed more evidences of fear or fright, but not more than any one would exhibit who had found his unusual sensations continued instead of disappearing as he had wished them. His letters show that he interprets certain sensations as "independent agencies" and on this account I could not obtain as clear an idea of what his experiences really are. But apparently some sensation of heat attacks his stomach and he then feels what he calls the air affecting him and he seems to be out of his body. Of this he is extremely afraid without being able to control his fear or state why he is afraid.

In the course of the conversation he told me that the other day he was driving Mrs. B.— out in the coach and found himself far above his body and could see large stretches of the landscape and that the condition frightened him and he had hard work getting back into his body. Last night, after he had gone to bed, this fluid, which he calls the sensation in the stomach, began to rise and he resisted it with all his might, claiming great will power. He saw an unrecognizable apparition standing by him with his hand resting on his shoulder and uttering urgently the words "Will power." In the course of time, through this help or suggestion he was able to overcome the other agency which he thinks wants to injure him, and was able to get to sleep. But he does not like the struggle that this involves and is terribly afraid of the repetition of this sort of thing every night.

Unfortunately, Hyslop wasn't able to meet with the coachman's employer that afternoon, so he had to make a second trip to her home three days later. It was then that he learned the cause of her distress. She expressed growing concern about her employee and explained to Hyslop that her gardener was becoming more and more deranged. She expressed the hope that if the professor would break off all contact with Henry, a better prognosis for his cure would be forthcoming. Hyslop did not report his reaction to this conversation in his final report, but he apparently did not concur with her suggestion and refused to break off contact with Henry.

This was a fortunate decision, for shortly after that meeting, Hyslop received two further and important letters from him. Both concerned the "fluid" that the coachman was feeling in his stomach and with which he was preoccupied. Reading them today, any student of religion would classify them as perfect descriptions of the kundalini.

The first of these fascinating letters was sent on November 12. It read:

N.J., Nov. 12, '07

My Dear Dr. Hyslop,—

Yours received. Thank you. I will manage to stay a short while longer without interruption and then spend the winter either in New York or go over to Germany during cold weather. I am a nervous wreck of a man compared to what I once was. But line out a kind of cure for me, please. I know just exactly what the trouble is. It is a *fluid*—proper place in lower *center* of body—it leaves its home *very easy*—it is a strain on me to hold it there by breathing in a certain way. When the fluid gets out and gets in head it is enough to set any one crazy. My nervous strength soon gives out. I am nearing a breakdown. With the fluid in proper place there is no trouble at all. The air-stream is either the agent or the guide to it. Advise me, please. I am afraid of experiments, the automatic brought this trouble out.

Very sincerely,

S— H—

Although this letter reads fairly coherently, it was followed within the week by a frankly psychotic communication. Despite the incomprehensibility of this second letter, several references to the fluid were spelled-out. The coachman continued to claim that the raps were persecuting him, and he still insisted that the fluid in his stomach was driving him crazy—especially when it reached his brain.

Hyslop published these two letters without comment, probably because in 1907 there was simply nothing he could say about them. But these letters are critical to the case since they actually offer us a coherent framework by which the experiences plaguing Henry can be explained. So perhaps we should break the strict chronology of the case again to examine what Henry was probably trying to communicate to Hyslop, who, as I said earlier, totally failed to appreciate the remarks.

For the sake of simplicity, the phenomenon Henry was probably experiencing can best be called by its Sanskrit designation. The kundalini is by tradition an energy of sorts that lies at the base of the spine. It is activated by special breathing techniques that were not generally known in the West until relatively recently. When the kundalini is properly activated, the student will feel sensations of heat rising up the spine toward the brain. These sensations are literally produced by the kundalini, which activates several psychic centers (chakras) in the body while creeping upward. The opening of these centers bestows psychic and spiritual powers upon the student. This process of unfoldment constitutes the goal of some systems of yoga. When the kundalini finally reaches the head, by tradition either of two reactions can occur. Divine ecstasy and enlightenment will be experienced if the kundalini has been properly raised. But sometimes the process misfires badly and the kundalini shatters the mind when it strikes the brain. For this reason, raising the kundalini can be dangerous, and several Eastern traditions warn the student against raising it without the supervision of a guru.

It would be easy to dismiss the concept of the kundalini as simply colorful folklore except for the fact that widely separate cultures have made similar spiritual discoveries. For example, the !Kung bushmen (who reside in southern Africa's Kalahari region) talk of a force identical to the kundalini; they call it the *n/um*. In a 1973 issue of the *Journal of Transpersonal Psychology*, Dr. Richard Katz—an acknowledged expert on the !Kung—published two descriptions of the *n/um* that he collected from his native informants. He later explained the doctrine in detail in his fascinating book *Boiling Energy*, and it conforms in every detail to what we know of the *kundalini*.

There exist several rich correspondences between the kundalini, the *n/um*, and the strange "fluid" that Henry believed he had discovered. Like the *n/um* and the kundalini, the coachman's "fluid" also resided in the stomach, could be controlled by breathing, and could travel to the brain—where it drove him crazy in the true tradition of the kundalini.

Of course, Henry wasn't practicing Eastern breathing techniques when he experienced the kundalini, and he certainly knew nothing of the dancing rituals the !Kung use to raise the *n/um*. So why was he suddenly and inexplicably being bothered by the kundalini? Can it ignite spontaneously?

Several transpersonal psychologists here in the West have come to recognize the spiritual reality of the kundalini. Some of them have even seen cases of kundalini-linked psychosis in their practice. It seems that on rare occasions the kundalini can rise up the spine spontaneously—to the complete surprise and shock of the experiencer, to say the least. Since few of these people tend to be students of religion or the paranormal, they usually have no framework by which to understand their experiences. They inevitably end up confused and terrified, and it often takes considerable psychological and spiritual counseling to properly explain the situation to them.

This may strike the reader as rank superstition, but several of these case reports are currently in print. Dr. Lee Sannella is a physician practicing in San Francisco who has been specializing in such cases, and he published several of them in 1976 in his short book *Kundalini— psychosis or transcendence?* Since that time, Dr. Stanislav Grof (a psychiatrist from Czechoslovakia who originally specialized in LSD research) has taken the reality of the kundalini a step further. He and his wife recently founded the Spiritual Emergence Network, which originally operated from the Esalen Institute in Big Sur, California. (The network has since been reestablished at the California Institute of Transpersonal Psychology in Menlo Park.) The purpose of the organization is to provide support for and referrals to clients experiencing spiritual emergencies: which would include kundalini experiences or psychotic responses to any form of spiritual practice or psychic experience.

I feel that the legendary raising of the kundalini is a conceptual model by which we can explain Henry's bizarre experiences. It seems clear that he had managed somehow to activate this power but was mismanaging the force badly. It also seems possible that the force might have been accidentally liberated while Henry was experiencing his OBEs. It is a curious fact that the techniques for raising the kundalini are very similar to the procedures taught in yoga for leaving the body. It is therefore reasonable to assume that experiencing one phenomenon may ignite the other. Either separately or jointly, these experiences may have literally driven Henry insane.

Looking back at the case today, it is apparent that the coachman needed a guru more than a psychical researcher. But gurus were in short supply in 1907.

So with all this information in hand, let's return to the climax and denouement of the case.

Discovering the strange force in the pit of his stomach didn't help Henry very much. His letters to James Hyslop during December 1907 were filled with anguish and confusion, and it was evident that he was getting worse. He was still certain that his experiences were the result of some sort of possession, and he was becoming progressively more delusional. By the end of the year he complained to Hyslop that he constantly felt rats crawling inside his head, and he began exhibiting other symptoms of full-blown paranoid schizophrenia. For all practical purposes, Henry was now completely insane.

Despite the perplexity of the case, Hyslop realized by February 1908 that he had an obligation to help Henry in any way possible. So toward the end of the month, he suggested that Henry undertake a series of trips to New York to meet with him personally. Hyslop planned to experiment with a unique form of cure using psychological suggestion as the therapy. Daily sessions were started at the ASPR, during which the professor hypnotized the disturbed man and encouraged him to forget his problems and delusions. He also offered him a series of posthypnotic suggestions to the same effect. He further urged him to sleep better and more soundly, in fervent hope that simple rest would help soothe his subject's mania.

Even though these treatments were extremely simple, the sessions worked wonders and the coachman gradually began to recover. Whether this recovery happened in response to the treatment or was simply a spontaneous emergence from his psychosis is debatable. But by the end of April, Henry was able to report back to Hyslop that he was completely well. He now realized that some of his previous experiences had been delusions, but he still insisted on the reality of his earlier psychic contacts and his out-of-body experiences.

It looked as if the case were over, and Henry continued to take charge of his own life. He proceeded to get a better job, entered into some business transactions, took up the flute, and began seriously studying psychical research.

Hyslop was encouraged by Henry's recovery and visited him for a final time the following December. "I found him in a very good mental state," he reported, "very different from what he was when I used suggestion to [sic] him last spring." Hyslop kept in contact with Henry until 1917 to make sure the cure was permanent. There is no reason to believe that it wasn't.

Hyslop never really knew what to make of this bizarre case; for some years he considered it a clear-cut case neither of spirit obsession nor of simple insanity. When he finally introduced the case to his readers, however, he was more sympathetic to the possibly paranormal reality of Henry's experiences. He felt that the subject's out-of-body experiences, for example, could best be explained as the result of some sort of incipient possession.

The researcher was not dogmatic on this point, though, and he ended his report with the following disclaimer: "I am merely putting on record a case which some day will be classified more assuredly than the skeptic will allow us to do at present."

CHAPTER 5

THE POSSESSION OF ETTA DE CAMP

By the time his research with Frederic Thompson and S. Henry was completed, James Hyslop realized that spirit obsession represented a double-edged problem. A person like Frederic Thompson could actively benefit from this bizarre form of psychic invasion. Even though the craftsman initially exhibited some substantial stress and anxiety when Gifford's (ostensible) influence first began invading his mind, this problem was relatively short-lived. Once he realized the psychic nature of his fixations and obsessions, he was free to use the influence to further develop his own artistic skills. He "survived" the process of psychic invasion, so to speak, and eventually learned to cooperate with Gifford's psychic presence. He apparently took advantage of the situation for several years.

But the case of S. Henry represented a different side of the syndrome, since nothing beneficial ever emerged from it. The psychic influences presumably raiding the coachman's psyche were devastating. They drove him to the depths of a complete psychotic breakdown from which he only gradually emerged.

The two cases couldn't have been more different. The creatively motivated Thompson stands in stark contrast to the coachman, who was nearly destroyed by his contact with the psychic world.

Despite the influence of these cases on Hyslop's thinking, the researcher refrained from further investigating the possible existence of psychic obsession for the next three years. There were simply too many other investigations that he was undertaking. Even during his involvement with the Thompson case, for instance, he had also been deeply involved with a case of secondary personality reported from New York. This case was very similar to the case of Ansel Bourne, the one that had first piqued the professor's interest in psychical research in 1889 and which led him to collaborate with the old American Society for Psychical Research. (See Chapter 2.) The curious case of Charles P. Brewin began in 1903, when this merchant/tailor from Burlington, New Jersey, simply vanished from the face of the earth. He suffered a prolonged fugue, during which he took up residence in New York under a separate identity. He lived his life peacefully as "Fred G. Johnson" until one fateful afternoon when he decided to sleep for a while and woke up with his previous memory back intact. He didn't know where he was and knew little of his life between 1903 and 1907. *The New York Times* carried the story in their July 1 issue and implied that the case could be a hoax. Hyslop disagreed and was soon busy tracking down the facts. He published a report on his investigation the following October.

Upon completing his work on the Thompson/Gifford and the Henry investigations, Hyslop threw himself back into his experiments with psychics and mediums. Toward the end of 1906 he had discovered a promising new sensitive who was gifted both with clairvoyance and with psychic writing skills. Mrs. Belmar's mediumship didn't strike the professor auspiciously at first, but during February 1908 he undertook a series of experiments with her in hopes of making contact with the deceased Richard Hodgson. While some evidence that Richard Hodgson was communicating through her was received, the experiments fizzled. Hyslop was undaunted by this failure and stepped up his research on mediumship over the next two years. He was constantly working with Minnie Soule in Boston every weekend while he was keeping watchful eyes on several promising psychics in New York. He left the coziness of the East coast, though, in 1909 to look into a provocative case in Toledo, Ohio, involving Miss Ada Bessinet (later Mrs. William W. Roche). She wasn't a conventional trance medium, since she was primarily a physical medium. Visitors to her darkened séances would see lights darting through the room; phantom forms would materialize, and voices would speak, whistle, or sing from the air. Miss Bessinet's psychic gifts had been developed by her spiritistically inclined aunt, in whose home the sittings were usually held. She was quickly becoming the darling of the Spiritualist community, and Prof. Hyslop undertook seventy sittings with her between 1909 and 1910. His final evaluation was that the young woman was unconsciously faking the phenomena while in a dissociated state. Some years later, though, he changed his verdict and conceded that some of her psychic lights and raps were probably genuine.*

After he returned home, Hyslop busied himself with local research and with the daily operations of the ASPR. It should be remembered that not only was he the secretary and founder of the organization, he *was* the ASPR. He ran the organization, edited and often wrote full issues of its publications. Sometimes he had little time for anything else, and even his family was often forced into the background.

Winifred Hyslop, one of the professor's two daughters, often commented to this effect in her later life. For example, she recalled this period of her father's career in some correspondence we shared in the summer of 1970.

"In 1910 I was sixteen-years-old and hadn't any idea what my father was doing," she wrote to me. "He tended to work at his desk when he was home about 16-18 hours a day, seven days a week when he wasn't investigating mediums in and out of town, reading the paper at breakfast and dinner."

Despite his fierce writing schedule, Hyslop cleared considerable time to continue his research with his favorite sensitives. During the months of September and October 1910 he worked constantly with Minnie Soule, who was bringing through regular and evidential communications from his deceased wife and father-in-law. He divided his time between that research and a crisis that threatened to compromise his professional life. This episode in his career is actually an amusing story in itself.

By 1910, the fame of Leonore Piper was becoming too widespread for the conventional psychological establishment to ignore. So while Hyslop was busy with Minnie Soule in Boston and the ASPR in New York, Prof. G. Stanely Hall, his former mentor at Johns Hopkins University, began undertaking his own research with Mrs. Piper. Most of these experiments were conducted in cooperation with his research coadjutor, Dr. Amy Tanner of Clark University in Worcester, Massachusetts, where Hall had since become president. The researchers were not impressed with with Mrs. Piper's mediumship and in 1910 Dr. Tanner published some ferocious criticisms of the psychic in her book *Studies in Spiritism*, which also vehemently attacked James Hyslop's lengthy

---

* He made this concession in his last book on psychical research, *Contact with the Other World*, published in 1919. Hyslop continued to refer to the psychic as "Miss Burton" in his reports even after her identity had become common knowledge.

1901 report on the sensitive. Hyslop was enraged when he read the book, for he found that Dr. Tanner had consistently misrepresented and even falsified his reports and personal evaluations. His outrage was so severe that he spent several weeks toward the end of 1910 writing a ninety-eight page rebuttal, contesting every word Dr. Tanner wrote concerning his investigation!

With all these investigations and rejoinders preoccupying him, it certainly wasn't odd that the subject of spirit obsession wasn't of central concern to Hyslop between 1907 and 1911. There was one significant exception, however. Sometime in 1910 (we don't know the exact date), he undertook a trip to Kansas City, Missouri, to visit the Temple of Light. The temple was actually a Spiritualist church that specialized in the treatment of the mentally deranged. The Spiritualists of this era believed that some cases of insanity were caused by spirit possession, and the Kansas City temple featured resident psychics who treated these unfortunate people by way of special séances. The sensitives would enter trance, contact the possessing entities, and then the sitters conducting the sessions would convince them to stop bothering their victims. The same procedures were being employed in the private homes of Spiritualists everywhere in the country, who often found their friends and mediums controlled by undesirable personalities. The Spiritualists claimed surprising success with the use of these simple procedures.

Whatever Hyslop witnessed during the trip profoundly influenced him. Perhaps the séances reminded him of the way Mrs. Soule and Mrs. Cleaveland had promptly "diagnosed" the Thompson/Gifford case. Whatever the truth of the matter, the Temple of Light's work planted seeds in the professor's fertile mind, and he began thinking that similar procedures could be cogently employed by physicians and psychiatrists.

These various research projects and investigations set the stage for Hyslop's subsequent work in psychical research. Between 1912 and 1918 several cases suggesting the reality of spirit obsession came to his notice. Some of them were similar to the Thompson/Gifford case, in which seemingly ordinary people suddenly developed remarkable creative skills.

Hyslop had been familiar with the case of Miss Etta De Camp long before he came to suspect that she suffered from some form of spirit obsession. The case was reported to him just after his work with Frederic Thompson and his possession by Robert Swain Gifford, and he later began experimenting with her with the help of Minnie Soule.

Miss De Camp* was probably destined to be a psychic. Her childhood, which she spent in Ohio, was filled with a succession of illnesses and physical problems which prevented her from enjoying her formative years. She managed to survive her tribulations and left the Midwest when her parents moved to Schenectady, New York. When she was ready to embark upon a career, Miss De Camp found employment in New York City, where she worked for *Broadway* magazine reading and evaluating submissions. Despite the fact the she worked in the publishing field, the young woman was never drawn to creative writing and didn't possess any apparent literary skills.

Miss De Camp did not claim any encounters or experiences with the psychic world during her childhood or early professional career. The only unusual event that Hyslop could trace in her family history was reported by her mother in October 1908, when the family received the disturbing news that Miss De Camp's brother was in the hospital. The young man had been living in Chicago, where he was diagnosed as suffering from tetanus, which in those days was usually fatal. Mrs. De Camp was extremely distraught and immediately booked passage for the Windy City by train. But a surprise was in store for her. During the long overnight journey, Mrs. De Camp suddenly felt the soothing presence of her late husband traveling with her. She sensed that he didn't want her to worry and that their son would survive the crises. When the elderly woman finally arrived in Chicago, she found that her son's condition was not hopeful, but sure enough, he survived the nightmare. Mrs. De Camp felt that his recovery was preordained, and she remained convinced that the spiritual contact she experienced with her late husband had been genuine. Despite her strong impression, however, she mentioned nothing about her husband's post-mortem presence to the rest of her family. But the incident would become a key link in the psychic drama soon to envelop her daughter.

During this family crisis, Miss Etta De Camp was still living in New York City. It was not until three months later that her interest in psychical research was sparked when she began reading some material on Spiritualism written by W. T. Stead, who was then a famous British journalist and social reformer. He had become a Spiritualist in 1892 after suddenly developing his own psychic gifts. He made a public pro-

---

*This was the woman's maiden name. She eventually wrote her memoirs under the name of Etta de (not De) Camp. Her married name was Mrs. Milton Snider.

nouncement to this effect a short time later in 1893 and during the early months of 1909 he was engaged in organizing a bureau where clients could book sittings with gifted psychics.

What had so impressed Stead was a series of communications he had received through his own automatic writing. The scripts purported to come from a deceased American newspaperwoman whom he had met previously in Great Britain. Etta De Camp was greatly taken with Stead's writings, so she began to experiment with psychic writing herself. She would make her consciousness blank so that her hand could write by itself. She was immediately successful, although at first her hand only produced scrawls. But even these productions didn't seem quite normal.

"I had a peculiar sensation in my arm," she later explained to Hyslop. "It was like a shock of electricity, a tingling sensation of the hands. I think I worked two or three days before I could get anything that looked like a word."

Miss De Camp was extremely lucky, since most people practice for weeks or months before developing this level of skill. The production of the writing was not easy, though. She often suffered excruciating headaches and earaches during this critical period of her psychic development. Often the pain would come when she tried to resist the urge to produce the writings and would force her to submit. This ordeal represented the first indication that some sort of psychic invasion of her personality was taking place. She eventually realized that she could avoid the discomfort by entering a trance state while producing the scripts, but she disliked the thought of losing control of her consciousness. She never submitted to the urge to enter trance and produced her writings while perfectly alert despite the pain.

These developments were so startling that Miss De Camp began confiding in her employer and friend, George F. Duysters. Duysters was an international lawyer in New York who often employed the young lady for proofreading and editing. One of his many business ventures was selling typewriters in the United States and Miss De Camp was also contracted to teach typing skills to prospective buyers. Duysters was a kindly older gentleman who had studied psychical research for some years, and he was personally acquainted with Hyslop. So it was natural for Miss De Camp to confide in him, and he eagerly encouraged her to experiment further. By this time she was experimenting every evening in her New York apartment.

Despite the fact that whole words and sentences were being written, Miss De Camp was not satisfied with the scripts. In fact, once she became so annoyed by their lack of coherence that she openly chided the "spirits" using her body.

"Whoever you are that is trying to write," she said one evening as she glared at her pencil, "if you cannot write bring me someone who can."

From that session and for several months to come, the writings began to make considerably more sense. Her first regular communicator claimed to be a discarnate Indian brave. (This development was right in keeping with the Spiritualist tradition of that era, when every psychic claimed colorful spirit guides.) Other purported communicators came and disappeared, but Miss De Camp was insightful enough to take their claims with a pinch of salt—a pinch roughly the size of Lot's wife.

The next phase in her psychic development came during one of these private sessions in March. She was receiving some communications from a discarnate who refused to provide any evidential information about herself. Miss De Camp was arguing with the persona, commenting caustically to the unseen presence upon receiving each of the discarnate's messages. The discarnate finally became frustrated with Miss De Camp and departed, whereupon the sturdy Indian brave continued with the writing.

"He will bring a man," her hand began to write, "a man who wrote; who is anxious to have someone finish the stories he left when he passed away."

Miss De Camp thought this message refered to stories the deceased author had previously conceived but had never succeeded in setting down on paper. But she was puzzled by why she was being chosen.

"I had never written a word in my life," she later explained to Hyslop. "While I have been a great reader and preferred to be with literary people, I have never had any talent that way, at all myself. My letters are just ordinary. . . . I never wrote a particularly bright letter unless I am in the mood."

The arrival of this new communicator was consummated the next evening, when Miss De Camp's pencil wrote that Mr. Frank R. Stockton was present and wished to communicate. The initial "possession" was anything but pleasant for the young woman. She wrote in her autobiographical *The Return of Frank R. Stockton* that "at that moment I was taken with an intense pain in the forehead between the eyes; and I felt a sensation on the left side of my head as though another mind was crowding into my own. For a few minutes the agony was so great that

I got up and walked the floor . . ." Miss De Camp found herself pacing while crying out loud that she couldn't bear the pain. She was also afraid that she was losing her mind.

"Fortunately," she also said, "it [the pain] lasted only a short time and was caused, it seemed to me, by the shock produced when Mr. Stockton's mentality first assumed control of my nerves, muscles or hand."

It was the beginning of a strange collaboration which bore an uncanny resemblance to the way Frederic Thompson's life had been similarly invaded by Robert Swain Gifford.

The writings of Frank (Francis) Richard Stockton are hardly remembered today, although they were extremely popular at the turn of the century. Stockton was born in Philadelphia in 1834. He worked first as a wood engraver before turning to journalism. He subsequently worked on the editorial staffs of several well-known publications, including the *Philadelphia Post* and *Scribner's Monthly* magazine. He began his literary career by editing periodicals, but he came to national prominence with a series of short stories for children. His trademarks were his humor and his wonderfully whimsical characters, whom he liked to place in bizarre situations. His most famous short story was "The Lady or the Tiger," which every schoolboy and girl still reads even in today's sophisticated times. The pure outlandishness of Stockton's writings is better represented, however, in his story "The Casting Away of Mrs. Lecks and Mrs. Aleshine." This wonderful story concerns two shipwrecked elderly ladies who try to marry off their male companion. Stockton produced dozens of these delightful books and stories between 1872 and his death in 1902.

The psychic return of Frank Stockton in 1909 caused considerable changes in Miss De Camp's mediumship. The communicator didn't particularly like the way she was practicing her skills, so he began instructing her in the procedures he expected her to follow! He explained in the scripts he produced daily through her writing that she was to get up early in the morning, drink some coffee, and then begin the psychic writing. It is clear that the presence didn't want her to produce the scripts in the evenings. The Stockton personality explained that he preferred that she follow this protocol since it matched the way he had worked during his earthly existence. The communicator assured the surprised Miss De Camp that by following these rules, the writings would be elicited more easily.

The prediction was correct, and slowly but surely Miss De Camp began writing a series of short stories, while her chronic headaches and related pain gradually subsided. (They returned only when the psychic refused to write when the Stockton personality beckoned her to work.) These stories did not, however, enter the psychic's mind while she composed them. She had no inkling as to where a particular story was heading until she read each subsequent sentence written by her pencil. Although she felt herself in direct communication with the Stockton personality while producing the scripts, the contact would break immediately if she ceased writing for any reason. This phenomenon convinced the young psychic that her unconscious mind was not responsible for the compositions.

"Days I have sat here with a pencil in my hand," she later explained to Hyslop, "and a telephone receiver at my ear.* When I lay the pencil down—if it is in the middle of a sentence—it is like putting down a receiver. Not a word comes to me. You know that does [away], to my mind, with all subconscious operation, because it seems to me that if it were the subconscious, I would have these flashes. When I lay the pencil down, I have no inspiration of what is to follow each sentence."

It is also interesting that, even though Miss De Camp could follow each story while the writing was progressing, she would forget the story's plot when the session ended. She had to refamiliarize herself with the story while typing the finished copy.

Between the months of March and May 1909, several of these stories were received and George Duysters was extremely impressed by their literary merit. They seemed to possess the wit and flippancy of Frank Stockton's published work. This growing enthusiasm encouraged Duysters to bring the case to limited public exposure, but he proceeded cautiously. The first person he approached with the material was Hyslop, who was immediately drawn to the case since it so forcefully reminded him of the Thompson/Gifford investigation. (That research had reached its denouement the previous December.) Duysters was also curious whether the stories were publishable, so he submitted them to *Harper's* magazine, explaining to its editor the strange conditions under which they had been written. The editor wrote back that he couldn't

---

*It is not clear whether this reference is figurative for her self-perceived contact with Stockton, or whether Miss De Camp talked on the phone to keep her mind preoccupied while the writings were being received. I personally think that the first explanation is probably correct.

publish them and warned the lawyer that Stockton's executors could bring a suit if they were published as examples of his writing, posthumous or not! He ended the note by saying that the stories were "very real," which probably implied that some genuine resemblances existed between Miss De Camp's stories and Stockton's own earthly compositions.

The prolific communications from Frank Stockton were not the only psychic activities complicating the psychic's life during these months, however. Two other developments contributed to her growing conviction that she had established contact with the spirit world. The first consisted of a series of incidents in which powerful psychic perfumes suddenly manifested in her presence. They would occur without warning in her apartment, while she was riding the subway, and sometimes even while she was visiting her friends. They had once manifested in George Duysters's home, and that time they smelled like lilies. The incident had been witnessed not only by Duysters but by his entire family. He was extremely impressed by the incident and made a verbal report to Hyslop on May 4, 1909.

But more impressive to Miss De Camp personally was the startling and unexpected arrival of a new communicator who briefly shared the scripts with the Stockton personality. Miss De Camp's father had died some fifteen years before in March 1894. While the Stockton communicator was writing so copiously between March and May, the father began writing through his daughter as if to commemorate the date of his death.

Miss De Camp later placed a chronology of the events leading to the receipt of her father's messages on record for Hyslop. This chronology differs slightly from what she later reported in her autobiographical notes, where she writes that these messages preceded the Stockton writings. Whatever the case, both sets of communications were obviously received during the same critical time. Miss De Camp's first contact with her late father occurred while she was finishing her office work one evening:

> Nothing vital came up that made me ask for my father and I thought it was best to wait and let them bring him themselves. Father and I were so closely connected and the rest of the family always thought that if Father could communicate he would reach me. I thought Father had gone too far. He had been dead fifteen years and I thought he had in

that time gone out of the reach of anyone. That was why I had not asked for him. I didn't know about the earth-bound spirits then. He came unexpectedly. I had just finished off a dozen business letters and laid them on the desk to be signed. There was no one in the office at the time and I just—you know, when thinking I suppose I had a pencil in my hand and there was the slip of paper on my desk. I sat there, with a pencil in my hand, looking out of the window, and somebody near it began to write. It called me by my baby name which my father always used— "Ettie." It said, "Ettie, your father is here and wishes to talk to you." It startled me so that I sat down and cried. It was so unexpected. I was not thinking of Father. There was nothing to make me think of him. After I recovered myself I took another piece of paper and took the message. I was so upset that I had to put my things on and go home. After the first shock was over I felt as if I had been weeping for weeks.

The contents of these scripts were never made public by Hyslop, but they were invariably addressed to Miss De Camp's mother. Mrs. De Camp was skeptical of the communications, but was surprised to find a special message included in the scripts. The self-purported Mr. De Camp explained to his wife that his presence had been with her during her trip to Chicago to see their son! This seemed to be an evidential communication since the elderly woman had never told her daughter about the presence she sensed during the journey.

Even though this communicator seemed capable of proving his identity, the persona did not preoccupy Miss De Camp's writing. He delivered six to ten scripts and then departed from the mediumship, explaining that his mission had been accomplished. There was simply no further reason for him to remain in contact with his family.

The stage was now set for more communications from the deceased Stockton, and for James Hyslop's own entrance into the case.

Hyslop first met Etta De Camp when the Stockton scripts were still being copiously produced. Their first meeting took place in May 1909, and they talked for a considerable length of time. Hyslop later asked the psychic to repeat her story to his secretary, who made a written report on their conversation for her employer's files. During these conversations with Hyslop and his secretary, Miss De Camp claimed that she had never read any of Stockton's books or other writings, with the possible exception of a single short story. She was also perplexed about the material she was receiving. She felt that the stories should be published, which was also the surreptitious wish of her communicator.

But she didn't want the public to think she was perpetrating a fraud to gain financially from Stockton's reputation. Prof. Hyslop was, in turn, impressed by the young woman, her obvious intelligence, and her critical attitude toward her burgeoning mediumship. He was also intrigued by the stories themselves. But he was also worried about Miss De Camp's state of mind, since the constant stress of producing the writings was taking a gradual and frightening toll. The young woman was beginning to show signs of a severe breakdown, and finally Miss De Camp took a leave of absence from her work in New York and returned to her mother's residence in Schenectady. She spent several weeks there during the summer of 1909 recuperating from her physical and psychological exhaustion.

It seemed to Hyslop that the case was a likely instance of postmortem influence. The case fit the pattern of spirit obsession cases that he had provisionally identified from his research with Frederic Thompson, even though nothing truly evidential had so far emerged in this case. But because of Miss De Camp's precarious psychological state, Hyslop decided not to experiment further with the possibility. The press had got wind of the story by this time, and publicity was beginning to leak concerning the psychic "return" of Frank Stockton. A story about the De Camp productions appeared in the *New York Herald* while the psychic was recovering upstate. The publication of this story probably didn't please Hyslop since it threatened to ruin any future research he was likely to carry out with Miss De Camp.

Despite the fact that Prof. Hyslop was keeping his distance from the case, Miss De Camp was progressively succumbing to some sort of psychic web of intrigue. This new development in her mediumship dates from September 1909 while she was still in Schenectady. She was still producing writings from Frank Stockton daily while sitting at a table in her mother's attic, which she had converted into a private and informal séance room. She would put the table in front of a window, place a screen behind herself, and wait for the writing to come. That way she could receive the communications from the Stockton personality in a rather secluded environment. Nothing could have been further from her mind than the production of physical (i.e., psychokinetic) phenomena, but her communicator had other plans.

"I can make the table move for you," the communicator claimed that fateful September morning.

Miss De Camp was intrigued by the sudden remark. The table she was using consisted of a deep and heavy tray that rested on legs fabricated by cross pieces of wood. She would set the tray upside down and place a writing mat on its surface before working. Since the tray was not really attached to the legs, the table was bulky and difficult to maneuver. Moving it psychokinetically seemed like the perfect task for a discarnate presence to try.

"Very well," said the excited and curious Miss De Camp. "Let me see you do it."

She laid down her pencil while speaking, stood up, and rested her hands lightly on the table. She was so excited by what happened next that she immediately wrote to Hyslop.

> By the time I had finished speaking the table began to squeak as if some one was trying to move it. . . .
>
> Then it began to rock back and forth towards me. Finally it *began to move* slowly at first and then began turning around. By this time my chair was pushed so near to the screen that, in order not to knock it over, I got up and stood with my hands on the table and it turned around and around as fast as I could move. By this time I had only one finger on the table and it fairly flew over the rough floor. I was so excited and delighted with this evidence of a force I could see that I went down and got my mother to come up and see it. She will testify to that fact.

Miss De Camp's mother did, in fact, testify to witnessing the incident, and she sent a short statement to Hyslop three days later. She even saw the table move when her daughter was touching it with a single finger.

But the day's table-turning session had hardly ended. After Miss De Camp returned to her chair, her pencil began scribbling more scripts.

"This is to prove to you that we are here with you," her communicator emphasized. "The chair you are in will move too, if you sit quietly in it. Try it."

But the young psychic was no longer in the mood. "I will try it some other day," she responded to the unseen presence guiding the writing. "I am too tired just now. But you can try to move the chair without me in it."

What happened subsequently was certainly impressive. It was a fitting encore to the previous demonstration.

> I stood up with the chair in front of me resting one hand on the knob at the top of the back. It began to move slowly and then suddenly spun around like a top on one of the legs.

The thing which interested me besides the moving of both chair and table was the feeling of lightness in both and the ease with which they moved about.

Miss De Camp continued these psychokinetic experiments for several days, keeping careful records of everything that transpired. She also found that she could move her writing pad by lightly placing her finger on it. The pad would then meander over the table's surface.

Whether any of these phenomena were really significant remains debatable, though. So before proceeding further, let's evaluate the De Camp/Stockton case from its inception to the following summer.

The skeptical reader could, in fact, probably build a case against the entire episode without even calling the good faith of its principle protagonist into question. It seems obvious that Miss De Camp would be drawn to the glamorous world of literature and publishing. She even admitted harboring these inclinations to Hyslop when they first met, although she claimed no personal talent for writing herself. But the subconscious mind can be a strange creature. It isn't hard to believe that Miss De Camp could have systematically (although unconsciously) learned proper writing skills while working as a manuscript reader in New York. She certainly had the opportunity to gain this knowledge through her wide reading. The appropriate skills could have gradually accumulated within her subconscious mind and broken loose only months later in the form of "psychic" writings.

This kind of dissociative behavior is not really a rare or delicate psychic gift. It is a potential possessed by many people, similar to the potential most people have for operating a ouija board or planchette. It is a skill that can be learned through practice or developed through hypnotic suggestion. Psychologists today believe that a breakthrough from deep within the unconscious mind can be double-edged potential, however. It can certainly contribute to the production of a full-fledged psychosis, but great creativity can be unleashed, too. Perhaps this was the case with Etta De Camp. Since she was basing her psychic practice on the Spiritualist traditions of her day, it isn't strange that the writings claimed to come from the world beyond. The scripts could have been a production of her own conscious expectations.

It is therefore a pity that Miss De Camp's "Stockton" stories are forgotten today by parapsychologists more concerned with ESP tests than with survival research. Computer technology has blossomed and grown tremendously during the last several decades. There are currently methods by which pieces of literature or possible literary forgeries can be computer analyzed. Each writer has his or her own peculiarities, primarily in the use of phraseology, punctuation, and even sentence length. A computer can be programmed to compare and contrast two pieces of literature, thereby evaluating whether they were written by the same person. This procedure has already been used successfully for detecting forgeries, and it would be fascinating to see what a computer would find by comparing some of the De Camp/Stockton stories to Stockton's own published work.

Of course, Etta De Camp produced more than merely the Stockton stories. During the period of their reception she was also receiving messages from her father. But whatever evidential information was contained in them could be feasibly traced to telepathy from her mother. Similar extrasensory sources could be postulated for some of the psychic's other scripts, which occasionally included paranormally derived information.

The ostensibly psychokinetic episodes Miss De Camp witnessed while in Schenectady can also be criticized. While they sound impressive from the reports, she never really saw the table moving by itself. She was always in direct contact with its surface. It is therefore possible that she was producing the phenomena herself, perhaps through some sort of subconscious muscular pressure—i.e., the same kind of pressure that works a dowsing rod. This possibility seems unlikely since the table's movements were so extraordinary, but the skeptic can't be faulted for suggesting this explanation.

Hyslop was certainly not blind to these problems with the De Camp/Stockton case. Concerning the writings the psychic was receiving from the deceased Frank Stockton, the professor wrote that "there was every reason to accept her veracity and that of her family and friends as to her character." But he emended this statement by stating that "the phenomena had an unusual interest, even tho[ugh] we did not admit any evidence for the supernormal."

The seasoned researcher was not impressed by the psychic's psychokinesis, either. "The contact of the hand spoils the incidents for evidence," he wrote in his final report, "but only because we insist on demanding that spirits must produce the movements of objects without human or other contact that is known."

Despite his cautious opinions on the case, however, Hyslop decided to personally investigate it the following November. Nine months had passed since he first learned of Miss De Camp's mediumship, but his current focus would be the psychokinesis and not the Stockton contacts.

Due to his reengendered interest in the case, Hyslop urged George Duysters to bring Miss De Camp back to New York for some controlled experiments. Duysters found the plan exciting, and he and Miss De Camp made the appropriate commitment toward the end of November. The psychic was provided with a room in a hotel near the ASPR, where Hyslop conducted a series of experiments between November 30 and December 1. The sessions were a curious mixture of limited success but technical failure. During their first sitting together on the morning of November thirtieth, Prof. Hyslop watched his subject work with a relatively light table, fourteen by sixteen inches square. She was able to set the table in motion, but only when she placed her hand on its surface. The professor wasn't impressed, even though he detected no evidence that she was deliberately pushing the stand. She was also capable of moving the table after Hyslop placed some paper under her hands, but he realized that even this experiment was unsatisfactory. As part of a third impromptu test, Hyslop required his subject to place her hands on his own, which he then placed firmly on the tabletop. But the stand didn't budge under these better controlled conditions.

Hyslop also experimented with Miss De Camp's purported ability to move a writing pad or magazine merely by touching it lightly. These tests were likewise inconclusive.

The professor conducted a second series of experiments the following morning, but they similarly failed. Despite the unsatisfactory outcome of the investigation, however, Hyslop did witness a curious phenomenon during his second visit.

Before the experiment, she told me that she had tried the table tipping last night after I left and I could not have been more than out of the hotel when it was perfectly successful. She tried the same this morning before I came and the table tipping was easy. She also said that she did not know how tired she was last night until she started to retire, when she felt tired and went to sleep immediately and slept soundly all night.

In the experiment this morning, before I came, she remarked that her skirt swayed out, backward and forward. When she tried the experiment with me, she observed it again and called my attention to it. I looked and there was a very distinct swing, backward and forward, of her skirt, toward and from the table, and I tried to get the evidence of the cause of this in her breathing and other bodily movements, but I could not find any movement whatever about her breast or waist due to the breathing.

But when the experiments were evaluated in their entirety, Hyslop considered them totally inconclusive.

Hyslop took a lengthy sabbatical from 1910 to 1912 from the case of Frank Stockton's psychic return. The researcher simply didn't consider the investigation important and found little reason to pursue it. The investigation was further complicated by the death the following December 1909 of George Duysters, who had been his liaison with the case. Miss De Camp and the professor simply went their separate ways, although they occasionally kept in contact. Etta De Camp returned to New York to regain employment in June 1910, but she ultimately found that retirement from the psychic world was impossible. She soon found herself once again preoccupied with her psychic practices and the Stockton scripts. It seemed that the ex-proofreader was also now receiving scripts from Duysters, who successfully finished a sketch through her hand that he had originally penciled for her during a picnic. De Camp was especially impressed by the drawing and immediately reported it to Hyslop, claiming that the sketch was beyond her skills to produce.

Hyslop was still reluctant to return to the case, however. His reticence was reasonable enough, for during these weeks Miss De Camp was once again exhibiting symptoms of a complete breakdown. She complained of chronic fatigue, suffered bouts of depression, and constantly felt that her surroundings were unreal (a syndrome called "derealization" by psychologists). These severe symptoms pointed toward a chronic depressive disorder, and Miss De Camp ultimately returned to the sanctuary of her mother's home.

During this same summer of 1910, Hyslop was becoming deeply involved in an unrelated but fruitful research project that drew him even farther away from Etta De Camp. Researchers in the United States and England engaged in psychical research were deeply saddened when William James died toward the end of August. The great psychologist and philosopher had been the field's most prestigious spokesman in the United States. Hyslop had personally known him for several years so was certainly hopeful that he would soon "hear" from his friend through the sensitives he was working with. Hyslop was probably very excited when the deceased psychologist began communicating to him through Mrs. Cleaveland in Virginia. She began receiving scripts from the purported James during the month following his death, and the same persona began manifesting during Hyslop's weekly sittings in Boston with Minnie Soule. Hyslop pursued these possible post-mortem contacts between September and December (1910), and then journeyed to Virginia the following summer to experiment further with the entity.

The results of these experiments were exciting and evidential, and Hyslop reported his findings in the *Journal of the American Society for Psychical Research* and later in his book *Contact with the Other World*. Toward the end of that summer, he also went to Pittsburgh to review a fascinating case of multiple personality. (This trip was the beginning of an exciting investigation that will be discussed in Chapter 7.)

Luckily, though, whatever problems were threatening to destroy Etta De Camp's mind were not permanent and the psychic returned to New York sometime in 1911. By the beginning of 1912 she seemed perfectly well, so Hyslop decided to conduct some final experiments with the case. His plan was to replicate the research he had previously begun with Frederic Thompson and the Gifford influence. He wanted to establish post-mortem contact with the deceased Frank Stockton, if possible, and see whether his communications would bear on Miss De Camp's plight and compositions. This plan wasn't difficult to implement, since the professor was still working consistently with Minnie Soule.

Before engaging in these sittings, though, the professor wanted to procure some expert evaluations of the "Stockton" writings. Getting such opinions wasn't difficult since one of the stories had been previously read by John R. Meader, the editor of *The Common Cause* magazine and an enthusiastic fan of Stockton's stories and books. Hyslop knew Meader personally, and in early February he wrote to him and requested his opinion on the De Camp/Stockton stories. The editor replied back:

Feb. 13th, 1912

Dear Dr. Hyslop:

You were correctly informed as to my having read the De Camp manuscript. I hesitate to give you my opinion because it is as yet very vague. There are lots of points in it in keeping with Stockton's thought and style. Yes [probably a typographical error for *yet*], as a whole, the story "The Pirates Three" is disappointing. If you were to take only certain extracts and paste them together I think that any literary critic would recognize the Stockton hall marks. If he had to read through the whole manuscript and take these places out for himself the similarity would not be so striking.

I have more definite ideas as to the possible genuineness of the manuscript but these have to do with theories, not facts, and probably would not interest you.

Sincerely yours,

JOHN R. MEADER

The editor clarified his remarks in a follow-up letter which he sent to Hyslop a few days later. There he wrote that "the one thing I can say is that there is no doubt in my mind that many of the situations introduced in the story 'The Pirates Three' might easily pass as Stockton's."

This guarded report was good enough for Hyslop, so later that month he took Etta De Camp to Boston for a series of sittings with Minnie Soule. Because some stories concerning Miss De Camp had been previously published in the press, Hyslop was extremely cautious about keeping the sitter's identity secret from the psychic. He registered her into a Boston hotel under a pseudonym and personally took charge of each of the six subsequent sittings. When they arrived at Minnie Soule's home for each séance, the psychic's maid would let them into the ground floor of the house. Hyslop would then proceed upstairs to Mrs. Soule's séance room and meet with the psychic, who would then enter trance. Miss De Camp would enter the room only after being properly signaled by the researcher, would sit behind the sensitive, and was instructed to say nothing during the experiments.

Hyslop booked their first sitting with Mrs. Soule for the morning of February 26. The sitting began on a promising note since the psychic entered the writing stage of her trance almost immediately. The very first writings she produced were certainly relevant to Frank Stockton's possible presence.

"I am trying so hard to write and I am not yet in full command," the first communicator wrote.

Hyslop was encouraged. "Yes. Be patient and you will be," he commented to the presence.

"How do you know?" replied the writing. "It wiggles so and is so hard to keep firm.* I am not . . . am . . . so new to this work but it seems to be different, different, different." The communicator seemed to be losing control of the writing but soon regained command.

"No one writes for me now," the entity continued. "They ought to I think but they point me to the task myself and so I must try and make no mistakes this time. Do you understand?"

Hyslop and Miss De Camp certainly did understand, since the young lady had stopped mediating the Stockton scripts.

Minnie Soule's hand ceased writing at this point in the sitting. A long pause followed, and finally the communicator signed his name. Slowly and at first tentatively, the name "Frank" was signed to the message!

It was not only the content of these first messages that impressed Hyslop. Even the handwriting of the communicator gradually began to match the writings produced through Etta De Camp. (The Stockton stories had been written in a different script from the woman's regular handwriting and resembled Stockton's earthly penmanship.)

The ostensible Stockton persona faded quickly during this first sitting and little more was heard from him. The scripts became extremely confused, even though the sitting continued for a considerable time. There was a brief moment when the deceased George Duysters tried to communicate, but he managed to scribble only his first name and middle initial before also losing control.

Despite the fact that neither the deceased Frank Stockton nor the late George Duysters seemed capable of sustaining control of the psychic, Hyslop was not disappointed by the session. It seemed that post-mortem contact had been provisionally established with the two most important people in Miss De Camp's life. Nothing could have struck the professor as more promising, so the two sitters returned to Mrs. Soule's house the next morning to resume the experiments. The same precautions were taken so that the psychic could not see or meet Miss De Camp, but the séance was a failure. This momentary setback didn't phase Hyslop, though, who knew from long experience that post-mortem contact was difficult to establish and stabilize. It was especially difficult, he realized,

---

*This communication was evidential in itself. Three years prior to the sitting, Miss De Camp had told Hyslop that she had noticed a similar phenomenon when she first began receiving scripts from the Stockton personality. "When I am writing, the pencil turned [sic] around and around," she explained. "Sometimes when I am writing, it is all I can do to hold the pencil. *It wiggles so* [emphasis added]. You can feel the writing in the pencil."

for a novice or callow communicator to properly channel through a sensitive, since successfully communicating from the other side of death seems to take considerable practice and skill.

But even though Frank Stockton didn't manifest that morning, Miss De Camp seemed to receive a psychic message from him the following evening. While resting in her room at the hotel, she felt some sort of presence trying to reach her. She mentally requested the entity to leave her alone, and she especially didn't want to produce any psychic writing. But she suddenly received an extrasensory message from the presence that instructed her to sit less closely behind the psychic. Miss De Camp instantly realized that her physical proximity to the psychic was probably interfering with Mrs. Soule's receptions from the spirit world, thereby causing the earlier failure.

Miss De Camp told this strange story to Hyslop while they drove to Mrs. Soule's residence the following morning. Hyslop felt that the suggestion was reasonable enough, and so they followed the advice.

This sitting (which was held on the morning of February 28) began with a surprise. When Prof. Hyslop first entered the séance room, Mrs. Soule was already picking up the purported communicator's presence. She told the professor that the name "Frank" had been popping into her mind that morning, and she felt that the name was being sent to her by her spirit guides. It certainly looked as if the session would be promising, but when the psychic finally entered trance, the subliminal stage was exceedingly long. By voice the Boston psychic referred to the communicator as a story writer who wore a ring—which was true enough, as Hyslop was to learn later. Luckily, though, it didn't take long before the Stockton personality commenced writing directly through Mrs. Soule's pencil—and he offered a message directly pertinent to De Camp, who was sitting silently behind the psychic.

"We are working for more than the present effect," the communicator began. "We are working for posterity and for the joy of working. It is great and wholesome as well. Do not let any one say I am overdoing it or that I will hurt her [the sitter]. I will not and I will supply whatever energy I use. I mean the one through whom I write my manuscripts . . . not the hand I am using now."

The communicator then proceeded to discuss the circumstances under which he had come to work through Etta De Camp, directly saying that he had been "brought" to her by other discarnate entities. This was certainly correct and corresponded with the report Miss De Camp had previously given to Hyslop in 1909. (See page 77.)

"I could have come before," the presence explained further, "but I was not sure that you wanted me and there are others around who helped me to do the work. I did not make her a medium, she was one and the people were already there and it was easy for me to work because the organized plan for work was already established."

The communicator then expounded in great detail concerning the procedures he was using to write his stories through his psychic scribe. He then chided Hyslop for making him write through a different channel!

"I know that I am able to write through my little friend's hand," the communicator wrote through Mrs. Soule's pencil, "and she knows it and that is quite enough for me at present. I hope you will not think I am not cordial to your work or that I do not appreciate your courtesy but this is so much more difficult for me than my work with her."

Hyslop politely responded by explaining that he was trying to help the communicator prove his identity to the world, but the communicator wasn't impressed by the professor's speech. He replied cordially that such evidence had previously been channeled through his regular scribe. When Hyslop restated his argument, explaining that the skeptics would probably be unimpressed by his post-mortem writings, the communicator responded in a truly Stocktonesque manner.

"What do I care about the skeptics?" wrote the purported Stockton.

"Probably nothing," concurred Hyslop.

"They are a bad lot and I am not trying to save them. . . . I do my work in my own way and I know and she knows and that is enough."

The communicator kept up this humorous train of thought as the sitting progressed.

"It [is] a funny thing," the writing through Mrs. Soule continued, "if a man can have no rest in heaven but must go on repeating for the sake of a lot of idiots that his name is John Smith or whatsoever it may be. I really have a desire to do a certain kind of work but deliver me from the class who cut up their relatives to see how their corpuscles match up."

The discarnate entity then referred back to his dissatisfaction with the experiments Hyslop was conducting through Minnie Soule.

"I think I won't do for your business, but personally I have no fight with you," the entity explained. "You can go on and save all the critics you can but don't send them to me when they die."

The communicator then began reminiscing about his previous life and work and started to fade, but not before signing his name to the preceding scripts. Mrs. Soule's hand fumbled through several false starts but ended by writing "Frank" and then "Stockton." Once these calling cards were written, Mrs. Soule's hand began to falter again and the pencil finally fell from her grasp. The Stockton personality had obviously left the sitting, and the séance came to a rapid conclusion.

Reading the transcript of this experiment today, what should the reader think?

This séance was in my opinion truly extraordinary for a number of reasons. Although it is true that the Stockton personality offered no verifiable information about himself, the scripts channeled through Mrs. Soule were filled with evidential information. Remember that the Boston psychic knew nothing about her sitter, who lived 235 miles away in New York. Even though every precaution had been taken to ensure the secrecy of Miss De Camp's identity, the spirit presence writing through Mrs. Soule seemed to know and realized why the sitting was being conducted. The purported discarnate explained in detail the reason for and manner in which he was creating stories through the sitter, and he even claimed to be the exact person Hyslop was secretly hoping to contact.

But another aspect of this sitting should strike the reader as even more evidential. Reading the transcripts of this séance even today, some seventy years later, Stockton's presence seems to literally jump right from the pages. His presence comes by virtue of the communicator's wit, cynical humor, and contemptuous flippancy.

This personal blueprint pervades the Soule/Stockton sittings, and its impact becomes even more obvious to anybody who has read Frank Stockton's books and short stories. His stories especially were filled with a specific style of humor. Capping the humor was the writer's wonderfully grotesque attitude toward his characters and their plights. Note that the same characteristics permeate the Soule sittings, during which the Stockton personality is often capricious and delightfully obnoxious. His total disdain for the situation in which he found himself while communicating with Hyslop would have been characteristic of the real Frank Stockton.

It is also remarkable how personally distinct the Stockton personality seems to be. The persona seems to be a living (!) personality, a personality totally independent of the psychic's own mind.

This was an important phenomenon that Hyslop liked to emphasize in his writings on the phenomenon of post-mortem contact. Each of the personalities that he contacted during his dozens of experiments with Minnie Soule seemed to be different. For example, just compare the Stockton personality with that of Robert Swain Gifford, who regularly communicated through Soule during the summer of 1908. The Gifford presence was serious and somber. Not even a suggestion of levity pervaded the sittings Hyslop undertook to establish contact with the painter. The Gifford personality seemed to pursue his work with Thompson and his communications through Mrs. Soule with a religious zeal. This sense of importance and urgency virtually infected each and every message communicated from him to the researchers. But this was certainly not the case with the Stockton personality, who was perpetually filled with whimsy and cynicism. His literal "go f— yourself" demeanor toward Hyslop and Minnie Soule stands in stark contrast to the (excuse the pun) deadly seriousness of Robert Swain Gifford.

It is therefore easy to sympathize with Hyslop's refusal to believe that such distinct personalities could be springing from the psychic's subconscious.

Hyslop conducted three more sittings with Mrs. Soule in order to establish contact with the departed Frank Stockton. These sittings weren't quite so lively, although considerable evidential information was imparted by the Stockton personality. The only surprise came during the last sitting, on the morning of March 6, when the deceased George Duysters placed a final *vraisamblance* by writing his full name through Soule. The personality seemed to be laboring to write, and the information he communicated wasn't extremely evidential. But the fact that a name so significant to James Hyslop and Etta De Camp was correctly communicated by the Boston sensitive was impressive enough.

Hyslop's investigation of the De Camp/Stockton case ended with this sitting, and whatever became of Miss De Camp and her mediumship isn't a matter of public record. The stories she wrote with the purported guidance of the deceased Frank Stockton were eventually published in 1913 when Miss De Camp's own book on the case was issued. *The Return of Frank R. Stockton* includes most of the stories written through her hand. The original records were filed with the American Society for Psychical Research. Miss De Camp later married and lived the rest of her life in relative obscurity.

CHAPTER 6

THE SEARCH FOR EVIDENCE

The work with Etta De Camp and Minnie Soule contributed further to James Hyslop's growing conviction in the reality of spirit obsession. He often referred to the De Camp/Stockton case in the same breath with the psychic return of Robert Swain Gifford. Of course, it may seem that Miss De Camp was simply a trance channel and that her rapport with the late Frank Stockton shouldn't be considered possession or a case of psychic invasion in the classic sense. But this remains a debatable point. Even though the young woman had been actively experimenting with possible mediumship when the Stockton personality first manifested, his coming was presaged by several discomfiting symptoms. She suffered from chronic pain, experienced two breakdowns, and could only retreat from this threatened insanity by doing the communicator's bidding. She became psychologically fixated on his writings and eventually permitted the Stockton persona to take limited control of her body and mind. She was literally invaded by the personality of Frank Stockton.

To the fertile intellect of Prof. Hyslop, the case carried the earmarks of psychic obsession. It struck him as certainly more complicated than simple mediumship. The professor considered a second characteristic of the case even more provocative. He was preoccupied with the specific evolution of Miss De Camp's experiences, from her first writings to the eventual appearance of the deceased Stockton through Minnie Soule. He pointed out in his final report that Miss De Camp's original writings were not very impressive from the standpoint of the psychical researcher. There had been nothing in her writings or experiences that couldn't be explained psychologically. In fact, the professor first favored a purely psychological interpretation of the case. But the six sittings he undertook in Boston proved that his first impressions had been incorrect. The fact that a personality calling himself Frank Stockton was successfully contacted proved, to his mind, that Etta De Camp's problems and scripts were genuinely paranormal.

The implications that he drew from this line of thinking were enormous, and he began to wonder what other forms of "psychological" experiences could be due to spiritistic influences: Dissociative episodes in general? So-called secondary personalities? Multiple personality? Perhaps even full-blown madness?

Such a list could be extended even further, and Hyslop soon threw himself into the study of abnormal psychology and its relationship to psychical research in hopes of clarifying their connections. Of course, some of the subjects the professor began studying were already familiar to him. He had even written a book partly dealing with psi and the far reaches of the disturbed mind in 1906 during an earlier phase of his career. This volume was entitled *Borderland of Psychical Research* and touched on such topics as dissociation and multiple personality. But in that volume Hyslop had taken a primarily psychological approach to those subjects. He now planned to return to the study of various personality disorders from a psychic and spiritistic standpoint.

The De Camp/Stockton case was still fresh in his mind when he undertook his next important investigation. This case, too, seemed to suggest that some common psychological experiences may be rooted in the paranormal. The investigation and its report by Hyslop were simple and uncomplicated, but the case further convinced him that the implications he had drawn from the DeCamp/Stockton and Thompson/Gifford cases were correct.

The case concerned a single incident that occurred sometime early in June 1912. Hyslop received a communication at that time from the witness who resided in New York. Mr. W. (the professor didn't even bother to give him a pseudonym) explained that he recently awoke from sleep to find an apparition standing in his room. The figure resembled a deceased friend, so the percipient asked the apparition to "prove" his identity. The phantom complied and referred (whether by voice or telepathy is not stated) to a game of cribbage and poker they had once played. The ghost then departed, and Mr. W. was left wondering if the experience was genuinely paranormal or merely some sort of hallucination.

This case was perfect for Hyslop's purposes. He noted in his written report that "the whole experience is liable to the objection that it was a hypnagogic illusion" and that "there is nothing supernormal in the information given, in so far as evidence of the fact was concerned." But the indefatigable professor wasn't willing to withdraw from the case, so he took the gentleman to Boston to sit with Minnie Soule. He hoped to demonstrate that a spiritistic influence lurked behind this "simple" case of post-sleep imagery.

Hyslop and Mr. W. conducted two sittings with Mrs. Soule on June 11 and 12—which was shortly after the incident occurred. The same entity who had so rudely wakened Mr. W. communicated during both sessions. The entity correctly referred to the card game and to the private club where the incident had taken place, and he offered a confused comment to the effect that he was influencing his friend's "dreams." No further experiments were conducted with the Boston psychic after these sittings since Hyslop believed that the spiritistic basis of his subject's experience had been adequately proven.

"We may some day come to the conclusion that spiritistic influences on human life are very extensive," Hyslop concluded on the basis of this experiment. And from that summer until his death eight years later, the founder of the ASPR was totally convinced that discarnate influences play a significant role in many psychological experiences. He also suspected that they probably play a predominant role in many psychological disturbances.

These suspicions were confirmed several times between 1912 and 1915, when Hyslop undertook three further investigations into the realms of spirit possession. The most curious and prolonged of these projects dates from October 1912, when he received a peculiar letter from a woman he called Miss Ida Ritchie in his report on her experiences. This remarkable woman claimed that she was receiving psychic messages from Emma Abbott, an opera singer with an international reputation who had died in 1891.* The original files on this case are still extant and catalogued at the American Society for Psychical Research in New York. They show that "Miss Ritchie's" real name was Ida Marie Rogers.

When she first wrote to Hyslop, Ida Rogers was living in the country outside Boston where she rented a room from an older friend. The young woman was an aspiring singer, but the death of her parents some years before had left her bereft of any financial support. Despite the fact that her late father's family had been Spiritualists, Miss Rogers did not

* Hyslop incorrectly gave the date as 1888 in his report.

follow the religion and had never frequented their meetings. But she did consider herself somewhat psychic, which led her to experiment with psychic writing in 1909. Since she was an aspiring but amateur singer, it is not surprising that her first spirit control was the late Emma Abbott, the greatly beloved soprano who had pioneered the performance of opera in English. Certainly anyone versed in psychology would probably posit that the lonely young woman's choice of control reflected her subconscious fantasies. But there was a unique twist to the case: Miss Rogers claimed that the singer was controlling her, coaching her, and helping her with her career! By the time she first wrote to James Hyslop, Ida Rogers was already successfully performing and giving local recitals. The stunning rise in her career struck many of her friends as inexplicable, since she had undertaken frightfully little formal training. She had consulted with Lillian Nordica, who was then this country's leading Wagnerian soprano, but had not really been coached or instructed by her.

There was, however, an important complication to the case. Even though Miss Rogers was receiving copious writings from the purported spirit of Emma Abbott, she was also receiving writings from her late mother. It seems that this second entity wasn't satisfied with her daughter's situation and kept warning the confused young singer to desist from engaging in any rapprochement with the deceased soprano! So when Miss Rogers first made contact with Hyslop, she was being pulled in different directions by her burgeoning mediumship. This situation was causing her no little personal stress. She would later explain to Hyslop,

> When Miss Abbott first came to me and I took up the automatic writing, it was a great help to me. After a time, my mother came to me, but instead of being a help she tried to hinder my progress in every way. She would use up all the time writing herself and running down everybody and everything, especially Miss Abbott. She told me not to have anything to do with her. She said Miss Abbott could not help me in any way. This went on from week to week until I found she was putting a stop to all progress. I would cry and give it up for a time.

This is an important passage, for the mother's communications would play a decisive and evidential role later in the case.

What probably piqued Hyslop's interest in the report was the fact that Ida Rogers also claimed that the late William James sometimes communicated through her pencil. Hyslop had spent considerable time the previous year in Boston and Virginia trying to establish contact with his former colleague. (See Chapter 5.) So the chance to verify some of the messages he had received through Minnie Soule and Mrs. Cleaveland was probably irresistable. Miss Rogers eventually sent Hyslop the scripts she had purportedly received from James, which consisted solely of two lengthy paragraphs. Hyslop was underwhelmed by them and commented in his report on the case that "there [were] a few recognizable touches, vague and general and interfused with Miss Ritchie's [Rogers's] mind, of thought that is like Prof. James, but whether due to chance or not is not determinable."

The only impressive feature of these communications, to Hyslop's mind, was Miss Rogers's claim that she was totally unfamiliar with William James or his writings. This is a claim that the professor took at face value, although he probably should have questioned it. He also overlooked the fact that Miss Rogers was obviously familiar with his own writings, which often referred to the former Harvard professor. So in this respect, it certainly looks as if Hyslop's personal bias got the better of him.

Despite the unimpressive contents of the scripts, Hyslop was ultimately drawn to the case for two other reasons. The first concerned his subject's burgeoning musical talent and rapidly developing career. Miss Rogers's musical abilities were surprisingly similar to the development of Frederic Thompson's skill at the easel and to Etta De Camp's sudden facility for writing short stories. Both of these subjects had been "guided," so to speak, by well-known public figures, whose presence and influence had been proven to Hyslop's satisfaction through Minnie Soule and other gifted sensitives. The professor couldn't resist the thought that Ida Rogers's experiences were also the probable result of a benign but severe post-mortem influence.

"Normal education is the usual explanation for any excellence whatever beyond original endowments," he explained in his report on the case. "But when excellence is greater than we find in the average person with the proper education and yet is not accompanied by the corresponding education . . . it becomes a phenomenon of some psychological interest, tho[ugh] it may not be in any respect miraculous. It is at least anomalous and perhaps sufficient so to harmonize with the hypothesis suggested by other more important and evidential facts."

Hyslop was obviously referring to his research on the Thompson/Gifford and De Camp/Stockton cases.

"All I wish to indicate in this statement of the facts," he concluded, "is that there is some apparent discrepancy between the girl's education and the degree of her singing."

This was a debatable point, though, since history has produced many self-taught singers who managed successful careers. Self-taught opera singers were, in fact, not rare during the nineteenth century.

But Hyslop was also drawn to the case for another important reason. It seems that Ida Rogers had seen an evidential apparition that directly related to her purported contact with the surviving soul of Emma Abbott. This provocative incident occurred sometime during the period when she was first receiving writings from the former singer. She was in her room when she saw the ghost in broad daylight. The figure first materialized beside her bureau and then turned and faced her. She was dressed in white, and her face was partially hidden by a veil. The phantom's sudden appearance so frightened the young woman that she moved into a different room in her landlady's residence!

Even though Miss Rogers was puzzled by the ghostly figure, she didn't discover any clues concerning its identity for several months. Then one day when she and her landlady were rummaging through some old newspapers and clippings, they found a brief report on the life and death of Emma Abbott that stated that the singer had been particularly partial to a veil she had found in Paris. It soon became her personal good-luck charm, and she had been buried with part of it covering her face. The other portion had been sectioned and given to her former colleagues at the Emma Abbott English Opera Company as remembrances. This information was enough for the impressionable Miss Rogers to feel that the wraith's identity had finally been established.

Hyslop was intrigued enough by this report that he researched the incident in considerable depth. He eventually learned that the critical clipping had been found in a collection of papers previously amassed by a relative of Miss Rogers. (These papers consisted of a potpourri of receipts, calendars, pieces of poetry, and so forth.) So it really did look as though the discovery of the report of Emma Abbott's death was purely accidental.

What Hyslop didn't know, however, was that psychokinesis was also breaking out in the singer's presence. Loud raps would often startle her when she was resting in her room, and they even broke forth while she was visiting her friends. The raps were heard by several witnesses, although Hyslop only learned of this peculiar phenomenon several months later.

From a purely evidential standpoint, though, the case was hardly impressive, even though Hyslop well knew that the Thompson and

De Camp cases had not begun very propitiously. During most of 1912 and 1913 he was spending considerable time each week in Boston working with Minnie Soule, so the course of action he took in the Rogers case was predictable. He arranged for her to visit the city for a series of sittings with the psychic between February and March 1913. Of course, these sittings presented a serious problem, since Miss Rogers had previously sung recitals in Boston. She was therefore something of a public figure, although there is no reason to believe that Minnie Soule knew of her. But Hyslop was nothing if not perennially cautious, so he employed his customary controls for the sittings, similar to those he had previously taken to keep Etta De Camp's identity from the sensitive. He refrained from informing Mrs. Soule that a new sitter was coming with him for his weekly experiments, and Miss Rogers only entered her sitting room after the psychic was deeply entranced.

Unfortunately, though, Miss Rogers turned out to be an exceedingly poor sitter. Several times she nearly spoiled the evidence received by Mrs. Soule by making leading and inopportune statements.

The general tone of these sittings was in stark contrast to the sessions Hyslop had held to contact R. Swain Gifford and Frank Stockton. These new experiments reflected neither the urgency of the Gifford communications nor the puckishness of Frank Stockton's flippant repartée. Several communications pertinent to Miss Rogers's life and situation eventually arose from the sittings, but they were delivered by a series of surprising and unexpected discarnates. In fact, the entire series constitutes a long string of surprises and unexpected developments.

The first sitting scheduled by Prof. Hyslop and Miss Rogers took place on the morning of February 24. Minnie Soule entered trance without difficulty, but whatever personality was trying to control her immediately experienced difficulties. The pencil fell from Mrs. Soule's hand twice before she began to produce scrawls. Several more moments passed before any coherent messages were received and delivered. Mrs. Soule's pencil finally began trying to write the word *my* and eventually succeeded in writing *my little Girl*. The production of this phrase immediately impressed Hyslop, since the same phrase had often cropped up in Miss Rogers's own scripts. (The phrase had often been employed by Emma Abbott when referring to her scribe.)

The next series of written messages produced by Soule seemed even more pertinent to the sitter.

Mrs. Soule's communicator: She needs me now as much as ever.
            Hyslop: For what?

Mrs. Soule's communicator:	For her work which I want done.
Hyslop:	What kind of work is that?
Mrs. Soule's communicator:	Spirit work.
Hyslop:	What is her work?
Mrs. Soule's communicator:	It is her work.
Hyslop:	Yes, but what kind of work is that? It should be on the paper here so that it will be evidence.

Hyslop was obviously trying to encourage the communicator to refer to the sitter's singing, but the entity didn't seem to understand his concern. The communicator began rambling endlessly, then finally succeeded in getting the knack of writing through Mrs. Soule. The ghostly visitor began by simply asking whether the sitter knew a person whose name began with the letter L. The communicator was obviously encountering difficulties focusing on the proper name when Miss Rogers made a *faux pas* that contaminated the remainder of the sitting. Miss Rogers fumbled badly by whispering Lillian Nordica's name to Hyslop before the professor could motion to her to keep silent, and there is every reason to believe that Mrs. Soule subliminally heard the comment. This mistake ruined the evidence when Mrs. Soule wrote the name "Lillian" three times later during the session. The incident could also have cued the psychic's subconscious that the sitter's expectations related to singing and music.

As the session progressed, the first of several surprise communicators made contact with Hyslop and the sitter. The (as yet unidentified) first communicator explained that the sitter's mother was present, and that they were working together to establish contact with Ida Rogers from the world beyond. This was an impressive "hit" by the communicator—who probably had only a faint notion that a second sitter was present in the room—since Mrs. Soule couldn't have known that the sitter's mother was deceased. The same persona then referred directly to the rappings that Mrs. Ritchie had been hearing in her room, claiming direct responsibility for them! This was an extraordinary reference, since even Hyslop knew nothing about the rappings during this phase of the investigation.* But by this time the communicator was tiring and losing

---

*Hyslop later contacted a friend of Miss Rogers's who corroborated the singer's claim. She explained to the professor that "Miss Rogers remained overnight with me and after we had retired my mother came into the room. She sat down on the bed for a little chat. We heard some very loud raps at the head of the bed by Miss Rogers's side. We told mother to get up, thinking her weight might have caused the noise. She

control of the psychic. The presence began to fade but ended with a flourish by writing the single word *singer* through Mrs. Soule's clenched fingers.

The sitting had not accomplished very much, but Hyslop was encouraged by the few clues that were uncovered through Minnie Soule's psychic skills. Hyslop was, however, extremely puzzled by this sitting, since it had been unlike any he had previously witnessed with Minnie Soule. The entity who had been trying to communicate with him couldn't even hold the pencil correctly. Hyslop later explained in his report that during this sitting Mrs. Soule either dropped or broke the pencil several times. She shifted her hand constantly in order to maintain her control of it. Toward the end of the sitting Hyslop even helped brace the pencil himself so that the communicator could continue with the writing.

The experiments didn't progress any better when Ida Rogers and Hyslop sat with Minnie Soule again the following morning. It was obvious that the sitter's mother was trying to communicate, but little more was forthcoming. The real surprise came during the sitting of February 26, which constituted their third attempt to make contact with the late Emma Abbott. This sitting commenced at nine o'clock in the morning, which was a bit earlier than usual for the Boston psychic. Mrs. Soule entered the writing stage of the séance immediately, and a new communicator soon began manipulating her hand and pencil—for the purpose of coaching the sitter on proper singing technique!

"You are a good man," the communicator commented to Hyslop.

"I hope so," replied the professor.

"I hope so too for you have my friend with you," continued the discarnate, who clearly knew Ida Rogers.

The pencil fell from Mrs. Soule's hand at this point. This type of interruption usually signified a change in control, but the communicator's silence was only momentary. The communicator immediately continued the conversation.

"I have been trying to come to her by some method you do not understand," the persona explained. "Does she know about deep breathing?"

Hyslop looked at Rogers who shook her head.

"I do not mean as a health measure," the communicator remarked, "but an exercise for better control of the voice. Answer me."

got up but the raps continued." It appeared that Miss Rogers was entering a trance, and the raps only ceased when the women began joking about the mysterious sounds.

The communicator seemed rather indignant, so Hyslop responded on behalf of the sitter. "No," he explained, "she has not engaged in it but I imagine you want that advice followed."

The professor's comment was correct and pertinent, and the communicator proceeded to launch into a speech on correct vocal production. "I mean the breath exercise for prolonging out rounding, rounding the notes," the presence explained. ". . . Short breath spoils beauty of tone. I am no lady. I am a man."

This comment probably came as a surprise to Hyslop and Miss Rogers, who likely believed that they were communicating with the spirit of Emma Abbott.

". . . and I have found a way to make good advance in the science of . . . my desires," the communicator went on to say. "I must ask for definite co-operation and she will not regret the association with us."

"I understand," replied Hyslop, "and I shall back you up all I can."

The communicator offered a few more comments and then signed his name to the writings, giving it as "Carl Meuhler." Hyslop responded by speaking to the communicator in German, since he himself spoke the language fluently. The communicator successfully managed to write a few words in the same language through Mrs. Soule, but soon faltered and lost control of the psychic. The rest of the sitting was taken over by an unknown communicator whose writings were not pertinent to the plight of Ida Rogers.

This critical session came as a shock to Hyslop and his sitter. Their original plan had been to establish possible communication with the late Emma Abbott. No evidence had ever come through Miss Rogers's scripts that a *group* of discarnates was influencing the young singer.

Unfortunately the importance of these jolting communications was compromised by the fact that Mrs. Soule's subconscious mind probably knew that her sitter was a singer. But the professor himself tended to dismiss the importance of this possibility. After years of work with the Boston psychic, he knew that her communicators and control were not usually influenced by leading comments blurted out by her clients.

Despite these problems and possibilities, Hyslop remained puzzled by the communicator's unexpected presence and possible identity. He had never heard of any Carl Muehler, and Ida Rogers didn't recognize the name, either. So shortly after conducting the sitting, Hyslop engaged in a short search to discover any extant records of his possible earthly existence. He began by checking general-information encyclopedias, but this search was fruitless. No better results were forthcoming until he consulted several music encyclopedias. The professor eventually discovered that a Karl Friedrich Mueller and his son (also named Karl) were singers who had served in the Duke of Brunswick's court. They later left the Duke's service to take up residence in Berlin. Even though the father had died in 1873, Hyslop was convinced that Mrs. Soule's communicator was probably the son. The professor could not, however, discover the date of the son's death, so he sent off inquiries to the University of Berlin. From the return response he learned that Karl Mueller had died in 1907, two years before Miss Ida Rogers suddenly began developing her musical skills. This peculiar coincidence encouraged Hyslop in his belief that he was beginning to successfully unravel the Rogers case.

Of course, Karl Mueller is a relatively common name, and the communicator hadn't even spelled it correctly. But Hyslop believed that the spelling produced during the sitting—i.e., Meuhler—was an archaic derivative of "Mueller."

Whatever puzzles resulted from the February 26 sitting were resolved during Hyslop's subsequent experiments with Minnie Soule. He returned to Boston the following March where he met with Rogers, who was staying in the city with friends. By this time the professor knew the communicator's possible identity, though Mrs. Soule still had no conscious knowledge that he had been secretly bringing a female sitter to their weekly sessions. Even at this late stage in the sittings, Hyslop had still been instructing his subject to enter (and subsequently leave) Mrs. Soule's parlor while the psychic remained unconscious.

Hyslop's sitting with the psychic on March 3, as customary, began promptly at ten o'clock in the morning. Shortly after Miss Rogers entered the room, Mrs. Soule grabbed a pencil and began scrawling. Karl Mueller's name was immediately and correctly written in bold print. The communicator specifically explained that his first name was spelled with a K and not with a C, thereby correcting the error produced during the previous week's session. Hyslop was eager for the communicator to establish his personal identity, so he pressed the entity in that direction.

"Thank you for what you have done here," he began by saying. "In order to strengthen the evidence I shall ask you what was your occupation in life on earth."

The communicator seemed prepared for the challenge. "That I will tell you," replied the discarnate courteously, "for I too am desirous of making the evidence as clear as can be."

The persona paused for a moment and then wrote the word *music*. Hyslop was delighted with the result, but the communicator had more surprises in store for him.

"Music was and is my theme," the persona continued through Mrs. Soule. "Berlin my . . . home . . . but not all my earthly life was spent there. Part of it in America and when I came to this state of life . . . I was not surprised for I had long been conscious of the attendance of spirits in my own life. I will bring nothing but good to her [the sitter] for I am intent [sic] of the expressions of the finer gifts through media."

The communicator did not, however, spend much more time proving his earthly existence, and the sitting took a new direction. During the first sitting with Mrs. Soule, the communicators writing through the psychic had suggested that the sitter's late parents were somehow implicated in her musical development. Starting with the March 3 session, the successful communication of this message to Ida Rogers began to preoccupy Mrs. Soule's controls. This theme was continued by the Karl Mueller personality throughout his conversations with Hyslop.

"Enough has been done of other types [of evidence] to satisfy me," the deceased Karl Mueller explained through Mrs. Soule's pencil, "and enough has been done of the type I desire to perform without any recognition of the source, and experiments are to be continuing with her. All this is with the knowledge and consent of her folks . . . who are with me today."

Nothing could have been more pertinent to Ida Rogers's situation and to Hyslop's plans for solving the case. Recall that the plan behind these sittings with Minnie Soule had been to shed light on Miss Rogers's belief that discarnate influences were guiding her career. By this fourth sitting it was clear that she and Hyslop were receiving information directly relevant to this possibility. But the situation now seemed to be more complex than either of them had first realized. It began to look as if the sitter's parents, who had deserted her by their premature deaths, were trying to rectify these circumstances from their side of the veil. They were apparently coordinating an effort to help their daughter by working with deceased vocal coaches and singers!

This situation promised to help Hyslop prove the spiritistic nature

of the case. Even more clues were delivered by Mrs. Soule's communicators later during the sitting.

"Her own desire and purpose helps us to the performance of the
work," explained the Mueller personality through Mrs. Soule's scribbling pencil. "I will take care of the tone if she will take care of herself.
She knows what I mean."

Hyslop encouraged the communicator at this point in the session,
hoping that the persona would offer more messages pertinent to Miss
Rogers.

The entity readily complied. "[She] is only too ready if she could
be told what to do," the communicator commented.

"Yes, I understand," replied the professor.

"Little excitement as possible," continued the communicator.
"Excitement brings tension and tension produces uneven action by us."

"I understand," repeated the researcher.

The communicator then continued his coaching. "Sleep, food,
exercise, air," listed the entity. "Air, practice and faith . . . and the
rest is our work. . . . Sooner than she dreams opportunity opens the
door and we . . . will take it for our work. Study German songs."

The communicator proceeded to turn his conversation toward more
metaphysical matters but then simply faded away. Some previous communicators privately known to Hyslop from his earlier work with Mrs.
Soule took over the pencil, encouraged the professor in his work, and
then ended the session.

Despite the fact that no communications were directly received
from the late Emma Abbott, it certainly looked as if Hyslop's experiments with Ida Rogers and Minnie Soule were leading somewhere. There
can be little doubt that Mrs. Soule's communicators knew a great deal
about the sitter, and they even seemed cognizant of Hyslop's plan behind bringing the singer to the sensitive. It was unfortunate that Miss
Rogers had slipped so badly by mentioning Lillian Nordica by name in
the psychic's presence. But it is unlikely that Soule's subconscious mind
could have developed such a pertinent scenario concerning the singer's
situation from this single clue. What is so impressive is, in fact, how
much the sittings *departed* from the expectations Hyslop and his subject
probably entertained before undertaking them. Hyslop's singular plan
had been simply to secure contact with the surviving soul of Emma
Abbott. His sittings in Boston were therefore identical in intention to
his earlier experiments with Frederic Thompson and Etta De Camp,

Minnie Soule, and Mrs. Cleaveland. If either the professor or his sitter dropped any clues about their mission during the sitting, they probably would have related to these expectations.

But what did Hyslop really receive? An entirely different story unfolded during the course of his experiments from what he expected. Perhaps it's ironic that no personality claiming to be the late Emma Abbott ever communicated during these first sittings.

The surprising nature of these sittings also shed some provocative light on the source of Mrs. Soule's mediumship and her spirit communicators. At the turn of the century, psychical researchers in the United States and England were hopelessly divided over the survival issue. Most of them couldn't decide whether gifted psychics such as Minnie Soule and Leonore Piper were genuinely contacting the dead or were simply gifted mind readers. They considered it possible that while in trance these psychics produced nothing but secondary personalities who only pretended to be spirit entities—but who used telepathy and clairvoyance to bolster their bogus claims. Such a facile theory could, for example, easily explain the Stockton messages that Hyslop had received through Mrs. Soule in 1912.

But this theory fails to explain the information Hyslop received during his experiments with Ida Rogers and Mrs. Soule. If Minnie Soule had been reading the minds of her sitters, she would have spun a scenario that included communications from the late Emma Abbott. But this just isn't what took place during the sittings. An entirely different story was expounded by the psychic and her communicators, concerning a deceased but traceable vocal coach who once lived in Berlin but who was currently guiding the sitter's career. Remember that Ida Rogers was an orphan, and she was perfectly indifferent to establishing contact with her late parents. This discarnate couple were, however, conspicuously present during the sittings, and their role in the sittings became more important as the session progressed. From whose mind could this complicated—but unfailingly consistent—information be coming if not from the world beyond the light? This is an issue to which we'll return later in this book.

But for now, let's return to Hyslop and his experiments.

Even though his sitting with Mrs. Soule on March 3 had been extremely evidential, Hyslop did not feel that the Rogers case had reached any resolution. He therefore scheduled five more sittings from March 4 and extending through March 12. The surviving personality of Emma Abbott did seem to communicate during the March 4 sitting, for when

Soule entered her trance, a communicator claiming to be an opera singer first controlled the séance. The communicator offered several names of well-known opera singers, but she encountered difficulties communicating her own. The most impressive evidence offered was the name "Brignoli," which meant nothing to either Hyslop or Miss Rogers, but they later learned that Brignoli was an Italian tenor who had sung with Emma Abbott early in her career. Unfortunately, any further evidence from the Emma Abbott persona was ruined later during this fascinating sitting by Miss Rogers. When the communicator tried to endorse the scripts, the sitter whispered the famous singer's name and it is conceivable that Mrs. Soule heard her.

The sitting Hyslop and Miss Rogers conducted with Minnie Soule on the morning of March 10 was equally evidential. Most of the séance was occupied by the presence of a new communicator who claimed to be the sitter's deceased father. Since this entity wasn't familiar with properly controlling the sensitive, his efforts to communicate were labored and only partially successful. But this promising sitting, too, was spoiled by Miss Rogers's behavior. She was totally uninterested in her father's possible return from the dead and refused to encourage him to write through Mrs. Soule. She was interested only in establishing person-to-person contact with Emma Abbott, so she rocked back and forth in her chair silently until Hyslop admonished her to stop. Hyslop realized that the communicator was becoming upset by his purported daughter's behavior and encouraged him to write further. He designed his speech to the entity as a signal to Miss Rogers that he wasn't happy with her attitude toward the communicator. This subtle reproof had little effect on the sitter, though, and Mrs. Soule's controls soon brought the session to a close.

"As soon as the sitting was over," commented the professor in his report on the case, "I told the lady that it was her attitude that spoiled the sitting." He lectured her further, but Miss Rogers maintained her complete indifference.

Despite his annoyance with his client, Hyslop proceeded with the sittings. The final sessions the couple held with Mrs. Soule elicited several more bits of evidential information pertinent to the earthly life of Emma Abbott, but Hyslop decided to take a break from the case at this point in the investigation to work on another project. He spent the rest of the month trying to determine whether Minnie Soule's controls could diagnose the illnesses of her sitters, either clairvoyantly or by long-distance remote viewing. Mrs. Soule had little experience with such research but cooperated in two experiments which produced curious but hardly clear-cut results.

By the end of March, then, the first phase of Hyslop's research with the Rogers case had been completed. The results struck him as a mixture of success and failure. It was clear that the information received through Mrs. Soule's mediumship was clearly directly pertinent to the client, but several loose ends were still crying for resolution. Hyslop also remained puzzled by the communications from the Karl Mueller personality, whose sudden presence was the case's most notable surprise. But what was so perplexing to him was his failure to reach the surviving spirit of Emma Abbott more directly. During the months when the sittings were being held, Miss Rogers was still receiving voluminous writings from the singer through her own psychic writing. She had also received several communications from her late mother, who was still warning her to keep her distance from Emma Abbott! Hyslop was willing to take Miss Rogers's scripts at face value, so he couldn't understand why the opera singer took a backseat during the sessions with Mrs. Soule. It certainly seemed that the diva's spirit wished to communicate with him, but only suggestions of her presence were being picked up.

Hyslop's furlough from the Rogers case was not permanent, however, and he kept in touch with the young woman for several more months. He learned the following June, for instance, that Emma Abbott's ostensible apparition had again appeared, this time during a church picnic. Miss Rogers described the encounter in a letter she posted to the professor.

A strange thing happened a few nights before I went away. I was invited with a lot of church people to a basket lunch about six miles from here. There were quite a few of the church people there when I arrived and on leaving the car you had to walk quite a distance through the woods and up quite a steep hill where the others had gathered. When we were all sitting down and had started to eat our lunch, the minister's wife turned to me and said: "Why Miss Ritchie, where is Mrs. B____ [Miss Ritchie's landlady]." I said: "She did not feel able to come to-night." It was then about 5:30. She then said: "Well, who was the lady that came with you?" I said: *"No one. I came alone."* She then said: "I distinctly saw a woman walking by your side as you came through the woods and up the hill." Again I told her I was all alone, and if you could have seen her face! It was as white as a sheet. Of course I knew whom she saw, but had I said so, I would have been asked to leave, for they (Baptists) are so against such things.

This development probably contributed to Hyslop's desire to resume the investigation. So in December 1913 he decided to conduct more experiments to contact Miss Rogers's spirit contacts. He requested that she return to Boston for further sittings with Mrs. Soule, and together they held a series of five sessions between December 8 and December 17. Since Miss Rogers only entered Mrs. Soule's séance room after the psychic was well into her trance, the Boston psychic never realized that her sitter was a repeat caller. In the meantime, Hyslop booked a private sitting with Mrs. Soule on December 22 to further explore the case.

Each of these sittings was extremely evidential. During the first sitting, for instance, Mrs. Soule's pencil correctly scribbled the name of Emma Abbott, who seemed to take control of the psychic. The medium was then thrown into a coughing fit by the communicator, which piqued the professor's interest since Emma Abbott had died during a bout of pneumonia.

The psychic's coughing was extremely severe. "I soon saw she was in [the] apparent death throes of one dying from trouble with the lungs," noted Hyslop during the sitting. "I placed the left hand on her forehead and a little later the right hand on her throat also. There was much coughing and struggling, as if she would lose her breath and die. Finally she calmed down and the face twisted a moment and became placid."

The communicator then relinquished control, and then—from the subliminal state of her trance—Mrs. Soule clairvoyantly explained to the sitters what had caused the discomfort.

Mrs. Soule: Am I dead?
   Hyslop: I guess you have been. It is all right. I think the person got too far in.
Mrs. Soule: What did they do it for?
   Hyslop: I do not think they intended it at all. It only happened by accident.
Mrs. Soule: Oh, oh. There must have been a dreadful pain in the lungs. Did you know it?
   Hyslop: Yes.
Mrs. Soule: Is that what made them do it?
   Hyslop: Yes.

Mrs. Soule: Oh, I wish you would put your hand . . .
    Hyslop: What?
Mrs. Soule: . . . where I cough.

Hyslop complied and placed his hand on his own chest for a few moments. The gesture inexplicitly helped Mrs. Soule. The sitting then continued.

Mrs. Soule: That's better. Thank you, that is better. It is just like having it
              yourself, isn't it?
    Hyslop: Yes.
Mrs. Soule: You don't know who it is, but it is a lady.
    Hyslop: Yes, I know.
Mrs. Soule: She stooped down and said, so sorry. It was just the sympathetic
              current, you know.
    Hyslop: Yes.
Mrs. Soule: I couldn't help it. Do you know if she ever had a green velvet
              dress?
    Hyslop: We don't know.
Mrs. Soule: I see this long velvet dress, a sort of olive green like a Marguerite
              costume.
    Hyslop: Yes.
Mrs. Soule: It looks like that . . . down the back, really a Marguerite cos-
              tume.* She is pretty in it. I don't think I can get this and the
              name. I kind of get them mixed. I can't tell you.
    Hyslop: Try.
Mrs. Soule: When I said it was Marguerite, you know she changed it and said
              the dress belonged to Elsa** and not to Marguerite. Perhaps you
              know now do you?
    Hyslop: Yes.
Mrs. Soule: Shall I tell you a little word she says?
    Hyslop: Yes.
Mrs. Soule: God bless my little friend.
    Hyslop: If you can, tell who she is.
Mrs. Soule: I think she is an actress, you know. I think so.
    Hyslop: Well, tell all you can.
Mrs. Soule: Well, I only think so. She don't tell me. I can't . . . Why yes
               . . . you know her.

    *This is a reference to the character of Marguerite in Charles Gounod's opera *Faust*, a role Emma Abbot often sang. Hyslop erroneously stated in his report that she never sang the role.
    **Elsa is the heroine in Richard Wagner's opera *Lohengrin*.

Hyslop: Who is it?

Mrs. Soule: Why, she has been here before. She would rather tell it herself.

Hyslop: She must tell.

Mrs. Soule: Why?

Hyslop: For evidence.

Mrs. Soule: I have forgotten her name. I have seen her in this room before but I don't remember the name. She put her hand on my forehead and won't let me remember. I ought to know. . . . She makes me think of that singer. You know what I mean.

Hyslop: Yes, you ought to be able to tell.

Mrs. Soule: Well, then she won't let me?

Hyslop: All right.

Mrs. Soule: I remember Emma, Emma, you know. Emma, Emma. Goodbye.

Hyslop: Goodbye.

Mrs. Soule: I didn't tell you did I?

Hyslop: No.

Despite this impressive series of communications, the focus of the sittings changed during the next week, when the sitter's mother became eager to communicate in order to explain the reason behind her daughter's psychic plight. During the sitting of December 15 she explained in great detail that she had been wrong in trying to keep her daughter from psychically communing with Emma Abbott.

This unexpected message came as a startling development in the sittings since it fully corroborated the contents of Ida Rogers's private scripts. This incident proved to Hyslop that the experiments were definitely on the right track. He realized, too, that the case now pointed— in every respect—to the psychic presence of the dead in Ida Rogers's life. Some sort of plan was obviously being orchestrated from the world of the dead to help the sitter in her career.

It seemed essential for Mrs. Soule's communicators to deliver this important message to the sitter, even though it often undermined Hyslop's personal goal of securing evidential information from the entities. In this respect the case was slightly reminiscent of the Frank Stockton case, in which the chief communicator also hadn't seemed interested in Hyslop's plan. (Despite the gentle cajoling of the professor, the Stockton communicator had been determined to get through only the information *he* felt was important.)

Hyslop emphasized this point in his report, for he felt that only the spiritistic theory could explain these developments.

The important thing to which I wish here to call attention is the fact that there was less interest by the controls in my scientific object in these experiments than there was in the lady's development and the exhibition of spirit power on which they were bent. My object to increase the scientific evidence was discarded in the interests of ethical harmony in the agencies desiring to use the lady for their manifestations. The process by which it was all effected was one with which we are gradually getting acquainted in our work, and that is to bring a recalcitrant spirit to a medium and to educate it in some way to harmonious action. Here the mother was to be convinced that her course was injurious to her daughter and that the great truth of spirit influences on the world was too important to be sacrificed to the fears of a mother who had not yet gotten beyond her earthly orthodox ideas. There is not the proof yet for the rigid sceptic that this psychological machinery is real, but it is accumulating and I have no doubt from what I have seen in other cases that it contains an important truth. Here it seemed more important that the lady's interests be protected, and the process had this additional importance, that the lady herself had cultivated much hostility to the return of her father and mother, and it is possible that this feeling was the cause of her mother's unwitting antagonism to her development. We do not know. But to get both the dead and the living into harmony seemed to be the primary object of the controls, even at the sacrifice of my object.

The professor was not to be disappointed, for—in true operatic fashion—the grand finale of the case came during the final sitting, which took place on December 22, when Hyslop sat privately with Mrs. Soule. Right at the beginning of this session, the spirit of Emma Abbott communicated promptly and wrote her proper name through the psychic. The discarnate then explained in great depth why she was helping Ida Rogers and why she had relinquished control of the sittings to the sitter's mother.

"I could not do what I wanted to do the other day," the communicator explained.

When Hyslop asked why, the entity elaborated.

"Because the influence of the mother was so strong and persistent," she continued. "She did not get her message all down as she desired and kept trying to do something and no one had the heart to put her aside. This may show that we are human beings still, and have feeling quite apart from mere duty. The sentiment of the situation appealed to all of us."

This conversation between the discarnate singer and Hyslop continued for several minutes. Eventually the surviving soul of Emma Abbott indicated why she had played such a small role in the first sittings. The critical factor had been Ida Rogers's strong resistance to hearing from her parents, who wished to communicate with her from the start of the Boston experiments.

"I can talk with you alone much better than when she was here with all her prejudice and feeling stirred by regret and pain and uncertainty," the communicator stated. "It was hard to keep still the first days but after that I found no trouble. I recalled the first time she came here and the influx of power which came to this place and I longed to go forward as I felt I would but . . . discretion was the better part of valor and so I waited for the mother to get her release if possible."

The deceased singer's control of the psychic grew as the sitting progressed, and finally took physical possession of Minnie Soule's voice. The legendary singer ceased writing through the sensitive's hand and soon Mrs. Soule began singing in French, trilling and vocalizing in genuine bravura fashion, much to Hyslop's delight.* She kept dropping the pencil while engaged in these vocal pyrotechnics, which Hyslop continually replaced in her grasp since he still hoped to secure more information from the communicator.

This unusual display continued for several moments, and then the pencil fell from Mrs. Soule's hand for the last time. She suddenly stopped singing and the sitting—and the entire case, as far as Hyslop was concerned—came to a close.

What became of Ida Rogers isn't known. She apparently didn't make a permanent mark on the musical world. Hyslop, on the other hand, spent several months during the following two years (1914–15) pursuing his research on psychopathology and spirit obsession. He eventually published brief reports on two further cases of psychic invasion, but neither of them displayed the strong evidential features of the Thompson, De Camp, or Rogers cases. Both concerned ordinary people who suddenly developed artistic skills, and both subjects were diagnosed as suffering from spirit possession by Mrs. Soule during subsequent ex-

---

* Readers without a background in vocal technique may not realize the significance of this report. Trilling (rapidly altering between two tones a step or half-step apart) with the voice is extremely difficult. Producing the effect is a skill, and even some seasoned opera singers "fake" their trills by the use of a wide rapid vibrato. If Mrs. Soule really did produce trills as Hyslop stated in his report, the performance would seem remarkable and evidential.

periments. But Prof. Hyslop's most important project during these months focused on a related subject. The researcher had long been fascinated by the strange phenomenon of multiple personality, and by 1914 he was beginning to think that spiritistic influences might be a factor in its occurrence. The opportunity to prove this theory finally presented itself that November, and Hyslop threw himself into the case with his customary zeal. It would be his final major contribution to the study of spiritistic obsession, as well as his most complicated.

CHAPTER 7

THE MANY FACES OF
DORIS FISCHER—PART 1

While James Hyslop was still conducting his research into the possible existence of spirit possession and obsession, the strange case of Doris Fischer was gradually coming to light. This case is so complex that only a summary of its main features can be given in this book, though it was the single case that eventually served as the cornerstone in the evidence Hyslop was collecting.

Doris (whose real name was Brittia L. Fritschle) was born in Pittsburgh, Pennsylvania, in 1889. During this era the city's major industries were mining and manufacturing. It was a restless time in Pittsburgh's history, with its population still smarting from the great economic crisis of 1873, which had resulted in the closure of several banks and business firms. The city saw railway strikes and riots in the late 1870s and would see more violence in the decades to come.

Doris was born of German stock and her childhood reflected the city's turbulence. Although her father was neither uneducated nor ignorant, he was prone to bouts of drinking and extreme violence. These problems eventually caused him to lose his executive job, which forced him to work as a common laborer while Doris was growing up. Her beloved mother also suffered endlessly at the hands of her drunken husband. She had come from a prominent family but entered into her marriage while still a young woman. She soon gave birth to several children. Her parents never approved of her choice and (perhaps justifiably) disowned her after she eloped with him. The couple endured a life of poverty in a poor section of Pittsburgh, where the beginnings of little Doris's problems exploded one tragic night in 1892, when the girl was only three years old. Mrs. Fischer was taking her to bed when her inebriated husband burst in upon them, went into a rage, and ripped the child from his wife's arms. Displaying the most insidious violence conceivable, he threw the helpless child to the floor.

Doris was not the same after she recovered from this incident. She successfully survived the physical affects of the incident, but she never overcame the psychological trauma that it produced. After that terrible night and for several years to come, Doris suffered from episodes of dissociative behavior.

Dissociation is a psychological phenomenon in which part of a person's personality "takes over" control of the consciousness and/or body. Psychological dissociation can manifest in a variety of bizarre ways. When someone is working a ouija board, for instance, he or she is practicing a minor form of (usually harmless) voluntary dissociation—the person is encouraging the subconscious to take control of some of the body's motor functions. But sometimes this same form of dissociation can become involuntary, the strange fugue that Frederic Thompson experienced when he discovered that R. Swain Gifford was dead (see Chapter 2) being an excellent case in point. The most complicated form of dissociative behavior is the pathological phenomenon called "multiple personality." This syndrome results when a person's personality is psychologically shattered, thereby giving rise to what are called secondary personalities. These secondary personalities possess their own desires, character development, and goals. Eventually each of these personalities even tries to take control of the victim's body. Even though this curious infighting can sometimes become vicious, the patient (the primary or original personality) usually isn't cognizant of the breaks within his or her psyche. He or she usually only experiences strange bouts of memory loss and/or finds him- or herself blamed for escapades for which he or she has no memory. These fugues can be brief (lasting barely beyond a few hours) or they can extend to several weeks.

When Doris was thrown to the floor by her disturbed father, one of these stereotypical secondary personalities was released from her mind. The cruel incident produced a split within her personality which would cause her endless problems for the rest of her childhood. Doris herself remained the primary personality. Plump, docile and reserved—she remained the stereotypical "good little girl," a role she fulfilled brilliantly. But behind this psychological facade emerged a personality who liked to call herself "Margaret." This pathological personality served as a storehouse for Doris's chronic psychological pain. She was extremely mischievious, possessed an extreme dislike for the "person" who shared her body and was constantly getting Doris into trouble both at home and at school.

Doris's sickness was typical of multiple personality cases in several other respects. The most important was that even though "Margaret" was perfectly aware of Doris's existence, Doris did not realize what was happening to her and spent her entire childhood suffering from strange memory losses when her secondary personality took control.

Despite the fact that Doris possessed two personalities fighting to control her mind and body, her problems were soon compounded further. Doris was a bright child who learned easily, but for some unknown psychological reason "Margaret" stopped maturing when she was only ten. She would invariably behave like a child when she controlled Doris's body, and her behavior often became downright embarrassing for her parents. This was especially true while Doris was a teenager. Sometimes she would come home from the domestic job at which she worked and would tell her parents of her day's activities. Then, right in the middle of the conversation, she would change personalities, plop down onto the floor, and start making paper dolls! Doris's parents were mystified by these strange episodes, but they never thought that their daughter needed professional care since she never seemed to be physically ill. Part of the problem was undoubtedly Doris's father, who was still prone to bouts of drinking, violence, and child beating. He was hardly a caring parent or capable of realizing that his daughter was suffering from a psychological disorder—a disorder for which he was solely responsible.

Even though Doris had to contend with a physically abusive and dangerous father, she was extremely fond of her mother. It was truly a tragedy when the woman died in May 1906. She had been sick for only a single day and Doris had to prepare the body for burial while her father lay nearby in a drunken stupor. The stress was too much for her, and she responded by relinquishing control of her body to her secondary personality. But not even little "Margaret" could contend with the situation, and so Doris underwent a second fragmentation. She gave birth to yet a third personality, who thereupon took control of her body. This personality came to be known as "Sick Doris" since she was born with no personal memories, and although her personality rather resembled Doris's, she believed herself to be fatally ill. This new secondary personality would eventually completely replace Doris as the girl's primary personality.

It is amazing, in retrospect, that Doris (or later "Sick Doris") ever managed to function in society at all with these splits complicating her personality. But function she did, the fact that she suffered from multiple personalities being carefully hidden by "Margaret." This secondary personality took care to keep "Sick Doris" from getting into trouble and gradually helped her overcome her lack of memory. She even educated her by feeding her information about Doris's past. She also helped "Sick Doris" deal with social situations by sending her "voices" telling her what to do when she became confused.

Now it may appear to the reader that "Margaret" was caretaking the body and helping "Sick Doris" develop her personal identity in a considerable and compassionate way. But this would be a misguided interpretation of the case, for the "Margaret" personality was nothing if not primarily selfish. She was really trying to keep Doris's secret hidden so that she could preserve her own existence, and she came to dislike this "Sick Doris" with the same vehemence that she previously projected onto their progenitor. This rivalry manifested in a variety of ways, but the worst was "Margaret's" physical assaults on "Sick Doris." When "Sick Doris" was controlling the body, the cantankerous secondary personality would control their brain so that the terrified girl would hit and scratch herself. She was especially afflicted by these vicious episodes when she tried to sleep.

Doris's miserable domestic life only disintegrated further over the course of the next two years, and even the normally docile Doris* began to realize that she had to escape her home to preserve what remained of her sanity. She was still being victimized by her father, who often came home from nights of drinking and beat her mercilessly. She usually fled the house when she heard her father returning, and the open streets became her sanctuary.

It was during February 1909 that Doris's life finally took a turn for the better. One day she was walking to the Methodist church where she usually worshipped, but she never arrived. She had recently undergone surgery on her foot and the walk was too much for her weakened leg. Instead, she stopped to visit the nearby All Saints [Episcopal] Church

---

*By this time "Sick Doris" was the primary personality. For the rest of this chapter, the name "Doris" will be used to designate "Sick Doris" unless otherwise indicated. Doris underwent a further break in 1907, but that emerging personality never completely formed and will not be discussed in this chapter.

where the Rev. W. Franklin Prince was rector. Dr. Prince and his wife (who helped run the rectory) had moved to Pittsburgh from New York in 1907 and were still settling into their new church and home.

For some reason Mrs. Prince was immediately drawn to the girl and struck up a cordial friendship with her. During the course of the next several weeks Mrs. Prince got to know Doris better and soon realized that there was something radically wrong with her. She didn't realize the severity of the girl's problems, but she noticed her moodiness and emotional detachment. These observations were eventually brought to the attention of her husband, but Dr. Prince didn't initially recognize the seriousness of the situation. He spoke with Doris, but she was suspicious of the clergyman and kept her distance. She was probably intimidated by the clergyman, having been so callously treated by the only other older man she knew.

It was fortunate for Doris that the Princes encouraged her visits to their church, which was located relatively close to her home. Doris joined the Sunday-school class at the church, and by November she was visiting the church regularly. Soon she was taking a daily meal there and usually visited the rectory sometime each day in order to catch up on her sleep. (She rarely slept at home because of her father's drunken behavior. Often she stayed awake at night and tried to hide from him, or she simply walked the streets.)

During these weeks Mrs. Prince began to understand the extent to which Doris was emotionally ill. During their many talks, Doris tried to convince Mrs. Prince that she suffered from tuberculosis and that she was a gifted painter. Both of these claims were blatantly untrue, and Mrs. Prince could not understand why Doris seemed to be so chronically deluded. But the kindly woman soon became more concerned about the girl's sleeping habits than with her curious claims. These concerns grew when Doris began to spend more and more time at the rectory sleeping. During the early months of 1910, Mrs. Prince became puzzled by the fact that Doris talked excessively in her sleep. She grew increasingly worried when she saw that Doris sometimes threatened and physically struck herself while resting. Doris's bouts of self-mutilation became so common that Mrs. Prince had to protect her by holding the girl's hands while she slept. These sessions became almost daily rituals at the rectory, and by January 1911, Mrs. Prince was simply too exhausted to protect Doris further and requested her husband's help. It was then that Dr. Prince began to watch over Doris's sleep, and he quickly realized that she was more disturbed than they had originally thought. He talked to the girl while she slept, and through her bizarre responses he first learned that a second personality was living inside Doris's body. Her case was finally beginning to make sense to him.

It was fortunate for young Doris Fischer that the Reverend Dr. W. Franklin Prince discovered the secret cause of her problems since he was probably one of the few people in Pittsburgh capable of helping her. So before proceeding with the history of the case, some background into the life of this remarkable man is necessary.

W. Franklin Prince was born in 1863, the second son of an old and proud New England family on his mother's side. His parents were deeply religious members of the Methodist church, and they instilled in their son a love for the spiritual. The couple were also fiercely devoted to proper education, and even before he was a teenager Franklin was reading and enjoying the classics. It almost seemed fated that Franklin would enter the clergy. He was first educated at Maine Wesleyan Seminary, and he graduated in 1881 at the ripe old age of eighteen, by which time he was already serving in several of the state's local Methodist churches. He married one of his parishioners in 1885, but his marriage to Lelia Madora Colman was childless. Despite this disappointment, the Princes were a happy and devoted couple and never parted. They moved among several parsonages in Connecticut over the next several years. Reverend Prince eventually began to feel that he lacked a proper college education, so he enrolled in Drew Seminary in Madison, New Jersey and in 1897 took his formal divinity degree.

These years were a turning point in the young minister's life. Although his great loves were religion and the study of history, Prince found himself becoming increasingly interested in the burgeoning science of psychology. His growing fascination with the outer reaches of the psyche led him to enroll at Yale University, where he worked toward a graduate degree. He received his doctorate in 1899 with a dissertation on—synchronistically enough—multiple personality.

W. Franklin Prince broke with the Methodist Church in 1904 and was subsequently ordained a priest of the Protestant Episcopal Church. He worked first in Brooklyn as an assistant rector at St. Anne's Church before being reassigned to Pittsburgh, where he remained for the next several years.

His studies in religion and psychology also brought the field of psychical research to Dr. Prince's notice, and he even joined the American Society for Psychical Research in 1908. His primary interest was in the society's proposed study of psychopathology, however, and he was not overwhelmingly interested in psychic phenomena during this phase of his career. This interest was to be sparked later.*

By 1910, then, Dr. Prince was in a perfect position to help Doris Fischer. Not only did he have the personal compassion and resources to help the battered child, but he was also a trained psychologist. This background helped the clergyman to appreciate both the psychiatric and the possibly spiritual dimensions of her problem.

The sheer complexity of the case with which he was dealing finally struck Dr. Prince on the evening of January 22, 1910. It was a dramatic and terrifying night. Doris showed up at the rectory looking exhausted and obviously in pain, but she managed to eventually fall asleep in Dr. Prince's study. Despite the love and care the Princes were devoting to her, Doris began to tear at her skin while sleeping. Dr. Prince tried to talk to Doris (who, unknown to the clergyman, was being physically controlled by her secondary personality) and exhorted her to stop. Doris's fit only became worse the more the clergyman tried to soothe her, so, realizing that "something" was in possession of the girl, he performed a makeshift exorcism. He told the personality controlling the child in no uncertain terms that he was "withdrawing" the former's power.

The suggestion worked. Doris's face gradually lost its harsh countenance and she simply woke up. She was exhausted by the ordeal, and she looked so dreadful that the clergyman thought she might be dying. The girl's pulse dropped to fifty-four beats per minute, and Doris herself began to think the end was near.

"She smiled peacefully," Dr. Prince later wrote, "as though glad both to go and to know that she was to be missed. She looked singularly unlike her afternoon self, the very shape of her face altered—it seemed thinner, as though she had passed through a period of sickness since. Under the spell of considerable emotion I was looking into her eyes, and presently her gaze fixed upon mine, and with parted lips she continued to look, not rigidly, but dreamily and peacefully, while she waited for the end which we thought so near."

---

*Fulton Ousler, the celebrated journalist and religious writer, wrote a brilliant portrait of W. Franklin Prince in 1935. He described him as "like a character out of Dickens. . . . There was something fussbudgety about him, something honest and out of fashion—sincerity in old clothes, a naive good humor, and a capacity for indignation which our shallow generation has lost. He made faces when he talked. His voice squeaked and barked and snarled and chuckled. And he thought of life as having mysteries still worth solving. . . . He was, in an old-fashioned sense of the word, a gentleman and scholar."

Dr. Prince's prognosis was misjudged, though, and Doris continued to stare into space. She seemed to be in some kind of trance.

Then the shocker came. When Dr. Prince bent over to examine the girl, a strange but powerful voice suddenly shouted from within her.

"You must get her out of this," commanded the voice. Dr. Prince was so compelled by the voice's presence that he began to shake Doris.

"Shake her harder!" the voice continued. "Hurry!"

The clergyman soon realized that Doris had fallen into a state akin to a deep hypnotic trance, and he tried to revive her. While Dr. Prince continued shouting and shaking her, the stricken girl gradually began to respond and move her eyes.

"Walk her! Walk her!" the voice continued to shout. The exasperated Dr. Prince obeyed without question even though poor Doris continually stumbled while he paraded her through the study. The personality controlling her continued to direct the clergyman, who kept walking and talking to Doris until her controller was content.

"She is coming to herself now," the voice finally stated. "She will be all right soon."

Just as these words were spoken, Doris became lucid and finally revived fully. She had little comprehension of what had taken place and Dr. Prince was just as flabbergasted. For the rest of the night there were similar episodes of possession, and sometimes the frightened girl had to be restrained by both Dr. Prince and his wife.

"Her strength seemed prodigious," Dr. Prince later recollected, "and at times I was nearly exhausted, even with the help of Mrs. Prince, in simply preventing mischief upon her body. Finally she fell into a state of lethargic slumber, and remained inert and speechless until nearly morning while Mrs. Prince and I continued to watch."

When the poor girl finally awoke, she was obviously still recovering from the ordeal. "She . . . . crept feebly home," according to the rector, "a pale and dejected figure, to get her father's breakfast."

By this time Dr. Prince fully suspected that Doris suffered from multiple personalities. But since he was a devout Christian, the Episcopal clergyman harbored provisional suspicions that some sort of possession might be playing a role in her problem, too. Never before had the clergyman's psychological and religious backgrounds come into such conflict, and it was a conflict he never completely resolved.

Dr. Prince's suspicions that his young parishioner might be possessed were reinforced when Doris returned to the rectory the following day. She went to sleep in the clergyman's study that night at eight o'clock.

She began massaging herself in her sleep, but sometimes called for the clergyman. Despite these movements, her slumber was relatively calm. She awoke briefly several times but did not seem to be sleeping fitfully. When she finally and permanently awoke she told Dr. Prince that for several months she had been hearing voices inside her head. The clergyman was interested in her comments and realized that her symptoms could be indicating either insanity or perhaps incipient possession.

Finally he decided to directly explore the possibility that a spiritual cause was lurking behind Doris's experiences. "Have you ever prayed against the voices?" he asked the bewildered girl.

Dr. Prince was startled when Doris reacted to the suggestion by flinching painfully.

"Remember that Jesus helped people who had trouble," the clergyman continued. But even as he spoke, Doris continued to wince and writhe. Finally her face took on a strange glare. She looked totally transformed and a shrill voice emerged from her mouth.

"What made you want Doris to pray?" the voice screamed. "I don't want her to pray!"

Dr. Prince held his ground in the face of the mysterious entity. "Why don't you want her to?" he challenged. "Do you dread prayer?"

"Yes," responded the personality controlling Doris's speech.

Upon receiving this response, the clergyman began to pray in a firm but compassionate voice. Doris reacted to the prayer immediately. Her hands fell to her chest, her head rolled over, and she fell into a deep sleep. Whatever personality was controlling her had obviously relinquished the girl's body.

It is unfortunate that Dr. Prince never commented on his own reaction to this strange episode in Doris's life. It is therefore difficult to determine whether the exorcism fascinated him more as a psychologist or as a clergyman. Nor is it clear whether he was willing to grant that Doris's problem was primarily spiritual rather than psychological. The fact that Dr. Prince suggested prayer in the first place suggests that, even as early as 1910, he couldn't fully explain the case psychologically. Even though he had a thorough background in psychopathology, it should be remembered that Dr. Prince was a clergyman first. (He was even a vociferous supporter of Pennsylvania's blue laws, which prohibited recreational events or entertainment on Sundays.) The extent to which spiritual factors played a role in Doris's sickness would constantly concern Dr. Prince, who tried to exorcise Doris a second time on the evening of January 24.

Doris came to the church that day to sleep, which by now was completely customary. She kept repeating the same words while submerged in a restless slumber, exhorting the minister to let her possessor return.

"I again tried the experiment of praying in her hearing," reported the clergyman in his lengthy report on the case, "that if an evil spirit was in Doris it might be cast out, and she rolled over almost on the floor, her head bent over into her lap, and her arm wrapped around her face, wincing as if whipped. Then I forcibly turned her up upon her back, for a short space she remained quiet, but then began to manifest viciousness."

The voice of Doris's possessor manifested again, this time more viciously than ever before.

"You'll lose Doris," the personality warned the rector, who was still fervently praying. "You'll lose Doris if you don't look out."

Dr. Prince responded by telling the entity that he would rather see Doris die than give up control of her psyche to the possessor. The invading personality then caused Doris to begin choking herself and Dr. Prince had to restrain her forcefully before the girl returned to her senses and reverted back to her primary personality.

These possessionlike episodes were dramatic and even somewhat convincing, but Dr. Prince was a shrewd enough psychologist not to take them purely literally. Only later did he fully realize the tragic truth that Doris suffered from multiple personalities.

By this time Dr. Prince was consulting with Dr. W. K. Walker of the University of Pittsburgh, and he was taking Doris to the psychiatrist for treatment. (Dr. Prince never explained what these treatments entailed, but they probably entailed some sort of hypnosis or waking suggestion.) It was also during this crucial period in the case that Doris's secondary personalities began revealing themselves more openly. Dr. Prince was growing increasingly concerned about Doris's memory lapses and dissociative behavior, so he began placing a pencil in her hands when she slept at the rectory in hopes that her subconscious would use it to write and communicate with him.

By the use of this technique the clergyman entered into a constructive dialogue with Doris's main secondary personality, who to this time had kept her identity something of a secret from him. The clergyman now knew of her existence within Doris's mind, but he did not realize that she possessed the power to take control and displace her entire personality. While she sometimes communicated with him through

Doris's voice, she was secretive when physically controlling the girl, even though she flaunted herself in front of the Princes. She just never let them know that she considered herself a different person from Doris!

Despite her secretive and suspicious behavior, "Margaret" began to trust Dr. Prince and had become more open with him by the following February. She realized that he was trying to help Doris and thus, vicariously, herself. She soon would "come out" openly in his presence, but her appearances were usually self-restricted to the evening hours.

The real surprise came when Dr. Prince discovered that Doris possessed more than a single secondary personality. He took Doris to the dentist on February 27, 1911, and she spent the rest of the day and evening at the rectory with the clergyman. It was a curious and frustrating day, since "Margaret" had kept coming out—though she was shrewd enough to pretend to be Doris. She didn't want Dr. Prince to know she could control Doris even during the daytime. Dr. Prince wasn't fooled by the masquerade and the secondary personality gave up the charade that evening, when she began controlling Doris's body more openly. She engaged in a spirited conversation with her friend, even though their talk primarily concerned her dislike for her weak rival. Finally the personality began to interrogate Dr. Prince.

"What do you want her to come for?" she commented snidely, referring to Doris.

"Because we love her," responded the rector.

"Do you love her?" she replied in a sneering but searching voice. She looked toward Dr. Prince with round, unflinching eyes while speaking. "You think it is Doris sometimes when it isn't."

Dr. Prince didn't know what to make of this enigmatic remark, but later in the conversation "Margaret" returned to the subject.

"You never saw the real Doris but a very little," she said, "when it was all Doris." When Dr. Prince pressed her to explain her strange claim, she responded by saying, "I will wake Doris so that she will be *all Doris* for a little while."

Dr. Prince was confused by the comment, but he complied by suggesting she go to sleep and bring forth Doris. The personality controlling Doris laid down on the couch in Prince's study and soon became temporarily dormant. She aroused herself within minutes, but it was now neither "Margaret" nor the Doris he knew that was controlling the body. It was actually the *original* Doris who awoke that evening ever so briefly, the Doris whose personality had been replaced by "Sick Doris" in 1906 and who had withdrawn into the girl's subconscious.

The clergyman did not understand the importance of this brief emergence of Doris's original personality. He could tell that this Doris was different in look and manner from his daily visitor. But not until later did he realize that the Doris he knew and was beginning to love *was a secondary personality herself and that he didn't even know the primary Doris*. When he finally did grasp the extent of Doris's multiple dissociations some months later, he began to diagnose his parishioner more cogently. He understood more fully now that hers was a classic case of multiple personality and less a case of possible possession.

Dr. Prince was not completely satisfied with this diagnosis, though. Later and while working to restore the girl's health, he discovered a fifth personality embedded within her psyche. Dr. Prince would often talk to Doris while she slept since she was capable of entering into a coherent and constructive dialogue with him while in that state. Dr. Prince learned through these conversations that "Margaret" had not been the only personality liberated from Doris's mind in 1892 when she suffered her original fragmentation. Some portion of her subconscious had become detached from both Doris and her mischievious secondary personality, but this personality only came forth when Doris slept. For this reason Dr. Prince called her "Sleeping Margaret," and she seemed to be more mature and wise than either Doris, "Sick Doris," or the regressive and cantankerous "Margaret." She was cognizant of each of the other personalities and seemed to be some sort of "higher self" within the original Doris's unconscious.

During the next several years, Dr. Prince held almost nightly discourses with this personality. He would sneak into Doris's room late at night to consult with "Sleeping Margaret" about Doris's condition and the best way to handle her problems.

Dr. Prince was continually impressed by "Sleeping Margaret's" maturity, psychological wisdom, and compassion for Doris. He could never explain her existence psychologically, and he came to believe that she was probably a spiritual entity of some sort, a claim that "Sleeping Margaret" eventually encouraged herself.* Dr. Prince understood that

---

*The study of multiple personality was in its infancy when Dr. Prince conducted his research. He therefore did not know what later researchers would discover, i.e., that many sufferers of multiple personalities possess such "higher selves." These personas do not seem to be genuine secondary personalities but represent stable and integrated parts of the patients' subconscious minds. They tend to be excellent sources of information, and there is evidence that they can be reached through deep hypnosis. Even nonpathologically disturbed people seem to possess them.

this was the personality with whom he had previously spoken in 1910 and who had exhorted him to "walk" Doris when she became entranced during his exorcism.

By this time the reader should have a grasp of the many complexities complicating the Doris case. There were more to come. The next phase of the investigation began in March 1911, shortly after Prince discovered the existence of Doris's several selves. It was growing clearer and clearer both to Dr. Prince and to his wife that the girl's home life was the primary cause of her continuing problems. Since Doris was spending every day at the church, the next step the clergyman took to help her was obvious. Doris came to live with the Princes and soon became their foster daughter. Living full time at the rectory benefited the young woman in several ways. Not only did the change remove her from the presence of her vicious father, it also gave Dr. Prince the opportunity to begin work on a cure. Nothing could have been more therapeutic for her, and she immediately began to improve in response to his care.

There is no need to go into the particulars of the clergyman's course of treatment in this book. Dr. Prince's report on the Doris case is 1,332 pages long, and the sections concerning her cure comprise over a thousand! Suffice it to say that Dr. Prince began therapeutic work with Doris in March 1911 and that by the summer he had removed "Sick Doris" from the girl's repertoire of secondary personalities. The girl's other problematic secondary personality was more recalcitrant, and dislodging "Margaret's" partial control of Doris was no easy task. But through suggestion, environmental factors, and wisdom from "Sleeping Margaret's" constant counsel, the clergyman was able to fuse Doris and fully reinstate her primary personality by April 1914. The only exception to the completion of the cure was the beneficial existence of "Sleeping Margaret," with whom Dr. Prince continued to commune while Doris slept. She was never fused into Doris's own personality and permanently remained the voice of the girl's subconscious—though Dr. Prince never completely concluded that she was part of Doris's psyche.

During the course of Doris's treatment and cure, the Prince family moved away from Pittsburgh. Dr. Prince was given a new parish in San Bernardino, California, where he devoted himself to his ministerial work while his wife and Doris operated a chicken ranch.

By his own frank admission, Dr. Prince was not primarily concerned with psychical research during these years, although his interest in the subject was sparked several times during his therapeutic work with

TABLE 1

The Doris Case of Multiple Personality

Date	Event
March 1889	Doris born in Pittsburgh.
———— 1892	Doris thrown to floor by drunken father. "Margaret" and "Sleeping Margaret" emerge from her mind.
May 6, 1906	Doris's mother dies; "Sick Doris" emerges and begins to replace the girl's original personality.
September 1907	Doris falls and strikes her head. "Real 'Sick Doris' " partially emerges from her psyche.
January 1909	Doris visits All Saints Church in Pittsburgh.
October 1909	Doris joins the Sunday school at the church, meets Dr. and Mrs. Prince, and begins visiting the church on a daily basis.
January 1911	Dr. Prince discovers that Doris possesses multiple personalities.
March 1911	Doris comes to live with the Princes, and Dr. Prince begins his attempt to cure her.
September 1911	James Hyslop visits Pittsburgh, meets Doris, and witnesses her changes of personality.
October 1911	"Margaret" begins to regress and enters the first phase of her eventual disappearance.
November 1911	Dr. Prince successfully removes "Sick Doris" as the girl's primary personality and reinstates her original personality.
———— 1912	The Prince family moves from Pittsburgh to San Bernardino.
———— 1912 through April 1914	Dr. Prince gradually restores Doris to mental health by fusing her personalities.
August 1914*	Hyslop explores the possibility of working with Doris.
October 1914*	Doris leaves California for New York.
November 1914 through December 1915*	Hyslop explores the nature of Doris's former problem with the psychic help of Minnie Soule.

* Material marked by an asterisk will be covered in Chapter 8.

his foster daughter. It was obvious that she was extremely psychic and that several of her personalities—including Doris herself, "Sick Doris," and the perennially mischievious "Margaret"—controlled similar paranormal powers.

Doris had always maintained that she was psychic, and her (presumed) powers were considerable seeing that they included clairvoyance, precognition, remote viewing, and visitations by phantom presences. Doris personally claimed that when she was a small child, she often experienced premonitions that later came true. She claimed further that these psychic experiences became more prevalent during her troubled adolescence. While performing domestic work in Pittsburgh, for instance, she sometimes would "see" her mother via remote viewing or "traveling" (long-distance) clairvoyance. By checking with her mother later, Doris found that her "visions" were usually correct. The most dramatic of these incidents occurred on May 5, 1906, right before her mother's death. Doris later gave the following account to her foster father.

> The last experience of the kind was on May 5, 1906. I was sitting at the machine, sewing, at [my employer's]—this was five long squares from home—and I saw, pictured in the glass panel of the door opposite, my mother lying on the lounge, with her face turned toward the wall. I supposed, of course, that she must be lying so really, as she had proved before to be doing what I had seen her do, and I wondered, because it was six o'clock in the afternoon, time for her to be getting supper, and Mr. F[ischer] was very cranky about having his meals ready just on time. But I did not at first think much about it. Then the picture came again, the same as before. And then I saw it a third time, and mother was now turned toward me, and she was white about the lips, but the rest of her face was flushed. I was alarmed and told [my employer] that I must go home, and would come right back. I ran home and found mother looking just as I had seen her, and lying with her face turned from the wall. But I inquired of Trixie [a hopelessly ill and crippled sister, lying in bed in an adjoining room in sight of the lounge through the open door] and found that she had been lying toward the wall, and had turned over a little while before. Mother was very sick, and was half-unconscious. Mr. F[ischer] was almost always in the house for his supper at that time, but he was not there.

By the time Doris came to live with Dr. Prince, these clairvoyant episodes had ebbed considerably. Vestiges of her psychic sense were still evident, but it was the "Margaret" personality who was most prone to display them. During the course of his work with this provocative personality, Dr. Prince recorded several instances suggesting that she could willfully employ psychic powers.

This possibility first came to his notice on April 23, 1911. Dr. Prince was reading and smoking a cigar in the rectory while Doris was playing on the floor nearby, fully controlled by "Margaret." The book Dr. Prince was reading was entitled *Bennett Divorce Case*, which chronicled the eccentric writer's many marital problems. While perusing the volume, Dr. Prince showed "Margaret" a picture of Dr. Bennett which served as the frontispiece of the book, but he said nothing concerning the physician himself. But "Margaret" later interrupted the clergyman's reading by giving a psychic "reading" of the writer. She began by asking whether Dr. Bennett was deaf—a remark that startled Dr. Prince since it was directly pertinent to the physician. The clergyman responded by encouraging his foster daughter, and "Margaret" reacted by offering a series of impressions relevant to Dr. Bennett: that he and his wife lived with his sister, who strenuously objected to the arrangement, that they had been once caught in a rainstorm while en route to New York, and so forth. These episodes were indeed discussed in the book Dr. Prince was holding in his hands. The clergyman's first impression was that either Doris or one of her fragmented selves had read the book, but this didn't seem likely.

"Curiously enough," commented Dr. Prince in his report, "Doris for two years thereafter was never known to take a book from one of the glass-fronted cases, though perfectly free to do so. She got books from the public library, she picked them up from the desk or table, she read what I recommended or handed her, but she did not take them from my shelves."

Dr. Prince witnessed several such displays during the remainder of 1911, and an even more impressive experience came to light on the morning of October 28. While eating breakfast, Doris recounted a curious dream to her foster father. The following is Dr. Prince's own report on this incident.

She dreamed that she and Mrs. Prince went to a cemetery on the side of a hill and beside a road, in order to take up the bodies of her mother and sister, and remove them to another lot alongside. They took up the coffins and dug one grave. Mrs. Prince said, "If we don't get home soon, my beans will burn; let's put one coffin on top of the other." They did so, and then the question came up where to put the tombstones. Mrs.

Prince said, "Put one at the head and the other at the foot," and this was done. While the dream was relating I was thinking that yesterday a committee of a historical society of which I am an officer was discussing a proposal to erect a memorial of Gen. Neville of the Revolutionary period, in the Woodville cemetery. One of the members said that the cemetery was around an old chapel, and that it was pretty full, particularly near the road which bordered it. While the old cemetery has been neglected, the bodies of county poor have been taken there and buried, one coffin on another. I asked if some of the bodies in front could not be removed to the rear, leaving room for the memorial. It was also suggested that the memorial be placed in the chapel instead. It was decided that the Committee should go out next Saturday and inspect the ground. I had never reported one word of this at home. I am positive and certain of this, and Mrs. Prince corroborates me to the extent of declaring that she had heard nothing about it.

Dr. Prince pointed out in his report that there were five specific points of similarity between Doris's dream, his previous meeting with the historical society, and his proposed visit to the cemetery.

1. Both the dream and the visit dealt with a cemetery.
2. The geographical setting (the road and hill) seen in the dream matched the physical location of the cemetery.
3. Both the dream and the meeting included the bizarre theme of coffins placed or stacked to preserve space and/or time.
4. Doris's dream corresponded to Dr. Prince's proposal to disinter the cemetery's silent residents.
5. Dr. Prince's proposal concerning a memorial stone was transformed by Doris's psyche into a concern about tombstones.

The process by which Doris psychically came up with this information is an interesting sidelight to the case. Dr. Prince discussed this incident with "Sleeping Margaret" later that day while Doris was sleeping in her room. During their conversation "Sleeping Margaret" explained that it was "Margaret" who had first drawn the information from his mind. She had subsequently sent the information to Doris by way of the dream. The specific reasons for "Margaret's" sending the dream to her sister personality were not explained, but "Sleeping Margaret" warned Dr. Prince that Doris's second self was a proficient mind-reader when she wished to be.

When his conversation with Doris's unconscious self ended, it was

"Margaret" who awoke in Doris's bed. The clergyman immediately checked "Sleeping Margaret's" information by asking her whether she wanted to visit Woodville Cemetery with him.

The girl's reaction was startling. For according to Dr. Prince, "her face took on a knowing and triumphant look."

"I saw what you were thinking of last night," she said. "You can't fool your baby." She shook her finger at her foster father while speaking, and she cocked her head playfully. "I saw a p'rade [sic] going through your mind," she continued.

Dr. Prince was intrigued by this claim, and he explored it with the personality in more depth. "I didn't know that I was giving myself away," he replied. "What did you see?"

"A graveyard," responded the secondary personality immediately, "an old graveyard and lots of stones. Some people buried on top of other people. And some of them are going to be taken up."

The mischievious secondary personality then proceeded to describe the cemetery in phenomenal detail.

Probably the most celebrated instance of "Margaret's" telepathic power, though, was witnessed by Dr. Prince the following winter. During the afternoon of November 29, he secretly wrote a letter to Dr. Morton Prince—who was a noted Boston psychologist responsible for curing a similar case of multiple personality.* The clergyman was curious to know whether the patient's cure had been permanent, but he refrained from making the inquiry in his note. Later that evening Dr. Prince was relaxing by a fire in his home while "Margaret" played by his side. Suddenly he realized that the girl was staring right at him.

"You wrote to a man named Prince today—to Dr. Prince," she stated flatly. "You wrote about Doris."

The girl broke into a giggle after speaking, implying that her telepathic demonstration was nothing but a game. She then continued by saying, "You asked him how someone was getting on."

What so impressed Dr. Prince was that he had only *thought* of making that specific inquiry. His foster daughter must have been reading his mind, he concluded, since she couldn't have gleaned the information from the letter.

---

*This was the celebrated case of Christine L. Beauchamp, which Dr. Morton Prince published in his classic book *The Dissociation of a Personality*. It was the most famous case of multiple personality of the day, and even Richard Hodgson personally studied the patient. Morton Prince was no relation to W. Franklin Prince. Miss Beauchamp's real name was Clara Fowler.

Several similar incidents came to Dr. Prince's attention as he worked daily to cure Doris of her shattered personality. He eventually became fascinated by the psychic side of her problem and soon began writing to James Hyslop in New York. These letters first engendered the professor's interest in the case, and he paid a visit to Dr. Prince and Doris on September 21, 1911. Hyslop was interested in working further with Doris, but he realized that her condition was too delicate.

Despite the professor's initial reluctance to explore the psychic side of the Doris case, Dr. Prince began experimenting with the girl after they moved to San Bernardino in the summer of 1912. His first experiments to see whether Doris could function as a spirit medium were conducted the following September, but the results were rather negligible. Even though these initial forays into Spiritualist practices were not paying off, Dr. Prince continued them between September 30 and October 8 and then sporadically thereafter until Doris was finally cured in 1914.

The failure of these experiments did not daunt Doris's psychic sense, however, and the cured patient received two visitations from her deceased mother the following November—further evidence that there was a psychic side to her life.

These two visitations marked the beginning of a third phase in the case. Although Doris's provisional cure by Dr. Prince in 1914 heralded the end of his detailed record of her sickness, it did not end his research with her. For that crucial year brought the direct involvement of James Hyslop in the case. While the psychological storm within Doris's mind was ebbing, a psychic storm was about to reach Boston.

CHAPTER 8

THE MANY FACES OF
DORIS FISCHER—PART 2

The Doris case evolved during a critical period in James Hyslop's work. By the beginning of 1914, the researcher had studied several cases of purported spirit obsession and possession. It struck him that, oddly enough, none of these psychic invasions had permanently scarred his subjects psychologically. Even though each of them had undergone episodes of some sort of dissociation, they had all totally recovered.

Despite the relatively benign outcome of these complex incidents, however, another important issue began to preoccupy Hyslop's mind. Each of his previous cases looked like instances of psychopathology— either simple dissociation, secondary personality, or dementia praecox (the 19th-century term for what we call schizophrenia today). Frederic Thompson, Etta De Camp, and Ida Rogers seemed to be going insane, and only Hyslop's intervention and experiments may have saved them from a complete loss of reason.

Frederic Thompson had even been formally diagnosed as a case of incipient paranoia or dementia, but Hyslop's psychic diagnosis of his problem through the mediumship of Minnie Soule had thrown new light on his inner world.

Because of these studies, Hyslop began formulating a radical theory in order to explain some cases of insanity. The Spiritualists in the United States, England, and France had long maintained that possession and spirit influence were the true causes of some psychotic states and phobias. Of course, this interesting theory predated the rise of the Spir-

itualist movement by several centuries. Similar theories had been popular during the Enlightenment. They had been most vocally supported
by the theological writer Johann Weyer (1515–88) in his famous book
De Praestigiis Daemonum. Weyer championed the demonic theory of
insanity even though he was the most enlightened and vocal critic of
the European witch craze, which was rife during his lifetime.

The Spiritualists were, however, going beyond theory and theology
and were trying to cure cases of insanity by conducting exorcisms as
part of their seances. By the turn of the century, such "rescue work"
was being conducted by both private and public Spiritualist groups and
churches throughout the country.

Even though Hyslop never considered himself a Spiritualist, he
grew increasingly sympathetic to their views on insanity during the 1910s.
He was not positing that each and every case of insanity was due to
spirit influence or possession, but he felt that the possibility should be
kept in mind. He also realized that his era's medical community was in
no position to evaluate whether psychic factors were playing a role in
their patients' illnesses.

This theoretical framework might strike the reader as nothing short
of far-fetched, but Hyslop was not proposing a radically novel conceptual model for the problem of insanity. Many psychical researchers had
come to believe in life after death by this time, and some of them were
probably silently sympathetic to the theories Hyslop was promoting. Even
during the months when he was grappling with the Thompson/Gifford
case, William James was seeing the implications of his own research
into the phenomenon of mediumship. As early as 1909, James was willing to write in a report to the SPR:

> The refusal of modern "enlightenment" to treat "possession" as a hypoth-
> esis to be spoken of as even possible, in spite of the massive human
> tradition based on concrete experience in its favour, has always seemed
> to me a curious example of fashion in things scientific. That the demon
> theory (not necessarily a devil-theory) will have its innings again is to my
> mind absolutely certain. One has to be "scientific" indeed to be blind
> and ignorant enough to suspect no such possibility.

Hyslop's research between 1907 and 1914 was leading in the same direction, but there was an important difference between their views. William James had been speaking purely theoretically, while Hyslop was
speaking more and more from personal experience. He was pleased to

see that Frederic Thompson's and Etta De Camp's psychological dispositions had improved after their sittings with Minnie Soule. He would later write of his investigations and discoveries in his book *Life after Death* that "the chief interest in such cases is their revolutionary effect in the field of medicine. It is probable that thousands of cases diagnosed as 'paranoia' would yield to this sort of [psychic] investigation and treatment. It is high time for the medical world to wake up and learn something."

It is important again to note that Hyslop was not suggesting possession and spirit obsession as the sole causes of insanity. He felt either that the syndrome explained *some* such cases or that the general process of psychological disintegration might somehow attract misguided or obsessing discarnates. He pointed to this possibility several times in his writings and would later state this concept in his *Contact with the Other World*.

> It is important to remark at the onset of the exploration of obsession that I do not mean this idea to be a substitute for hysteria, dementia praecox, paranoia or other maladies, nor is it a rival explanation . . . hence that we are not to set aside organic and functional trouble in body and mind when acknowledging that obsession by spirits is an accompaniment of the trouble. It is quite conceivable that any disturbance to healthy functions, bodily or mental, might create conditions in which accidental connections with the discarnate would be established and would open the way to all sorts of voluntary and involuntary invasions.
>
> It must be thoroughly understood that we are not controverting psychological or psychiatric explanation. The only revolution that we wish to introduce into medicine is the denial of the limits ordinarily assigned to causes of disease and methods of treatment. The terms hysteria, dementia praecox, paranoia, manic depressive insanity, and epilepsy are largely descriptive; the causes are revealed only by autopsy and other such methods. Obsession does not displace other causes, but adds to them another factor.

By acknowledging such a possibility, exciting new avenues for future experimentation opened for the researcher. Could some people suffering from insanity be cured by going to gifted psychics? Does exorcism really work? Hyslop believed that these issues should be explored.

This then was Hyslop's state of mind as he embarked on the last phase of his thirteen-year work on the problems of spirit obsession. Remember, too, that the American Society for Psychical Research, which the professor still operated with determination, constituted Section B of the extensively scoped American Institute for Scientific Research. The first section of this organization was to be devoted to the study of psychopathology. Hyslop's great hope was, in fact, to combine the study of psychical research with conventional psychology, and it is unfortunate that the first section of the institute never went beyond paperwork. So it was somewhat predictable that, toward the end of his long and productive career, Hyslop should be drawn back to the field of psychopathology.

It should also be kept in mind that, even despite his Spiritualistic sympathies, Hyslop was no novice in the field of psychology. Even though Hyslop's primary studies were in philosophy and ethics, he had studied psychology with such pioneers as Wilhelm Wundt and Gustav Fechner in Germany. Shortly after completing these studies he taught the subject at Smith College in Massachusetts, filling in for a teacher who was on sabbatical leave. Hyslop was thoroughly versed in the psychology of his day, had deeply contemplated the field's contributions to the study of man, and wrote a textbook on the science in 1895. Psychology was still an infant science at the turn of the century, and the points of connection between psychology and parapsychology were not yet clearly drawn.

So the professor was, by the standards of his day, no rank beginner. Nor was he a flailing-armed Spiritualist who saw discarnates behind every subject's sneeze or phobia.

But Hyslop was not willing to remain solely a theoretician; he was primarily an empiricist and an experimentalist. He wasn't satisfied simply to posit theories concerning the secret nature of psychopathology, for he was willing to put his views to a critical test.

Shortly after he had formulated his beliefs about insanity, just such a test case came to his notice. We don't know very much about this case, since Hyslop never published a complete report on it. He mentioned it only briefly in his final book, *Contact with the Other World.* But shortly after the conclusion of his research with Ida Rogers and Etta De Camp, he began looking into a case of paranoid schizophrenia. The focus of the investigation was, according to the researcher, "a young girl just entering womanhood. She had suddenly become withdrawn to the point where she wouldn't respond to the people talking to her rationally." The girl's problem had been formally diagnosed by two physicians, both of whom considered her insane. Hyslop suspected, however, that she might be suffering from spirit obsession—i.e., some form of partial possession that was short-circuiting her mind and personality. The professor immediately implemented sittings with two psychics, and both of them successfully established separate contact with the purported spirit invader. During these sessions Hyslop exhorted the spirit being to leave the patient and to seek guidance from within his own realm beyond the veil.

"We had not the means to continue the work until we obtained a perfect cure," explained Hyslop in his book. "But there was unmistakable evidence that the phenomena [psychopathology] were of foreign instigation, though affected by the subconscious of the child."

Hyslop was eager to follow up on such leads, and his constant search for evidence finally led him back to the Doris Fischer case, to which he had been introduced in September 1911.

Even after his earlier withdrawal from the case, Hyslop had maintained close contact with W. Franklin Prince through correspondence. He had long wanted to experiment with Doris in the same manner that he had investigated the strange preoccupations of Frederic Thompson, Etta De Camp, and his other cases of possession. With the cure of the girl's problems completed in the early months of 1914, it was finally appropriate for him to return to this original plan. So the following summer, he wrote to Dr. Prince in California suggesting that his colleague and Doris undertake a trip east to take part in a series of mediumistic sessions. The proposal did not strike them as feasible. Neither the clergyman nor his foster daughter were interested in the plan, and Doris was particularly disinterested in the psychic aspect of the proposal. She was, however, interested in the prospect of a trip back to her childhood home, but her enthusiasm was countered by Dr. Prince, who was reluctant to leave his wife in sole charge of their chicken farm.

Even though Dr. Prince wrote to Hyslop expressing his reservations, "Sleeping Margaret" eventually intervened on the professor's behalf. The very night Dr. Prince expressed his reservations in his letter to Hyslop, she spoke of her own interest in the plan during Dr. Prince's consultation with her (while Doris's primary personality slept). She pointed out that Doris was capable of undertaking the journey by herself and that she, "Sleeping Margaret", would take good care of the girl. This plan struck everybody as satisfactory, and Doris left for New York on October 24.

Exactly what Hyslop hoped to prove by taking Doris to Minnie Soule isn't clear, although it seems likely that he suspected that some sort of spiritistic influence had played a role in her previous problems—

though perhaps without precisely causing them. This possibility seems clear from the introduction to his report on his experiments with Doris that the professor later wrote. "In my examination of [the case] some years ago, with a view to finding indications of obsession," he explained, "I had to admit there were none and I had no reason to suppose I would find them in this experiment. . . . Every feature of it seemed overwhelmingly against the hypothesis of instigation by spirits, so that there was nothing to suggest my experiments except the hazard that I might find traces of spiritistic influences which we should not expect and certainly some interesting psychological phenomena."

The researcher added, though, that "the temptation to try the . . . experiment was too great and the duty too imperative to neglect it."

When Doris was finally ready to sit with Minnie Soule in Boston, Hyslop was even more cautious than usual about keeping her presence in the city a secret from the psychic. Since a great deal of information on the Doris case was in print by 1914, the professor had to be doubly sure that the psychic had no way of knowing her sitter's identity. The safeguards he used were similar to those he implemented during the De Camp/Stockton and Rogers/Abbott experiments, so they need not be repeated in this chapter. With these safeguards in place and scrupulously adhered to, Hyslop and Doris began the sittings on November 9, 1914, and they continued with them regularly into 1915 (with an interruption of several months due to Hyslop's failing health). These sittings were phenomenally successful in many respects despite the caution with which they were conducted. So much evidential information concerning Doris's case and childhood was communicated that even a reasonable summary would be too complicated to include in this chapter. During the very first sitting, for instance, the full and correct name of Doris's brutal father was communicated—which was a piece of information that had never been publicly revealed.

Over the course of the next several sittings, three primary communicators presented themselves to Doris and Hyslop. Each of them seemed preoccupied with delivering specific information or sorts of information.

The most important communicator was the purported spirit of Doris's beloved mother, who recounted reams of information concerning her daughter's childhood. Most of this information was later verified by the professor and Dr. Prince, although the information did not bear directly on whether Doris had been suffering from spirit possession or not. Because this information was only peripheral to Hyslop's goal in planning these experiments, it will be bypassed in this chapter. However, a brief table sampling some of the chief communications offered by the purported spirit of Doris's mother appears on pages 144–5. The interested reader might wish to examine this chart in order to get a general feeling for these evidential communications.

The second primary visitor during Hyslop's sittings with Doris and Minnie Soule was a drop-in communicator.* During some of their experiments the professor and Doris were bothered by a shadowy character who called himself "Count Cagliostro," thereby claiming to be the great romancer, occultist, and charlatan of the eighteenth century who had been the scourge of the French court and whose real name was Giuseppe Balsamo. Hyslop tried to ignore this particular personality and spent most of his time convincing the entity to leave them alone. (Several decades later, the information communicated by this personality would be checked, and it would prove to be surprisingly correct. This information will be discussed in the concluding chapter.)

The final communicator in the Doris case was a sprightly self-professed Indian girl who claimed to be influencing Doris—and who thereby fulfilled Hyslop's suspicion that Doris was suffering from more than psychopathology.

For the present time, the focus of this chapter will be on the communications received from this funny character, since they represent the only information procured by Hyslop that bore directly on the possibility that Doris suffered from spirit possession.

The fact that Doris Fischer suffered from this syndrome first came to light during the sitting of November 19, the sixth in a series of sessions that had been dominated by the presence of Doris's deceased mother. It should be remembered that Prof. Hyslop was dividing his time among several similar projects during this phase of his career. He was, for example, still engaged in experiments to establish contact with the deceased psychical researcher Richard Hodgson. (See page 46.) The purported personality of the deceased psychical researcher habitually showed up, drop-in style, at several of the sittings Hyslop was undertaking with his many clients, and the professor welcomed his manifestation. Sometimes he specifically requested it. So it wasn't surprising when he showed up during the sittings with Doris.

---

*Drop-ins are spirit entities totally unknown to either the sitters or the psychic. They usually manifest suddenly in order to deliver a simple message. They are rarely heard from at subsequent sittings, but they usually offer verifiable information regarding their earthly lives.

TABLE 2

Some Representative Communications Received From Doris's Mother During the Soule/Hyslop Sittings of November 1914 *

Date	Information Furnished Through Minnie Soule	Verification
November 11, 1914	Mrs. Fischer's spirit explains that her daughter didn't play with other children and that there was something wrong with her.	Doris had previously explained that her personality changes confused her playmates, who thereupon refused to play with her. Her mother was her chief companion during her childhood.
	She explains that Doris often ran away from home for extended periods of time, and that she (the mother) worried that the girl would accidentally drown.	When "Margaret" took control of Doris's body, she would often slip out of the house and disappear. She liked to swim, even when it was dangerous to engage in such adventures, and Mrs. Fischer constantly worried that Doris would drown.
November 16, 1914	Mrs. Fischer mentions a "trinket" she left at her parents' home and later identifies it as being a ring.	Hyslop learned that after Mrs. Fischer eloped, she had been totally disowned by her parents, and her father refused to send her a ring she valued. Many years later the ring was found by her aunt, who sent it to her.
	Talking about her parents and their home, Mrs. Fischer describes the lilies that grew there, referred to the couple's religion as being Methodist, and talked of a curl she once cut from Doris's head as a keepsake.	Doris later explained to Hyslop that her mother often referred to the lilies bordering her childhood home. Mrs. Fischer came from a strict Methodist family, and the incident concerning the curl had occurred when Doris was a child.
	Doris's mother correctly gives two of her pet childhood names for the sitter.	

Date	Information Furnished Through Minnie Soule	Verification
November 17, 1914	Mrs. Fischer describes a swing by their home in detail where Doris liked to play.	The description was correct.
	She and Doris liked to play croquet together.	Correct.
	Mrs. Fischer described a pink bonnet Doris once possessed, which she often wore when they visited somebody who lived down the street from their house.	Doris explained that the bonnet had been given to her by an elderly lady who lived in the neighborhood. She invariably wore it when visiting the kindly woman.
	Mrs. Fischer refers to a place where they liked to cut daisies, and how somebody's pet used to follow them back home.	Doris and her mother used to visit some old estates in Pittsburgh to pick daisies. Someone's pet cat would invariably follow them, and they constantly worried that it would become lost.
November 30, 1914	Mrs. Fischer explains that Doris's problem was the result of a terrible accident, which occurred when the girl was being taken to bed.	This was correct. It was the incident that first caused Doris's frequent dissociative episodes.
	Mrs. Fischer refers to a tin cup in which pennies were kept. She explained that she and her daughter used the pennies to buy little personal things and that they "had to save some for Sunday."	This information was also correct. Doris's mother gave her some of the pennies to take to Sunday school.

*This table includes only a few of the dozens of evidential statements offered by Doris's mother through the trance mediumship of Minnie Soule. Described also were incidents from the girl's life, the names of her relatives, and so forth.

The sudden appearance of the Richard Hodgson persona on November 19 came at the beginning of the sitting, when Mrs. Soule first entered the writing stage of her trance. The information he wished to deliver was vital, as far as Hyslop was concerned. The specific message he delivered certainly came as a surprise.

"I will do what I can on this side to help on the case," the communicator wrote through the psychic. "I believe it as important as any M.P. ever had."

When Hyslop pressed the communicator further, the entity explained that he was referring to Dr. Morton Prince and his work on the Christine L. Beauchamp case (which he correctly named). So even from his side of death, it seems that Richard Hodgson knew that Mrs. Soule's sitter represented a case of multiple personality!

Hyslop was even more intrigued when the communicator explained that the sitter's case was more complex than the earlier one.

"The secondary self with all the multiple equations is not the cause of what is going on," the Hodgson personality continued.

Nothing could have been more apparent to Hyslop, and it now looked as if his former colleague was diagnosing Doris as a case of possession rather than multiple personality. The deceased but informative Dr. Hodgson continued by saying that the departed soul of a child was complicating the sitter's life and partially controlling her body.

The professor was both excited and puzzled by the results of this particular sitting, since no information pointing to a spiritistic cause of the sitter's problems had been communicated by her deceased mother. Clearly the sittings were beginning to move in a different direction.

The entity first described by the Richard Hodgson personality began channeling information through Minnie Soule and her spirit guide during the next sitting, conducted on the morning of November 30. This colorful and enigmatic personality came to dominate several of the sessions from November to December 1914. She claimed—either by sending her thoughts to Mrs. Soule's control or by directly taking possession of the psychic—that her name was "Laughing Water" (Minnehaha) and that she had long been influencing Doris and causing many other problems. Of course, Hyslop had a difficult time taking the entity seriously, especially since her self-professed cognomen seemed borrowed from Henry Wadsworth Longfellow's famous poem *Hiawatha*, published in 1855! But the professor also knew from past experience that some spirit entities liked to encrust themselves with spectacular or playful claims. So the communicator's silly pronouncements didn't imme-

Professor James H. Hyslop, who pioneered the study of spirit obsession and possession.

Mrs. Minnie Soale, one of Professor Hyslop's favorite mediums, who collaborated with him to depossess several of his clients.
(Courtesy of the American Society for Psychical Research, Inc.)

One of the critical sketches made by Frederic Thompson and left in Professor Hyslop's possession.

An unfinished painting by R. Swain Gifford that matches the Thompson sketch previously shown to Hyslop.

A sketch of some gnarled oaks that haunted Thompson's mind when Gifford began "obsessing" him.

The actual location on the Elizabeth islands previously sketched by Frederic Thompson from his visions and described at a sitting with Mrs. Soale. (One of the branches had been broken by sheep and was placed artificially back into position.)

The "real" Doris Fischer.
(Brittia L. Fritschle)

Doris Fischer, while exhibiting her "Sick Doris" personality.

Top: Doris Fischer while exhibiting her "Margaret" personality.

Bottom: Doris Fischer while exhibiting her "Sleeping Margaret" personality talking with Dr. Prince.

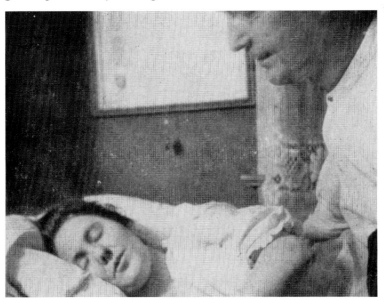

Above: Dr. and Mrs. Carl Wickland, who pioneered the Spiritualist treatment for mental illness.

Right: Dr. Walter Franklin Prince, who cured two cases of spirit obsession through exorcism.

Above: Dr. Elwood Worcester, the founder of the Emmanuel Movement in Boston, who realized that some mental health problems could be complicated by "spiritistic" influences.
(From a painting by Pollack-Offendorff.)

Left: Miss Etta de Camp, who wrote several short stories while "possessed" or "obsessed" by Frank Stockton.

Dr. Titus Bull, the eminent New York neurologist who came to believe that spirit obsession was a complicating factor in mental illness.
(Courtesy of the American Society for Psychical Research, Inc.)

diately make him suspicious of the entity's psychic reality. But whatever the truth of her claims, the communicator knew a great deal about Doris, who merely sat in Mrs. Soule's parlor during the sittings without saying a word. The communicator described correctly even the terrible incident that had caused Doris's problems. The curious visitor to Mrs. Soule's sittings also recounted several incidents from Doris's past and took credit for getting Doris into trouble with her parents and friends. She even called Hyslop by the pet name (calling him an "old monkey") that "Margaret" had given him in 1911!

What was Hyslop to make of these bizarre claims, coupled as they were with evidential information concerning the sitter seemingly emparted by her deceased mother? The professor grappled with the interpretations of this personality through several sittings and finally came to the conclusion that she was, indeed, independent of the psychic's mind. He didn't stop at that, though. The eventual upshot of the experiments was that Hyslop came to believe that this strange little character was somehow linked to the sitter's "Margaret" personality. He even toyed with the possibility that "Margaret" had not been a secondary personality of Doris's but rather a possessing spirit—*the same possessing spirit with whom he was now communicating through Minnie Soule.*

Things became even more complex as the sittings continued. Mrs. Soule's band of spirit protectors communicated regularly, often usurping control from Doris's deceased mother and "Laughing Water" to deliver their messages. They explained to Hyslop that the sitter suffered from more than simple obsession, and they were eager to clarify the situation in great detail.

"They were not content with proving that a spirit was at the bottom of the Margaret personality," Hyslop wrote in 1918 in his book *Life after Death*, "but took up the task of showing that she was but a mere tool of a group that was more important than she was."

Who were these spirit presences camouflaged behind Doris's complicated psychopathology? Mrs. Soule's controls told Hyslop that they were an organized band of evil influences that was trying to compromise the girl's life. They additionally told the professor that Doris's case was similar to other cases that occurred every day—cases of insanity that were perfectly curable through psychic exorcism.

It was only after these important messages were delivered that a strange and shadowy character began popping up during the Boston séances. Mrs. Soule's controls eventually forced this persona to reveal himself to Hyslop, who received several direct communications from the self-professed Count Cagliostro. (The historical Cagliostro, whose real name was Giuseppe Balsamo, had been one of the most colorful personalities in the history of Western occultism.*) Hyslop had little patience with this entity, and reasoned with him to stop bothering the sitter.

What occurred during (and as a result of) this makeshift exorcism can best be told in Hyslop's own words.

> When he found himself trapped, he was rather angry, but, after trying to commit violence on the medium by twisting her to pieces, was cajoled by the controls into further communications. He was finally persuaded to give up the life he was leading, and to abandon the organization of which he was the head. One after another of these disorder[ly] spirits was brought to the bar for confession, and shown their evil ways. Some were willing and desirous of escaping the hell they were in, but a few were very obstinate. They yielded, however, in most cases after much effort and pressure. The removal of Count Cagliostro made them leaderless, and they were utterly unable to carry out their plans without his help.

The researcher continued,

> Throughout all this revelation of the agencies at work, the controls displayed their higher objects in such work, and outlined the method of treating such cases, which was to thwart the purposes of the evil "spirits" in any special instance, to extort confession of their deeds, and then to remove them from contact with the living victim. They asserted the doctrine of obsession with all emphasis and endeavored to give the facts which proved it.

The researcher also experimented to see if he could cajole Doris's "Sleeping Margaret" personality into communicating through the psychic, but this experiment (conducted on December 18, 1914) failed completely.

Despite this last and perhaps revealing failure, the belief that Doris was in part possessed grew stronger in the professor's mind as the sittings continued into 1915. By the end of the year Hyslop was fully convinced that Doris had been partially possessed from the beginnings—or that some sort of spiritistic "overshadowing" had been behind her many person-

---

*Balsamo lived from 1743 to 1795. He began his career in science in a Catholic order. He left it to become a charlatan skilled in deceiving his patrons by faking magical effects. He died in a French prison, exposed and disgraced.

alities. After he reached these conclusions, Hyslop retired from the case and Doris Fischer returned to Dr. Prince's chicken farm in San Bernardino. Her life there was uneventful and she served successfully as the vice-president of a poultry association in the county, presiding over the group's meetings with intelligence and coolness.

While Hyslop wrote on this case several times between 1917 and 1919, he withdrew from it entirely after the Boston experiments. He had little more dealing with it professionally, although Doris would always think back fondly of him.

Unlike the fascinating cases of Frederic Thompson, Etta De Camp, and Ida Rogers, the disturbing case of Doris Fischer and her several selves did not conclude with the completion of Hyslop's investigation. Several more complicated chapters in her life followed her trip to Boston and Mrs. Soule's revelations about her past condition.

It was difficult, in fact, to know just what to make of Minnie Soule's communications about Doris's problems. By the end of his long career in psychical research, Hyslop was prone to take the phenomenon of trance mediumship rather literally. He had the utmost confidence in Minnie Soule's spirit guides. It didn't bother him that Doris's self-styled possessors claimed ridiculous names and personal identities, since he felt that he could easily explain their flippancy and boastfulness. He had long stopped suspecting that Mrs. Soule and other psychics could reach into his thoughts and create bogus spirit presences based on the contents of his own mind. Remember that at the turn of the century the phenomenon of telepathy seemed even more mysterious than it does today and it seemed to be a weak and unfocused power. But can we be so sure today that Mrs. Soule's unconscious mind *wasn't* reading Hyslop's thoughts and capitalizing on his suspicions in the Doris case?

This problem is the key issue which the contemporary student of psychical research must invariably confront when studying Hyslop's imposing body of research on spirit possession. The Doris case is even more frustrating since we have a double mystery to explain if we want to completely solve the case. We have two challenging problems: explaining the presence of Mrs. Fischer's surviving personality at the Soule sittings, who communicated many bits of confirmed evidential information concerning her daughter; and explaining the frankly ludicrous spirit entity whose existence (suspiciously?) fulfilled Hyslop's suspicions about the psychic cause of Doris's past psychopathology.

Untangling these components of the Doris case isn't easy, but no explanation of Doris's complicated problems would be complete unless we succeed. We'll return to these and related issues in Chapter 14.

Prof. Hyslop's experiments with Doris Fischer and Minnie Soule opened up a fresh chapter in the girl's personal psychic development. Psychic experiences had long played a role in her life, and some of them, such as her propensity for seeing phantoms, cast a spiritistic light on her powers. The spiritistic side of Doris became even more prominent upon her return to mental and physical health, and it was a constant source of study for Dr. Prince.

The clergyman didn't write much on the case between 1914 and 1916, probably for personal reasons. He underwent his own partial breakdown in 1913, which took the form of a severe depression. He began to reevaluate his life and found himself immersed in an existential vacuum in which his very soul seemed sick. Since he was approaching his fiftieth birthday when the depression first struck, perhaps his problem would today be diagnosed as a midlife crisis. This peculiar syndrome was hardly known to the psychiatry of the 1910s, but Dr. Prince eventually resolved his problems by relinquishing his parish work in California in 1916. He moved his family back to the east coast, where he engaged in psychotherapeutic work at St. Mark's Church in New York. He worked there for close to two years before joining the staff of the American Society for Psychical Research, where he became Hyslop's personal assistant and chief researcher.

The suspicion that Doris might have entered into contact with the world of the dead again came to Dr. Prince's notice toward the beginning of 1918, when he moved his family into a house in the fashionable suburb of Upper Montclair, New Jersey. The residence was then owned by Hyslop's secretary and there was certainly no prior indication that the house was haunted. But no sooner were the Princes settled into the three-story home than strange noises began to plague it. Doris, who was now going by the name of Theodosia Brittia Prince, was the first family member to notice these noises, and she took detailed notes on them.

"About a week after we moved into [the] house," she wrote of her first experience, "I began to hear noises on the stairs leading to the third floor. I did not pay much attention to them, as we were very busy. After getting the house in order I noticed that I heard the noise on the stairs, especially in the morning. It sounds as if a man were coming slowly down the stairs. I say a man because it is a heavy step and seems as if there must be a slight limp, as one step is much heavier than the other and sounds as though the one foot remained on the step until the other was brought down beside it."

Doris was not the only member of the household to hear the odd noises, which sounded as if a stranger were stumbling through the place. Mrs. Prince first heard the sounds in January 1919, and her description corroborated her daughter's earlier one.

> As I was down cellar fixing the furnace fire in our home at 202 Bellevue Ave., Upper Montclair, Jan. 10th, 1919, somewhere between 4 and 5 o'clock in the afternoon, I heard some one in the front hall walking. I thought it was my husband and wondered why he had come home so early. I hurried upstairs and was surprised not to see him, as I felt sure he came in. I went upstairs into the chambers, saw no one, wasn't satisfied, so went up to the third floor and looked all about, but saw no one.
>
> While in the kitchen about 6 o'clock I heard a noise in the cellar as if some one were walking over the coal. I wondered at it.
>
> Dr. Prince, my husband, did not come home for dinner. I was sitting alone in the living room. At about nine o'clock I heard the same sound in the cellar as if some one were walking over the coal, then the coal ran down the bin. It made me some nervous and I said to myself, "I won't go down to fix that furnace fire till Dr. Prince comes home." Soon I heard a noise as if some one was moving about in the cellar, then I heard a very distinct cough coming up the register. I was very startled and would not go down to attend to the furnace. When Dr. Prince did not come on the 10:30 train I knew my fire would go out if I did not attend to it, so I mustered up courage and went down. I looked all about, but saw nothing and the coal didn't look disturbed. No one could get into the cellar, as the door was fastened. I told Dr. Prince about it when he came home at 11:30 that night.

Mrs. Prince heard two loud raps the very next morning, which seemed to emanate from inside her piano.

The residence certainly seemed to be haunted, and it soon became obvious to Dr. Prince that the phenomenon focused on Doris. She was particularly sensitive to the psychic outbreaks and started receiving visitations from the apparition of her deceased mother the following March. These visitations usually occurred in her room when she was trying to sleep.

Doris saw an even more puzzling apparition three months later, when she returned home at 9:35 P.M. on the evening of June 12, 1919. She decided to relax before retiring, so she placed a record on the Victrola and sat back to enjoy it. She was startled when, moments later, she heard an upstairs door slam shut. She decided to investigate the incident, so she walked up two flights of stairs to a study where Dr. Prince kept a wooden desk. She didn't light the room upon first entering, but while sitting at the desk she saw a ghostly form build up by the window. The form represented a gentleman sitting in a wooden chair. Doris tried speaking to the figure, but he merely turned his head and chuckled.

"I felt piqued," Doris later explained, "and was going to leave right off, but discovered that I would have to step over his feet to get down the stairs, so I decided to stay. He looked towards the direction in which I was sitting and again gave the laugh. He then disappeared."

The figure had been neither ghostly nor transparent and Doris concluded her description of the episode by saying, "I could almost hear the chair creak when he moved, he looked so real."

The phenomena began to plague the house in earnest the following September when paranormal raps—loud wooden or metallic bangs—erupted throughout the structure. They were loud enough even for Dr. Prince to hear them despite his growing deafness. He was not willing to stand casually by and record the events, though, since he wanted to find the psychic cause of the uncanny outbreaks. This preoccupation led him right back to his foster daughter and her burgeoning paranormal powers. Since Doris seemed to be so psychic, Dr. Prince encouraged her to make contact with the entities purportedly infestating their home. She complied by sitting for psychic writing beginning in September 1919, and several scripts were produced stating that the phenomena were being engineered by two separate discarnates. Their names were given through Doris's automatic writing, but even though one of them insisted that she had known the clergyman when he was a child, Dr. Prince didn't recognize her. Whatever the truth behind these messages (which were never verified), the raps persisted through October and November and were heard every few days. Later they spread to Dr. Prince's office at the American Society for Psychical Research, where they were heard by Hyslop's secretary.

But that wasn't the end of the problem. The phenomena escalated even further the following month when Doris's bed began to shake while she was resting. The dramatic upshot of these incidents came three months later, when the presence infesting the house became still bolder. The critical incident took place on the night of March 31 and severely upset Doris.

I awoke about 1:45 in the morning with very bad cramps. I arose and got some medicine. About two o'clock papa came home, and after about 15 minutes he retired for the night. I lay there awake, when I became suddenly alert and felt as though there were some one in the room. I looked and saw nothing (my room is very light from an electric light across the street). I then felt my bed jerk as though some one had lurched against it once, twice, and then a third time. I waited, and the covers began to be pulled. I knew they were pulled, because I tuck my covers in and they cannot possibly slip. I held on to them and yelled for papa. While I was holding on as tight as I could it seemed as though there were one person on each side of my bed holding the covers just as tight as they could be held. I let go of the covers and, after getting up some nerve, put my hand down to where it seemed the covers were held. I felt nothing, but just then the covers were pulled to the floor. I got very nervous and fled into father's and mother's room. Papa came in and slept in my bed and I slept in his. There were knocking, scratches and raps in papa's room after I settled down. I was fast asleep when the table next to the bed (I was facing the other way) fell over or was pulled.

Mrs. Prince shared in this psychic episode. She woke up at 3:45 in the morning when Doris entered her room to complain of the activity in her own room.

The talk awoke my husband, Dr. Prince, and she told him. She said, "It seems more like a human being than ever before. I could feel the hands clutch the bedclothes. I put out my hand to try and see if I could touch the hand, but it kept moving farther down." Dr. Prince said he would like to go into her bed, and he did, she getting into his bed. I thought I would not go to sleep, but listen, but just got to sleep when I was awakened by a noise sounding like some one scratching loudly upon the door. I listened after it stopped and in a few moments I heard it much louder. I sat up in my bed and looked at the bed Theodosia was in, next to mine in same room. I thought she might have put her hand out and made the noise in her sleep. Her hand was in the bed. She immediately sat up and said, "Mother, what was that?" I said it sounded like some one scratching on the door. Did you touch the door? She said, "No, I was asleep. It sounded to me as though it was on the floor." All was quiet again and I fell asleep again to be awakened by a rap apparently on the bureau at the side of the room. After awhile I went to sleep to be awakened again by a louder noise as if something was thrown down. Theodosia also awakened and very nervously said, "What was that, I am shaking all over." I reached out my hand and found that a little table which is between the two beds and at the head of the beds was not in its place. It had an alarm clock and two other small things on it. I felt down between the beds. It was tipped over on its side.

Dr. Prince spent the rest of the night sleeping in his foster daughter's room but didn't witness the curious psychokinetic effects. "I went to sleep almost at once after entering [Doris's] room," he commented dryly in his report, "and was not disturbed. Nor did she have any more trouble after she returned to her room."

Later, Dr. Prince learned of an earlier occurrence in the house. He discovered from the owner that Etta De Camp (see Chapter 5) had visited the house either in 1917 or in 1918. She had experienced a similar episode which, despite her own psychic past, had terrified her.

With the discovery that the phenomena predated his tenancy in the house, Dr. Prince came to feel that perhaps the place was conventionally haunted and that Doris's presence was not, as he had originally suspected, instrumental to the manifestations. But his opinion soon changed. The rector bought his own house in the city at the beginning of 1921, and his family moved there at the end of February. The same phenomena soon broke out there! There were mysterious footsteps in the house, raps broke out continually, beds were shaken, and their little cocker spaniel even became frightened of the events.* In March 1923, Mrs. Prince began seeing a phantom stalking through the house, similar to several that Doris was seeing during the same months. Dr. Prince kept careful notes of these outbreaks between 1919 and 1925, and he published his diary of the events in 1926.

By this time, however, several changes had occurred in the clergyman's life. Lelia C. Prince, the researcher's wife, died in 1924, and Doris took over the domestic responsibilities of the house. She was passionately devoted to her foster father and cared for him conscientiously for the next several years and never married. The critical standards of the American Society for Psychical Research began to deteriorate at this time and Dr. Prince relinquished his post as research officer there also in 1924. Some of his colleagues founded a similar society in Boston, and it was under their aegis that his *The Psychic in the House* was pub-

---

*The poor creature refused to enter a room where Doris once saw a ghost in 1923 resembling Dr. Prince's deceased mother. She also cried and whimpered when she espied the phantasmal forms.

lished in 1926. Dr. Prince and Doris then moved to Boston, where he became the chief research officer for the Boston Society for Psychic Research. It isn't known whether the raps followed the Prince family to Boston, and the publication of the proceedings was the last report he issued on his foster daughter and her puzzling life. (The remaining years of her life will be discussed in Chapter 10.)

So in conclusion, was Doris Fischer the victim of spirit possession or not? The reports issued on the case make for fascinating reading, but it is difficult to reach a firm conclusion on the basis of them. By the end of his lengthy investigation, Dr. Prince personally felt that a spiritistic element was present in Doris's life, but he wasn't sure that it had ever been behind her multiple personalities. He certainly came to believe in the reality of life after death, and he genuinely believed that his foster daughter was capable of contacting the dearly departed. This possibility only contributed to his suspicion that Doris's "Sleeping Margaret" was independent of her unconscious mind, though he always stopped short of positively stating she was a spirit entity. So the enigmatic case of Doris Fischer will probably always remain a baffling psychological and parapsychological mystery, just as it was to W. Franklin Prince sixty years ago.

It is unfortunate that James Hyslop never lived to see these later developments in the case, which would have corroborated his suspicions of its spiritistic basis. His sittings with Doris and Minnie Soule in Boston constituted his last major investigation into the dark world of spirit possession. He never lost interest in the subject but grew increasingly less interested in publishing the results of his studies. During the summer of 1970 I corresponded briefly with Hyslop's younger daughter, and she confirmed my suspicion that the problem of spirit possession continually preoccupied him during the final phase of his career.

She wrote to me in this regard on August 9 from her home in Rochester, New York. "I do know that a year before my father died he came back home from his regular weekly experiments with a trance medium in Boston," she explained to me, "where he apparently was trying to persuade a departed spirit to leave some one alone. Supposedly the spirit threatened to make my father ill."

The denouement to this unpublished case was curious, to say the least. "He [Hyslop] kept on and apparently the spirit succeeded for a number of weeks," she continued. "I was home from college then and took care of him."

Unfortunately, we will never know the background behind this provocative story. Hyslop's health was never exemplary, and he suffered a debilitating stroke toward the end of 1919. He lingered for several months and finally passed over the infinite boundary on June 17, 1920.

PART II
Successors in the Work

CHAPTER **9**

The Work of Dr. Titus Bull

Dr. James Hyslop's psychic journey led him through several strange avenues of exploration. He conducted research for over a decade before coming to a series of conclusions about the nature of spirit obsession, its manifestations, and the prognosis for its cure. Through his work on the Doris Fischer case, he came to believe that spirit obsession could manifest in such a way that, to the unsuspecting clinician, it was indistinguishable from common forms of mental illness. This was an important conclusion, and it was natural for Hyslop to wonder whether such cases could be cured. Only toward the end of his life, however, did he finally outline "a method of dealing with the problem," as he termed it.

This therapeutic strategy was a natural outgrowth of his research on the Doris case. Hyslop felt that the best way to cure cases of spirit obsession was by contacting the entities causing the problem. This could be accomplished by working with a trance medium. The entities could then be dislodged by reasoning with them and encouraging them to progress spiritually in their own realm. This strategy was not really original, since it was no different from what many Spiritualists were practicing at the turn of the century.

Spiritualists, both in the United States and Great Britain, had come to the same conclusion years before, which led to the institution of a curious practice called the rescue circle. During these proceedings, the Spiritualist group would try to contact "low" and ignorant spirits whom they believed commonly possess the living. As I pointed out in an earlier chapter, it was common to bring people suffering from unusual mental symptoms to these séances. Their alleged obsessors would be invited to control the psychic in charge of the sitting, and the members of the group would then exhort them to leave or would call upon the psychic's guides to help dislodge them.

Hyslop was undoubtedly influenced by these practices, and his own suggestions were probably modeled after them. As I also pointed out earlier, sometime in 1910 Hyslop made a trip to Kansas City to visit the Temple of Light, a Spiritualist church that specialized in this sort of rescue work. He was impressed by what he had witnessed there, although unfortunately he left no written record of his trip. It is, nonetheless, interesting that he began promoting the mediumistic treatment of mental illness shortly after the trip. It is also interesting that, independently of Hyslop's work, other psychic researchers were coming to similar conclusions about the causes of mental illness. One of these researchers was even putting into practice what Hyslop was only suggesting. So before continuing with Hyslop's psychic legacy, let's turn our attention to the researcher who pioneered the psychic treatment of mental illness.

There is probably no more enigmatic figure in the history of psychical research than Dr. Carl Wickland (1861–1945), who was the first medically trained researcher to practice the Spiritualist treatment of the psychologically deranged. He was born in Sweden but emigrated to the United States in 1881. He married in 1896 and subsequently moved to Chicago to study medicine at Durham Medical College. He graduated in 1900 and worked in private practice before turning his skills to psychiatry. Nine years later, he became chief psychiatrist at the National Psychopathic Institute in Chicago, where he remained for several years before moving to Los Angeles in 1918. There he founded his National Psychological Institute at 2208 North Eleventh Street while maintaining his own residence in the then-fashionable suburb of Highland Park. The building that housed the institute is still standing and is currently occupied by seamstresses in the garment industry.

Long before James Hyslop dreamed he would be studying cases of spirit obsession, Dr. Wickland was coming to the conclusion that psychic factors play a hitherto unrecognized role in clinical psychopathology. He carried out his work independently of the parapsychological establishment of his day. But no less a figure than Dr. Isaac K. Funk, a prominent editor, psychical researcher, and a friend of Hyslop's, called public attention to his work as early as 1905. For example, he wrote about Dr. Wickland in the March 30, 1905 issue of the *Chicago Daily Tribune*.

Like Hyslop, Dr. Wickland believed that the most practical way to help patients obsessed by evil entities was to contact them through a medium. This presented little difficulty for Wickland since his wife was a gifted trance psychic. But unlike Hyslop, Wickland believed that the evidence for spirit obsession should be based on the efficacy of the cures obtained through psychic treatment. He did not consider it worthwhile trying to get the obsessors to prove their personal identities while simultaneously exorcising them. In fact, Wickland explained in his writings that obsessing entities often fail to supply such evidence, even when pressed for it. (He believed that this was due to their confused state of mind.) Because he was not primarily concerned with this issue, Dr. Wickland's major opus *Thirty Years Among the Dead* (1924) is totally lacking in this respect—i.e., the physician reports no cases where the possessing entities communicated information concerning their terrestrial identities or lives that properly checked out upon investigation. He claimed that he had encountered such cases and information, though. He also claimed that the possessors occasionally spoke through his wife in foreign languages that were totally unfamiliar to her. But no specific details regarding these potentially important cases were given in his book.

This does not mean that Wickland's work is worthless or devoid of any documentation. Several years after initiating their work, a Congregational minister from Ohio became interested in the Wicklands. Rev. E. Lee Howard attended several of their séances in the 1930s after the couple had moved to Los Angeles, which he chronicled in his book *My Adventure in Spiritualism*. Reverend Howard was impressed by the rescue sessions he visited, although he did not share his hosts' flippant attitude toward corroborative evidence. He therefore kept a lookout for any evidential incidents that might occur during the experiments he observed. He later wrote,

> A gentleman whom I came to know quite well had a daughter under treatment for a particularly obstinate multiple obsession. Among the entities removed from her and allowed to control Mrs. Wickland long enough so that something might be learned of their history, was one whose influence had been especially harmful and that proved to be the spirit of a suicide. Skillful questioning obtained the name, approximate date and other facts. The patient's father, who was present, made careful notes

and at once undertook a personal investigation. A search of the coroner's records quickly verified that name and date. The mortuary firm supplied additional information. A visit to the address where the suicide had been committed by gas asphyxiation completed a story which corroborated in every detail the one given by the entity itself.

Reverend Howard also notes that,

> A remarkable instance of verification occurred unexpectedly in November, 1931. Dr. Wickland received in his mail one day that month a letter from a stranger residing in the Mississippi Valley. The writer stated that he had just been reading a copy of "Thirty Years Among the Dead," and on a certain page, which he designated, had found the report of an experience in which the obsessing entity—according to the definite biographical data—was unmistakably a cousin of his father.

But for now, let's look at the precise methods the Wicklands used in their rescue work.

The Wicklands' methods were an outgrowth of some private mediumistic experiments they conducted in Chicago in the 1890s with some of their friends. By 1905, Dr. Wickland had witnessed enough Spiritualist phenomena to know that the dead could influence the living in sometimes harmful ways—by disrupting a victim's mind, behavior, and even physical health. These observations led him to wonder if some cases of mental (or even physical) illness—especially those that resisted conventional treatment—would respond to Spiritualist treatment. With this possibility in mind, he began conducting séances with some of his patients in which his wife served as the trance channel. The patient would first be given a shock of static electricity to dislodge the obsessing entity from his or her body or aura. The departing entity would then subsequently control Mrs. Wickland, and the physician would reason with the personality.

Dr. Wickland claimed remarkable success curing conditions ranging from drug use to dissociation and even to criminal behavior by using this simple procedure. He eventually published detailed transcripts of several of these sittings in his book and in its sequel *The Gateway of Understanding* (which appeared in 1934). The only unfortunate aspect of Dr. Wickland's work is its purely anecdotal quality. He never offered any data concerning those patients who didn't respond to treatment, nor elicited follow-up reports from his cured patients. So we simply have no idea if his cures were permanent or not.

The use of electrical shock was probably the most unusual aspect of Dr. Wickland's work. By passing a static current through his patients, he believed their symptoms could be removed. Momentarily dislodging a spirit presence was the very least it successfully accomplished. Dr. Wickland employed a Wimshurst machine for these experiments, a curious contraption that created a charge of static electricity when cranked up. By touching its terminal the patient would receive a strong but harmless shock.

Because the Wicklands spent so little time corroborating the life stories offered by the obsessors they contacted, their research is little more than a fascinating footnote in the history of psychical research. Their work cannot be ignored, but any judgment regarding it must be suspended. Suffice it to say the Wicklands continued with their therapeutic work for several years, both in Chicago and later in Los Angeles. Mrs. Wickland died in 1937 (the same year that Minnie Soule died in Boston), which prompted Dr. Wickland to visit Great Britain in hopes of finding a replacement for her. He especially hoped to recruit Bertha Harris, one of England's most celebrated platform clairvoyants and trance psychics, but she turned down his offer. Dr. Wickland himself died in 1945. His work has been virtually forgotten today, although his *Thirty Years Among the Dead* remains constantly in print.

This background material will give the reader a rough overview of spirit therapy and how it was practiced by the Spiritualist community in the United States. Hyslop's specific accomplishment was in taking the practice out of Spiritualism and placing it within the realms of parapsychology and psychiatry.

Even though Hyslop never publicly acknowledged the Wicklands' work, we know that he was certainly aware of it. Shortly before his death in 1920, he began planning to establish a clinic for the psychic and spiritistic treatment of the mentally ill. His only problem was in finding a suitable successor to carry out the plan. His eventual choice was an old friend, the prominent New York neurologist Dr. Titus Bull. Dr. Bull's work opened up a new chapter in the search to prove the existence of spirit possession.

Titus Bull was born in New York in 1871. He graduated from New York University and Bellevue Medical College and was a member of the American Medical Association and the American Association for the Advancement of Science. To the New York community of his day, he was a highly respected physician and neurologist who lived in a fashionable section of the Upper West Side. He lived, in fact, directly across the street from the Hyslop family on 149th Street. He was a man of culture and etiquette and possessed a critical and talented medical mind. He was a portly man who sported a neatly trimmed mustache.

Dr. Bull practiced neurology, psychiatry, and general medicine at a time when little was known concerning the workings of the mind. Even Sigmund Freud's work was barely known outside small medical circles in Europe. Dr. Bull, like other physicians working in this era, had only a rudimentary understanding of the causes of mental illnesses. Psychopathology was usually explained as the result of both neurological and emotional causes, but this insight didn't help them successfully treat most of the cases brought to them. Many of their psychotic patients wound up incarcerated in public institutions with little hope of ever leaving.

It isn't clear just how and when Dr. Bull first became acquainted with Hyslop and the American Society for Psychical Research. They probably met professionally, since in 1906 Hyslop was still hoping to reorganize the ASPR by combining it with an institute for the study of psychology. We know that Hyslop consulted with Dr. Bull during his early research on the Thompson/Gifford case. (See page 39.) Dr. Bull was not then a member of the ASPR, though he joined shortly after working on the case. Since Hyslop and Bull lived so close to each other, it is reasonable to believe that they discussed the subject of spirit obsession between 1907 and 1919, the years during which Hyslop became preoccupied with the subject.

We know little about Dr. Bull's early work in the field of psychical research, but we do know that he was fascinated by the phenomenon of psychic diagnosis. He conducted some experiments along these lines (probably in the late 1910s) with E. Margaret Harvey, a psychic from England who could clairvoyantly diagnose the physical problems of her clients by giving them psychic "readings".* He never issued a report on these experiments, however. It is possible that Miss Harvey helped Dr. Bull with his early studies on spirit obsession, since by 1918 he was already experimenting with exorcism as a cure for some forms of psychopathology.

The fact that James Hyslop ultimately asked Dr. Bull to continue

---

*Miss Harvey played a prominent role in an anonymously written book published in 1920 entitled *The Unseen Doctor*. (The book's British title was *One Thing I Know*.) It was written by Ella Mabel Storr, who had been a hopeless invalid before being cured by the psychic and her spirit guides. Miss Harvey's identity was concealed in the book, where she is consistently called "Miss Rose."

his own clinical research on spirit possession is significant, since it is well known that Hyslop was extremely cautious about the colleagues with whom he worked. He must have been very impressed by Dr. Bull's critical judgment and standards. The only criticism of Dr. Bull I ever personally heard, in fact, came from Dr. J. B. Rhine—the founder of modern experimental parapsychology—who visited him once in the 1920s. Dr. Rhine told me (when I visited him in Durham, North Carolina, in the summer of 1973) that Bull was a little "too believing"—i.e., too credulous—for his taste. However, Dr. Rhine was basing his judgment on a fifty-year-old memory.

Whatever the case, Dr. Bull was sympathetic to Hyslop's request and—side by side with his conventional practice—spent the next twenty years exploring the spiritistic basis for some cases of psychopathology in which either ignorant or obviously evil entities seemed to be overpowering the patient's life. Dr. Bull initially worked by himself and treated these patients with psychological suggestion, hypnosis, and the laying-on-of-hands. Sometimes, though, he consulted a clairvoyant when working on his cases. He found that these various procedures provided excellent therapy for removing his patients' more problematic symptoms. These extraordinary studies were at first undertaken only sporadically, and psychic healing was only employed in those cases where traditional therapy was clearly failing.

Dr. Bull's research received a major impetus in 1925, when a young woman named Mrs. Carolyn C. Duke began working with him. She was a relatively young psychic who came to Dr. Bull under rather strange circumstances. When they first met, she told the physician that she was in contact with the late James Hyslop! Mrs. Duke continued by relating that the entity had urged her to contact Dr. Bull and to offer her services to him. Dr. Bull was impressed enough with the story to retain her as a medium-in-residence to help him with his psychic work. She had previously been a teacher.

That, at least, is the official story behind her meeting with Dr. Bull. The real story may be more complicated.

The career of Mrs. Duke represents somewhat of a puzzle. She was instrumental in Dr. Bull's work, though he never gave his readers any information about her background. Nor did he reveal that the name "Mrs. Duke" was possibly a pseudonym. Her real identity may have been a closely guarded secret. Based on clues buried in psychical research's literature, it is *possible* that she was really Mrs. Caroline Randolph Chapman, who later became a prominent and well-regarded New

York trance medium whose career lasted until her retirement in 1969. She was psychic from birth, but she never planned to capitalize on her powers. But then her husband went blind after suffering a head injury in Cuba, where the couple lived for some years on a plantation. This crisis and their return to New York exacerbated her psychic capabilities, and she was soon receiving visitations from the ghosts of her deceased mother and daughter. These experiences were so disturbing that she feared for her sanity and rushed to consult with her family doctor. Fortunately, the Randolphs' family doctor was none other than Dr. Bull. When he heard Mrs. Chapman's story, Dr. Bull explained to her that she was not psychotic, but probably psychic. He told her about James Hyslop's research and promised to help her confront and unfold her powers. During the 1930s the American Society for Psychical Research regularly sent clients to her, and she became well known for her work in helping other people develop their own psychic senses.

The psychic collaborated with Warren Weldon in writing her biography upon her retirement. This book was published in 1970 under the title A *Happy Medium—the life of Caroline Randolph Chapman*. The episode concerning Mrs. Chapman's meeting with Dr. Bull is mentioned in the book, even though the physician's identity is not revealed. Weldon discusses the psychic's work with a few cases of possession, but again Dr. Bull's work is bypassed.

The enigma of Mrs. Duke's possibly disguised identity will probably never be solved to everyone's satisfaction. Since my possible identification of Mrs. Duke with Mrs. Chapman is partially based on speculation, I will use the name "Mrs. Duke" throughout this chapter.

Dr. Bull was also able to hire Mrs. Helen Lambert, a wealthy woman from St. Louis who had been a friend of Hyslop's, as a full-time secretary and collaborator. She was in charge of keeping records on his cases and researching some of them.

Dr. Bull's Spiritualist techniques were simple, like the procedures Carl Wickland was simultaneously using in Los Angeles. Only when one of his patients failed to respond to conventional medical treatment would he resort to psychic and mediumistic treatment. He would invite the patient to a sitting with Mrs. Duke, who would diagnose his or her problems through a psychic reading. If the reading pointed to possession, she would bring through the personalities bothering the patient for Dr. Bull to deal with.

Dr. Bull was primarily interested in curing his patients and not with conducting research. Although he kept careful records of his several cases, he didn't possess Hyslop's zeal for publishing them. Very few of his case studies are therefore available to us today, and we have re-course only to summaries of their main facts.

The case of Mr. C. E.

While working with Dr. Bull, Helen Lambert published a complete summary of one of his more provocative cases in 1928. The patient was called Mr. C. E. in the report, and in some respects the case resembles that of Frederic Thompson, the case that had originally sparked Hyslop's interest in the problem of spirit obsession.

The patient first wandered into Dr. Bull's clinic suffering from some form of progressive dementia. He seemed to be prematurely senile and severely dissociated, and he couldn't stop ranting about his paintings and inventions. He also claimed that he was being invaded by a spirit who was forcing him to paint. He also complained, from what Dr. Bull could glean from his confused speech, of seizures and compulsive sexual thoughts. The patient went on to say that the entity possessing him was a deceased Austrian painter by the name of Josef Selleny, who had once been befriended by the Emperor Maximillian in Mexico.

By current standards, the patient would today probably be diagnosed as suffering from an acute schizophrenic episode, paranoid type.

Dr. Bull was intrigued by the obviously spiritistic elements complicating the patient's complaints and focused on them. His first course of action was to interest Helen Lambert in checking on the confused client's claims. She began by sifting through several European art encyclopedias in search of the historical painter. She later wrote in her analysis of the case,

> When I first read the Selleny communication I was rather skeptical. It seemed too glib and precise to be genuinely supernormal and I thought it would prove to be a subconscious memory on the patient's part, of a passage seen in a book; or else one of those utterly spurious messages, so prone to exact detail about some purely fictitious charactor. In the New York Library I found three encyclopedias containing short biographies of Joseph Selleny. (The name in the automatic script was spelled Josef. A friend in Vienna informs me that Joseph is spelled with an F in Austria so it would seem that the entity spelled his own name correctly and that the encyclopedias are at fault.) Of these three books, one was in English,

one in French and one in German. The statements made in the script are verified in each volume except that in the English and French biographies no mention is made of the Emperor Maximillian. In the German account Selleny is said to have accompanied Maximillian to Northern Africa and Brazil. Mr. C. E. is too ignorant of these subjects to know that these slight errors would strengthen the evidential value of the message, and he reads neither French or German. However, the most interesting discovery that I made, in view of the fact that it was under this control that the patient became violently deranged is that the artist, Selleny, died insane.

Mrs. Lambert listed as her sources the *Allgemeines Künstler-Lexicon* by Hans Wolfgang Singer, Bénézet's *Dictionnaire des Peintres, Sculptures, Etc.*, and *Bryan's Dictionary of Painters*.

Mrs. Lambert also became interested in the paintings that the patient was producing under the control of the alleged Selleny.

The early work is in pencil, and has intricate and lovely designs. One drawing covers a large sheet of paper two or more feet square, with delicate spirals and spider-web designs in one unbroken line. The pencil has not been lifted from the paper. In the crayon work the lurid and repulsive predominate. The colors are heavy, and the figures are monsters with heads like gargoyles which have no bodies but are set on what appears to be a mass of viscera. In spite of the ugliness these figures are far from being without artistic merit. The drawing is bold and effective and the leering, vicious faces are extraordinary.

Two of Mr. C. E.'s attempts at oil painting when not under control are landscapes of the crude sort which anyone with a little sense of color and perspective might achieve. The brush-work is clumsy and heavy, and they look like the work of a beginner or of a clever child. I have seen only one of the paintings done under the Selleny control,—the last, over which the final conflict occurred. It is a canvas about twenty-eight inches long by twenty inches, and represents a lonely lake with masses of forest foliage around it. There are distant mountains in the background. It is almost impossible to believe that this picture was painted by the same hand that executed the two crude pictures which I mentioned. Perspective, coloring, and detail show astonishing technique. Hidden in the masses of foliage are the heads of animals, which C. E. did not discover until they were called to his attention by automatic writing in which he was told of the symbolism in this picture. During the conflict which took place as the painting was completed, Mr. C. E. was impelled against his will to paint out a delicate sky by covering it with a lurid red.

Mrs. Lambert was not the only researcher impressed by the paintings. Dr. Henry McComas, a psychologist from Johns Hopkins University in Baltimore, investigated Spiritualism in the 1920s and issued a scathing report in his book *Ghosts I Have Talked With*. He was unimpressed both by Dr. Bull's work, and by the sitting he undertook with Mrs. Duke in October 1926. He saw the paintings executed by Mr. C. E., however, and was extremely impressed by them. They were still hanging in Dr. Bull's office when the psychologist paid his visit.

Since the patient was so incoherent when he came to the center, Dr. Bull immediately called in Carolyn Duke to see if she could clairvoyantly perceive the basis of his problem. She presumably met the patient and gave a detailed reading for him and Dr. Bull. Most of the information Mrs. Duke communicated concerning the patient's background proved to be correct. Formal corroboration was secured through conversations with the patient subsequent to the reading.

It turned out that Mr. C. E. had previously suffered a head injury severe enough to cause his hospitalization, which marked the beginning of his problems. The patient's later seizures stemmed from this injury, which led to what Dr. Bull called the client's "moral deprivation." (This probably referred to Mr. C. E.'s compulsive sexual thoughts and excessive masturbation.) While he was undergoing these seizures, the patient first felt a separate "stream of consciousness" beginning to control his mind. This problem was soon exacerbated further. When the patient began experimenting with a ouija board, this separate element within his mind began exerting itself more forcefully. He found that automatic writing and painting suddenly came easily, but the results soon turned sinister. He began to paint grotesque figures while his "separate self" compelled him to paint in a totally different style. This war between his inner selves finally became debilitating and Mr. C. E. suffered a total collapse. That's when he was first institutionalized. He recovered from this psychotic episode while incarcerated but regressed upon his release (which frequently happens with people suffering from schizophrenic disorders). It was never clear why or how Mr. C. E. was finally directed to Dr. Bull.

Since the patient specifically claimed that he was possessed, Dr. Bull lost little time conducting a Spiritualist exorcism. He undertook a series of forty sittings at his office, during which Carolyn Duke purportedly contacted the entities troubling Mr. C. E. During these sittings, the patient was simply instructed to lie on an operating table and remain silent. Mrs. Duke never became fully entranced but relayed the messages she picked up from Mr. C. E.'s tormenters to Dr. Bull. She sometimes permitted the obsessors to communicate through her for short periods, but she refused to relinquish control of her body to them. Unfortunately, we do not have the full transcripts of these sittings, but Helen Lambert offered a summary of them in 1928 in her book *A General Survey of Psychic Phenomena* and in a paper she published in an issue of *Psychic Science*, an English Spiritualist publication, from that same year.

Dr. Bull and Mrs. Duke realized early on in the proceedings that they were in for a real fight. During the second séance, one of the possessing entities unexpectedly took control of Mrs. Duke and grabbed Dr. Bull's throat. That was only the beginning of a lengthy and tiring ordeal. The primary entity possessing the patient turned out to be a Moslem priest who was full of hatred for Dr. Bull and his client. Several other obsessors were uncovered as the sittings progressed. This band included a senile old man, a sexually disturbed spirit (whom the patient had picked up while participating in a séance), a self-styled Mexican, and several secondary entities. The first seven sittings were devoted to talking to these obsessors, and Dr. Bull could see that the patient's symptoms improved the more he interacted with the Moslem priest personality. This led the physician to suspect that the "Moslem priest" was instigating Mr. C. E.'s insanity, so the subsequent twenty sessions were devoted to cajoling him into departing. Then the sittings became even more complicated, for the loathsome entity brought forth the other possessors in a frantic effort to retain control of the patient's mind and body. Luckily, Dr. Bull was able to displace most of them from the patient by reasoning with them. He encouraged them to find spiritual satisfaction in their own realm, but some of the obsessors proved to be stubborn. These personalities were genuinely evil, and Dr. Bull finally had to invoke Mrs. Duke's spirit controls to help. He (or they) were eventually successful in ejecting the possessors.

Helen Lambert personally witnessed these bizarre proceedings—proceedings shockingly and surprisingly similar to those that Dr. Wickland was simultaneously witnessing in Los Angeles. Mrs. Lambert observed that the patient usually remained calm and silent during most of the verbal fisticuffs between Dr. Bull and his client's psychic tormenters. But when the interactions became more violent, his body would begin to tremble.

Helen Lambert stated in her book that Dr. Bull succeeded in fully curing the patient with Mrs. Duke's assistance. This is certainly a remarkable claim since long-standing schizophrenic behavior is particularly resistant to cure. Such behavior usually doesn't respond to conventional psychotherapy, and only taking antipsychotic drugs seem to help these unfortunate people function properly. It should be remembered, though, that Mr. C. E. had a history of spontaneous recoveries; and since there is no evidence from the records that Dr. Bull kept in touch with him after the sittings, we don't know if the cure was permanent.

The case remains extremely interesting, but it also presents a major paradox: Dr. Bull never established contact with the Josef Selleny persona during the sittings, so Mr. C. E.'s primary claim about being possessed was never corroborated through Mrs. Duke's mediumship, despite his cure. Mrs. Lambert came to believe, though, that the senile old man persona brought through by the psychic probably was the surviving painter—perhaps still suffering from the insanity that plagued the end of his life.

The case of Mrs. K. L.

The case of Mrs. K. L. was one of Dr. Bull's first successes and a summary of it was published in 1927. Mrs. K. L. originally came to Dr. Bull's clinic near the end of 1924 when she was thirty-seven years old. She was married and had been previously diagnosed by a psychiatrist as suffering from manic depression. (People suffering this well-known syndrome tend to jockey between periods of profound depression and frenzied hyperactivity). Some of the patient's problems derived from her early childhood. Dr. Bull later learned that when the patient was a child, her nurse had been badly frightened by a thunderstorm. Her reaction was so severe that she had hidden in a closet and had taken the patient with her. This was only the beginning of Mrs. K. L.'s problems. Some years later she was victimized by a rape attempt, but the assailant was (thankfully) frightened off before he could do any real harm. The patient's serious mental affliction began, however, after her marriage and the birth of her three children. She began suffering fits of rage and depression that soon incapacitated her.*

Dr. Bull treated the patient first through the laying-on-of-hands and with more conventional forms of physical/psychiatric treatment. This course of therapy continued for several weeks, but when no improve-

---

* It is interesting to wonder if Mrs. K. L. was suffering from postpartum depression, a common syndrome not fully recognized until relatively recently.

ment was forthcoming, he changed his strategy. Soon he recruited Mrs. Duke to work on the case. It only took them five sittings to uncover the root of the patient's problem and to cure her to their satisfaction.

During the first sitting at Dr. Bull's office, Mrs. Duke received a series of communications that bore on several traumatic episodes from Mrs. K. L.'s early life. Of course, Dr. Bull had told the psychic nothing about them. Despite the fact that Mrs. Duke was kept in the dark about the patient's past, she soon established contact with the patient's disturbed nurse-babysitter. This entity had somehow latched on to the young woman and was possessing her. The ensuing dialogue between Dr. Bull and the obsessor—speaking through Mrs. Duke—seemed to outline the basis of the patient's illness.

Mrs. Duke (speaking clairvoyantly):
Lady here now, and she limps; went across in straight line, hair grey but dark, iron grey. This lady used to manage things, actions, lots of pain, but works just the same. Lady is outspoken. Why don't she buck up and start things. Never was one to lay down on the job myself.

Dr. Bull:	Do you think you are competent to manage the affairs of this woman?
Obsessor (speaking through Mrs. Duke):	I did when she was a little girl. I am not afraid of anybody.
Dr. Bull:	You helped to make her sick.
Obsessor:	I do not think I made her sick.
Dr. Bull:	You might go away and leave her to us to care for.
Obsessor:	I do not know whether I will or not.

During the second sitting Mrs. Duke's controls communicated directly with Dr. Bull and confirmed that the patient was suffering from spirit obsession. They warned him further that the obsessor would be difficult to handle. The psychic next correctly received the clairvoyant impression that the primary obsessor's name was Margaret or Mary.

With this background now revealed, Dr. Bull spoke directly to the obsessor again, who was permitted to control Mrs. Duke. Dr. Bull didn't consider this procedure dangerous since he believed that the entity was confused more than really evil. He soon convinced the confused discarnate to stop bothering the patient, but this initial victory didn't resolve the case. During the following two sessions, Dr. Bull and Mrs. Duke discovered that their patient was also possessed by several secondary entities—and that some of them were definitely malicious. They had remained behind the scenes, so to speak, while Dr. Bull was fighting the patient's deceased nurse. Originally they had taken partial control of the young woman after the nurse "opened the way" for them by initiating her own possession. For example, one of these particularly unpleasant entities broke in spontaneously during the fourth sitting, while Mrs. Duke was communicating some information to Dr. Bull. Its speech was short and pointed. "She is mine, and I am going to keep her. You keep out of this," the persona threatened. "I can make her do things."

Bull's fight to usurp these secondary presences came to a climax during the fifth sitting. This same obsessor chimed in through the psychic, and he seemed angrier than ever before. "I came in of my own accord," he stated. "You or your gang cannot do anything with me." The psychic's arms contorted while the obsessor spoke, and her face grimaced in obvious pain.

Since it was clear that this entity couldn't be reasoned with, Dr. Bull responded by invoking Mrs. Duke's controls and requesting that they pull the obsessor away. This invocation had the required impact, and the entity immediately became more manageable.

"You know," it grumbled, "when I get thinking about women I can't think of anything else? They [the psychic's spirit controls] tell me to keep away from this woman. I don't know whether I can or not."

Mrs. K. L.'s possessor had finally come to realize his own pathetic situation and departed immediately.

Mrs. Duke also psychically discovered yet another spirit partially possessing the patient. This entity never communicated through her, and Mrs. Duke did not believe that this discarnate was necessarily evil. Her impression was that she was only accidentally possessing the patient. She had died in terrible psychological distress, Mrs. Duke clairvoyantly realized, upon being deserted by her fiancée, who had given her a venereal disease. Dr. Bull merely spoke to this entity by talking to her through his patient, and the persona was swiftly released from Mrs. K. L.'s mind and body. The patient seemed cured once this final entity was dispatched. Two years later she wrote to Dr. Bull that "I have never felt so well and happy in my life, and I will never forget what you did for me."

The case of Mr. J. D.

While they were grappling with Mrs. K. L.'s problem, Dr. Bull and Mrs. Duke were simultaneously treating a much more elaborate and recalcitrant case. The records concerning this matter are reasonably extant, since they were published by way of a three-part series in the *Journal of the American Society for Psychical Research* in 1928. This patient, too, was identified in the report only by his initials to protect his privacy.

When he first came to Dr. Bull for treatment, Mr. J. D. was suffering from a well-defined psychosis, chronic hallucinatory type, resulting from his chronic drinking problem. This diagnosis is interesting and challenging even by modern standards, since this type of problem is organic rather than functional in nature and usually results from brain damage. So it would be the least likely case to respond to anything but proper medical treatment. The patient was of Irish descent, forty-one years old, and had emigrated to the United States when he was sixteen. He was employed as a milkman before he started to drink excessively when he was twenty. He had married in 1906 but became a widower in 1919. This crisis apparently exacerbated his difficulties. Finding himself companionless after thirteen years of marriage took a severe psychological toll on his life. He fell into a severe depression, which only encouraged his heavy drinking. He seemed to overcome his problem in the summer of 1920 when he decided to stop drinking, but his sudden sobriety resulted in severe repercussions. For the very morning that he stopped drinking, internal voices began threatening him in violent and obscene language.

Mr. J. D.'s case history is not difficult for us to understand today, since similar symptoms typically result from sudden alcohol withdrawal. These symptoms often mimic those of paranoid schizophrenia. But they continued plaguing Mr. J. D. for a prolonged period of time, and they became even worse when he suffered an accidental blow to his head. The voices began threatening to kill his children while they also claimed to be in control of his deceased wife, whose apparition began visiting him.

While he was still recovering from his wife's death, the patient had become interested in the possibility of contacting the dead, and he became a Spiritualist in 1924. When he first approached Dr. Bull for treatment, however, he didn't realize that the physician sometimes took a Spiritualist approach to mental problems. Since he didn't expect to receive such treatment, he was surprised when it was suggested.

Dr. Bull began treating Mr. J. D. toward the end of 1924 with conventional medications. The patient failed to respond, so beginning in January 1925 the physician initiated the first of several consultations with Mrs. Duke in hopes of curing him. Eventually, sixty sittings were scheduled to flush out the cause of his problem, and the several obsessors who seemed to be controlling the patient's life were contacted. Mrs. Duke received considerable information from the entities relating to the patient's earlier life and present problems. She clairvoyantly felt that the primary obsessor was a recently executed criminal. His name and the case in which he was involved are mentioned in the report, but I have not been able to trace any information about it. The crime was apparently given some play in the New York papers when it originally occurred. She also picked up information concerning his cohorts and the slum areas where the entity had preferred to socialize before his death. This information was later corroborated by the psychic, her husband, and Dr. Bull by visiting the locations. While working on Mr. J. D.'s case, Carolyn Duke also psychically discovered that the patient suffered from a urinary problem, which was verified when Dr. Bull encouraged him to undergo a medical examination.

But even though Dr. Bull's spiritistic treatment and exorcisms removed some of the patient's symptoms, the case was never fully resolved in the long run. Mr. J. D. remained curiously uncooperative during the sittings since he never believed that his problems were spiritual rather than psychological. He conceded to Dr. Bull that Mrs. Duke's clairvoyant insights were strikingly accurate, but he preferred to believe that she was simply reading his mind. He became disenchanted with Dr. Bull's course of treatment and gradually became critical even of his former Spiritualist beliefs.

Dr. Bull kept track of the patient's subsequent history nonetheless. Mr. J. D. was later treated at the New York Neurological Institute and, beginning in 1927, at the Vanderbilt Clinic. Despite the efforts of their best clinicians, the patient's condition was never completely cured.

Procuring the services of a psychic such as Carolyn Duke enabled Dr. Bull to carry out the very research plan originally suggested by James Hyslop before his death. He could now directly contact the obsessors invading his patients' minds and speak with them. By 1927, after two years of such research, Dr. Bull was ready to turn his formal professional practice over to the problem of spirit obsession.

He began by incorporating the James H. Hyslop Foundation in the State of New York. The foundation was run partly by a board of directors consisting of seven people (none of them physicians) and offices were secured at 430 West 116th Street in Manhattan. The foundation offered memberships to the general public, but this membership steadily declined during the Depression. Despite this problem, Dr. Bull eventually collected an operating budget of $130,000, which was somewhat of a small fortune in those days. Some of this money probably came from Dr. Bull himself, who initially took only a modest salary of $2,000 a year. Private donors also contributed to the fund and the foundation operated well into the 1930s, by which time Dr. Bull's salary had grown to $14,000. The process of setting up the foundation must have been complex, since Bull resigned his position as chairman of the ASPR's publications committee to devote himself to the project full time.

It is not as well known that Dr. Bull later relied upon the services of three other psychics while engaged in his research. Since he felt that it took a special type of psychic to confront the dangers of spirit obsession, he found it necessary to train his own psychics to best prepare them for the work. During the late 1920s and early 1930s, he discovered and trained two such psychics—Grace Gause and a Mrs. Conklin. Grace Gause was probably the more interesting of the two. She had been married to a clergyman in New York who was familiar with and interested in the Bull work. She had also been one of his medical patients. For some reason Dr. Bull recognized that she was a potentially gifted psychic, and he soon convinced her to train with him. She developed both psychometric skills and trance mediumship under his direction.

When I met her in 1972, Mrs. Gause was probably the last surviving link with Dr. Bull's work. She was living in Los Altos, a small, beautiful community south of San Francisco. She was a stately, white-haired woman unfortunately confined to a wheelchair, but she was still practicing her mediumship.* She also radiated the strongest personal magnetism that I have ever felt from another person. It was a sort of "power" that I could feel almost physically emanating from her. I felt this force the moment she opened the door to her small home, and I have never experienced anything like it since. Whether this sensation was due to suggestion, to her psychic powers, or to some other unknown factor remains a mystery, but it was an unforgettable experience.

I know relatively little about Mrs. Conklin except for what Grace Gause told me during our conversation. She said that Mrs. Conklin had been incarcerated in a New York mental institution and that Reverend Gause and Dr. Bull both suspected that her problems were psychic and not psychopathological. They were able to obtain her release into

---

*A small book containing some of her channeled communications was published in 1969 under the title *The Profit and Loss of Dying* by Clyde Irion.

their care, and together they implemented a cure by depossessing her. Dr. Bull then went on to train her for his own work.

It should also be noted that Helen Lambert gradually developed her psychic skills while working with Dr. Bull. She not only served as his secretary but became a third psychic upon whom he sometimes relied.

None of these sensitives worked directly with any of Dr. Bull's patients, however. That sort of contact was reserved solely for Carolyn Duke whom Gause once described to me as a psychic of "incredible personal power" and unfailing capabilities. Mrs. Gause, Mrs. Conklin, and occasionally Mrs. Lambert served only as psychic information gatherers for their employer.

This terminology may strike the reader as a bit strange, so let me explain Dr. Bull's procedures in some detail.

When Dr. Bull was initially approached by a potential patient, he would begin by taking a complete medical history. If he suspected that the patient was suffering from possession, he would immediately institute sittings with Carolyn Duke to contact the troublesome entities. But the cautious researcher was sometimes unwilling to take Mrs. Duke's revelations at face value. So he would independently and privately call in either Mrs. Gause or Mrs. Conklin (or both) and ask them to psychometrize (receive psychic impressions from) personal objects belonging to the patient. Neither of these psychics were ever allowed to meet the patient, though. Dr. Bull would later compare the information obtained from these three sources to see if it was mutually corroborative— which it often was. By using this technique he could prove to himself that he was on the right track with the mediumistic sittings.

Mrs. Gause explained to me that Dr. Bull was very careful to keep information about his patients from her. He usually wouldn't even give her feedback as to whether her readings were on target or not, a situation she found constantly frustrating. She told me that in all the years she worked with the New York physician, she never once met any of his patients. Dr. Bull would only begrudgingly tell her that he regarded her work highly.

But did Dr. Bull really succeed in curing his patients? Or even some of them? We still face this issue today when evaluating his experiments. The same problem will also haunt us in the following two chapters, in which the work of two of Dr. Bull's colleagues will be presented.

The crucial issue is that people being treated for mental illness sometimes respond for any number of various and unknown reasons. Often it's impossible to determine exactly why one person improves while another doesn't, even when both are being given the same therapy—whether it be chemotherapy, psychotherapy, or electric shock therapy. Patients suffering from depression, psychotic episodes, or other syndromes also sometimes undergo alternating periods of regression and improvement even if they receive no treatment at all. So determining whether a specific treatment strategy actually worked in any particular case is extremely difficult, since the patient's improvement could always be purely coincidental. What we need is quantitative (i.e., statistical) data concerning the efficacy of Dr. Bull's work before we can pass judgment on it. We need to answer such basic questions such as: What was his success rate compared with his failure rate? What was his success rate compared with that of other therapists using more standard forms of treatment?

Dr. Bull did, in fact, attempt to offer his colleagues just this sort of data. In October 1929 he reported in his foundation's annual report on twenty-three cases that he was treating using Spiritualist therapy. Included in this tally were three cases of depression, one case of hysterical paralysis, and several other cases. The conventional prognosis for these cases was usually poor, owing either to the ages of the patients and/or to their prior psychiatric histories. Despite these two problems, Dr. Bull claimed that his methods had resulted in eight cures—including six cases of multiple personality, one case of depression, and a single case of incipient paranoia. Eight other cases were listed as "improved," while Dr. Bull fully acknowledged five failures. (Most of these failures, Bull explained, involved patients who had left treatment before its completion.) If this data is correct, then Dr. Bull could boast a good therapeutic record. But it strikes me that most psychiatrists in private practice during the 1920s probably claimed a similar success rate. (Psychiatrists are not the most humble people when it comes to discussing their successes and failures!) The problem we still face, however, is that Dr. Bull never explained the criteria he used to evaluate his cures. Did he base his evaluations on his own impressions, or did he employ any objective measurements? Nor is it clear if he stayed in contact with his patients to see whether their cures were permanent.

It is clear, though, that Dr. Bull never claimed perfect success in exorcising his patients; nor was he naive when it came to the difficulties inherent in psychic work, which he felt almost guaranteed occasional failure. "During the interval between treatment," he explained in his report, "patients are at the mercy of their environments. . . . The wonder is, that we have accomplished anything, under such conditions."

He also explained that "many patients come to us with the wrong idea. They seem to think that, if they are obsessed, and we have the power of the spiritual realm at our command, it ought to be a simple matter to make them well. This is entirely wrong. . . . It is equally true that the obsession is only a part of the problem." The implementation of spiritistic treatment takes time, he added, "and the length of time taken depends largely upon the duration and type of illness and also upon the individual under treatment. Thus you see, it is not the simple matter some may think."

From these excerpts, it is clear that by 1930 Dr. Bull had come to some firm conclusions concerning the nature of spirit obsession. So just what did he eventually come to believe?

Dr. Bull published his views on the possession syndrome in 1932 in a booklet, *Analysis of Unusual Experiences in Healing Relative to Diseased Minds and Results of Materialism Foreshadowed.** It is a curious and singularly provocative work in which Dr. Bull further developed James Hyslop's theory that psychic invasion rarely causes psychopathology but usually serves as a complicating factor in its development. Dr. Bull felt that spirit obsession only became possible when there already existed a weakness in the patient's nervous system—a preexisting weakness capable of breaking down the person's normal insulation against paranormal influences. What would cause such a problem? Dr. Bull believed he knew the answer. He thought that this weakness usually resulted from a severe trauma of either a physical or an emotional nature. Such a shock to the body or psyche could result in psychopathological behavior by itself, but Dr. Bull believed that the trauma could also "attract" discarnate entities to the patient. "While the writer does not feel that [spiritistic factors] are the only etiological factor," Dr. Bull explained, "he does feel that it plays an important part in the fixity of those conditions once they become rooted in the life of an individual." In other words, spirit obsessors could reinforce and contribute to a patient's psychotic or phobic behavior.

Toward the end of his life James Hyslop had come to believe that spirit obsession was sometimes a composite phenomenon in which several interacting personalities overshadowed the victim's thinking or behavior. This, too, was a position Dr. Bull came to respect. He believed that the process of obsession was an ongoing problem and that more

---

*This was followed in 1933 by *Nature, Man and Destiny* and in 1936 by *The Imperative Conquest*. These works were primarily philosophical.

and more entities could gradually become linked to the patient. In fact, Dr. Bull believed that the primary obsessing entity in any given case could be usurped by more malicious personalities.

As a result of his discussions with Carolyn Duke's controls—as well as with the spirit obsessors themselves—Dr. Bull also came to believe that the syndrome works in a predictable fashion on the body. The possessors tend to attach themselves to the patient at his or her brain, solar plexus, and genitals.

But why does spirit obsession and possession occur in the first place? Dr. Bull came to realize, just as the Spiritualists of his day were teaching, that many spirit entities fail to understand that they have passed on when they die. Ignorant and confused, they tend to link up with the first person they encounter, thereby becoming "caught" in his or her aura or psychic atmosphere. Dr. Bull also accepted the Spiritualist belief that people who were morally depraved in life will deliberately seek to victimize the living. These entities will seek out people with dispositions similar to their own in order to vicariously enjoy or express their depravities. The end result of both processes will be the same, suggested Dr. Bull, no matter what originally motivated the spirit obsessor. "They are alive and active and clamor for expression," Dr. Bull explained in his booklet, "therefore, the libido of the neurotic is the magnet which draws the spirit to the mortal and the physical body is the thing through which desired expression is attained. Such possibilities often end in complete domination of a mortal."

Dr. Bull's work and views were hardly conventional, and they had practically no effect on the psychiatric establishment of his day. There were hardly any attempts made by other psychiatrists or physicians to evaluate his work or methods. The only exception was the work of Dr. Geoffrey Burns, a prominent New York psychiatrist in private practice who spent considerable time studying Dr. Bull's records in the mid-1920s. He was mainly interested in evaluating the efficacy of his colleague's procedures. Dr. Burns never published his findings in a conventional scientific or medical journal, but he issued a sizable analysis of Dr. Bull's work in the *Journal of the American Society for Psychical Research* in 1928, in which he came to a series of positive conclusions about Dr. Bull's work. He felt, for instance, that his colleague had undoubtedly cured several of his patients. He even conceded that some of Dr. Bull's patients had overcome syndromes or psychological problems that had never responded to conventional or institutional treatment. He was also impressed by the number of times Carolyn Duke correctly diagnosed the problems of Dr. Bull's patients with her psychic faculties.

But at this point Dr. Burns parted company from Dr. Bull. For as Dr. Burns correctly pointed out in his report, Dr. Bull had successfully treated many of his patients with conventional medical treatment as well as with Spiritualist treatment. Perhaps, he suggested, it was the care and sympathy Dr. Bull showed his patients that had resulted in the cures and not his psychic exorcisms. Perhaps it was all something of a complicated placebo effect. Dr. Burns felt further that although Carolyn Duke was no doubt a talented psychic, the communications she received from the patients' obsessors were probably spiritistic fantasies engendered by her own mind—but that she reinforced them with brilliant flashes of clairvoyance.

Even though his opinions were carefully qualified, however, Dr. Burns was hesitant to dismiss the therapeutic value of his colleague's work. "It is true that the [spiritistic] theory has not been proved," he stated in his lengthy report on Dr. Bull and his cases. "We cannot accept either the claim that this patient was obsessed by evil spirits or admit that there were spirits aiding in the treatment of the patient. Such experimentation as this may not attain the desired goal. It may never prove the survival of the personality after death. It may not be able to prove that the old idea of a devil possessing humans was right. Yet, surely such work as this deserves encouragement, if earnestly and thoroughly carried on with a singleness of purpose but, yet, with a willingness to follow leads wherever they may indicate will surely result in something of worth."

Unfortunately, Dr. Titus Bull was never able to follow up on many of the leads uncovered by his years of research. His work ended tragically in 1942, when he suffered a stroke that left him paralyzed and speechless. His wife, Eva, cared for him for over four silent years before he died. Most of his extensive files were left to the American Society for Psychical Research, while portions were taken into the custody of his son Louis, who also became a physician. I learned from Grace Gause in 1972 that Dr. Louis Bull was never particularly interested in his father's psychic work and was usually unwilling to discuss it.

A recent search of the ASPR's archives failed to uncover these important files. This loss is a tragic one to psychical research and psychiatry.

CHAPTER **10**

FROM CLERGYMAN TO EXORCIST

Dr. Titus Bull wasn't the only physician exorcising his patients in New York. The psychic legacy left by James Hyslop extended much further.

Before his death in 1920, Hyslop had come to appreciate Dr. W. Franklin Prince's cool and critical standards, as well as the clergyman's compassionate and painstaking work on the Doris case. When he moved back to New York in 1916, Dr. Prince's connections with the American Society for Psychical Research grew steadily. Perhaps it was inevitable that James Hyslop would invite him to join the society's staff in 1917. Dr. Prince immediately relinquished his position at St. Mark's Church, where he had been engaged in counseling work, to begin his formal career in psychical research. Over the next seven years he devoted himself to several research projects and field investigations but relatively little to the problems of psychology. He was too preoccupied with such phenomena as psychic photography, spirit slate writing (in which mysterious writings suddenly appear on previously blank chalk slates), and poltergeists. He found little convincing evidence for the reality of these phenomena, and he remained skeptical of psychokinetic effects for most of his life. But when James Hyslop died in 1920, Dr. Prince was his likely successor and became the ASPR's principal research officer.

It was clear that his work as a psychotherapist, which had exclusively engaged him at St. Mark's, was coming to a close. Because of his background in psychology, however, Dr. Prince never lost his fascination with the power of suggestion. It had been through self-suggestion that Prince cured himself of the depression that incapacitated him in 1913. (See Chapter 8.)

   This depression had marked a turning point in the clergyman's life and thinking. He was unhappy and miserable in San Bernardino, unknown to the world of science, and the clergyman considered himself a total failure. His depression and sense of isolation became progressively more severe and brought on blinding headaches that immobilized him. Dr. Prince realized that something was wrong psychologically, and with no other hope in sight, he finally determined to cure himself. The starting point for this cure came from the writings of William James, who was probably the first psychologist to promote the power of positive thinking. This great psychologist once suggested that our lives could be enhanced easily enough if we merely focused our thoughts on the virtues of the world and ignore its corrupt and evil facets. Dr. Prince immediately saw the possibilities within this simple philosophy.

   He later stated in a lecture to some colleagues,

> In accordance with my teaching and mental habits, I resolved to make a careful, honest experiment which should be as carefully and honestly recorded. I decided to limit the period of conscious effort to one month, as I thought this time long enough to prove its value or its worthlessness to me. During this month I resolved to impose certain restrictions on my thoughts. If I thought of the past, I would try to let my mind dwell only on its happy, pleasing incidents, the bright days of my childhood, the inspiration of my teachers and the slow revelation of my life-work. In thinking of the present, I would deliberately turn my attention to its desirable elements, my home, the opportunities my solitude gave me to work, and so on, and I resolved to make the utmost use of these opportunities and to ignore the fact that they seemed to lead to nothing. In thinking of the future I determined to regard every worthy and possible ambition as within my grasp. Ridiculous as this seemed at the time, in view of what has come to me since, I see that the only defect of my plan was that it aimed too low and did not include enough.

Dr. Prince didn't have to wait long for his cure, for after eight days the experiment was obviously working. The headaches dissipated, he found himself overcome by happiness, and important changes started coming in his life.

   This story is important to keep in mind. Because of his work on the Doris case and his self-cure, Dr. Prince became increasingly fascinated with the powers of the psyche—both its power to heal and its power to destroy. This fascination with the unconscious mind became increasingly important when he began encountering cases of possible possession while working in psychical research.

Since Dr. Prince's position with the ASPR primarily involved investigating and evaluating cases, his involvement with Hyslop's research on spirit obsession was minimal. But he soon found himself caught up in similar studies. While working at St. Mark's, Dr. Prince had undertaken to cure a professional man he later called Leonard Tyrrell in his report on the case. The gentleman suffered from inebriety and Prince was able to cure him through psychological counseling and hypnosis. Despite short lapses between 1916 and 1918, the cure seemed to be relatively permanent. This cure wasn't permanent, though, and Dr. Prince received a phone call from the patient early in 1919. Soon afterward they met in Dr. Prince's office at the ASPR. In his report Dr. Prince explained that the gentleman's distraught manner and obvious embarassment were puzzling. The clergyman was finally forced to ask him point-blank what the problem was, and Mr. Tyrrell responded by pulling two sheets of paper from his pocket. Both were covered with writing that he had produced during profound states of dissociation. Tyrrell explained that, a few days before, he had simply been sitting by a table with a pencil in his grasp. Some paper was there, too. He sunk into a reverie, and after he revived he found the paper covered with messages . . . which was certainly a surprise! The content of the writing was spiritistic and purportedly consisted of several loving messages from the spirit of his favorite niece, who had died four months previously. If this weren't enough, Tyrrell went on to say that the same thing had occurred the night before! These scripts encouraged Tyrrell to write even more and his communicator urged him to consult with Dr. Prince. The gentleman found the situation shocking and was concerned for his sanity.

Dr. Prince was impressed by the story since the episodes seemed so bizarre.

"I knew the man, owing to the methods by which I had treated him, involving at times hypnosis, better in his inmost soul than most people who saw him daily," wrote Dr. Prince some years later. "He had full confidence in me. By casual queries from time to time I afterward drew from him that while of course he knew that spirits were supposed to communicate, he associated the claim with spiritualist meetings which he had never once attended. So far as he could recollect he had never read a book or article on the subject, though of course he may have forgotten reading one, and he must have casually glanced at articles of the kind in magazines or at least newspapers. But he appeared to have no conscious knowledge regarding such a thing as automatic writing."

In order to explore the etiology of the writings further, Dr. Prince booked an appointment to see his former patient a few days later. His main goal was to watch Tyrrell produce the writing before passing judgment on it.

His experiment was both successful and enlightening. Tyrrell returned to the ASPR on the scheduled day, promptly fell into trance at Dr. Prince's direction, and wrote feverishly for forty-five minutes in the researcher's presence. The writings again purportedly came from the gentleman's niece, and they contained a stern warning. The communicator revealed that a previous personal enemy of Tyrrell's, currently deceased, was trying to kill him! It was hardly a comforting message and Dr. Prince didn't know whether to reveal it to Tyrrell—who had remained completely unconscious during the production of the script.

Dr. Prince decided to encourage the writings despite the disturbing effects they might incur within the patient's mind. These subsequent sessions elicited more messages from his niece claiming that this enemy was trying to draw Tyrrell back to drink. The poor man once experienced a brief but terrifying hallucination while emerging from trance, when he saw his enemy's face superimposed over Dr. Prince's body.

These experiments were conducted over a protracted period of time, and Tyrrell was consistently kept ignorant of the content of the scripts. Dr. Prince provided his client with copies of only the comforting messages offered by his niece, and Tyrrell never consciously realized that a discarnate entity was supposedly causing his problems. Dr. Prince maintained this practice throughout his work on the case, which extended from April to June 1919. He lost contact with his frightened client that summer but resumed his experiments in December and January 1920. By this time the patient, through Dr. Prince's firm support and sound psychology, was beginning to accept his own burgeoning mediumship. No longer did he worry about his sanity, and the gentleman actually became rather disinterested in his sessions with the researcher.

Dr. Prince heard nothing further from Tyrrell until early in 1922, when his former patient returned to the ASPR in a more disturbed state than ever before. He explained that he was currently working as a businessman but that his work was being disrupted by strange spells of confusion. These incidents were so severe, he complained, that sometimes he could barely speak. Dr. Prince was concerned and responded sympathetically with further treatment (probably by using hypnosis), explaining that he still didn't think his patient was crazy. He didn't understand that Mr. Tyrrell's problem was more complex than he realized, but for the time being Dr. Prince felt it best to withdraw from the case. He didn't return to it for several months, during which time a curiously similar case came to his attention.

This case dated from the first week of May 1922, when a well-dressed and fashionable woman visited his office. "Her very walk and general bearing announced refinement," Dr. Prince later wrote in his record of the case. "She proved to be a lady of culture and social standing."

Dr. Prince was probably surprised when the lady calmly asked him if he believed in spirit obsession. Despite his knowledge of James Hyslop's work on the subject, Dr. Prince responded to Phyllis Latimer (his pseudonym for her) cautiously, explaining that he neither believed nor disbelieved in the phenomenon. The researcher willingly conceded that some evidence pointed to the reality of the syndrome, but he didn't want to interpret it. Dr. Prince's curiosity was kindled by Mrs. Latimer's inquiry, though, so he ended his speech with his own inquiry, for he was naturally curious *why* the lady was so interested in spirit obsession. She replied ever so calmly that she believed herself to be possessed.

Dr. Prince must have been surprised by this response, since Mrs. Latimer certainly didn't seem crazy. She had spoken calmly and with restraint throughout the meeting. Dr. Prince had a pressing schedule that day, unfortunately, so he couldn't talk further with his visitor. He had to excuse himself but requested that Mrs. Latimer return to the ASPR in a few days, and it was during this second meeting that the researcher learned the truth behind his client's strange preoccupation.

While still in her youth, Phyllis Latimer had been friendly with one of her male cousins. He became like a brother and for years frequently visited her. These social interactions came to an end upon his death sometime around 1920.

Within a few days of his death Mrs. Latimer began hearing her cousin's voice speaking to her. The voice initially sounded like it was external, but later it spoke directly within her mind, expressing unremitting hatred. The voice promised to make life miserable for her and said that there existed good cause for his hatred.

The entity's threats weren't empty, either. The persecutions had been continuous for two years and were making Mrs. Latimer's life a living nightmare. The voice's most common complaint was, "You made me suffer and I will make you suffer." Mrs. Latimer couldn't remember any slight to her late relative, but the voice eagerly reminded her of the incident that enraged him.

"It was related," recorded Dr. Prince, "that on a certain occasion when he was in her home and she had left the room, his eye fell upon a letter which she was writing and which contained a statement about him which bitterly hurt his feelings. This was very shortly before his death. Upon being told this she remembered the occasion, the letter and the remark to which he could easily have taken exception. She had never, so far as she knew, suspected that he might have glanced at the letter and read the obnoxious sentence."

Phyllis Latimer's possessor was also annoyingly fickle. For example, the entity would chide her but then take pity on her. Or sometimes he would even make predictions regarding her future. Mrs. Latimer told Dr. Prince that these prognostications invariably came true, which further convinced her that her cousin's presence was genuinely haunting her. Sometimes her cousin's surviving spirit seemed cognizant of information only he could have known. She was reprimanded, for example, for not sending flowers to his funeral. This claim upset her since she had sent roses to be placed on his coffin. But spurred by the voice's claim, she checked and found that the roses had been ignored by the people in charge of the ceremony.

Even though she always displayed a calm demeanor in front of Dr. Prince, Mrs. Latimer's private life was a study in terror. She would wake up screaming, the voices threatened her daily, and they tried to prevent her from seeing Dr. Prince.

It was a horrible story and Dr. Prince responded with ministerial compassion. But as a psychologist he realized that his client was probably suffering from paranoia. It appeared to be a classic case of the disorder complete with persecutory voices, a history of disappointing personal relationships, and (not summarized here) a succession of unfortunate events that she was desperately trying to explain. Dr. Prince also realized that Mrs. Latimer would be difficult to cure since her symptoms were so protracted. He was especially pessimistic because of his prior experience as a psychologist. While working as a therapist at St. Mark's he had often dealt with people suffering from all sorts of psychological complaints, mostly common phobias, neurotic symptoms, or problems with their day-to-day living. Such patients usually responded to counseling, suggestion, or spiritual ministrations. But cases of extreme paranoia represented a different kind of problem, and the psychiatrists of the 1920s usually failed to treat them successfully. He therefore doubted whether he could cure Phyllis Latimer, nor did he consider it likely that she was genuinely possessed.

But what if he were to counsel the lady by treating her as if she were possessed? This idea kept nagging at him, and Dr. Prince eventually decided to perform an exorcism. He hoped that such a powerful form of suggestion might work in her case.

Dr. Prince undertook this curious experiment during Mrs. Latimer's second visit to the ASPR on May 5, 1921. He told her how (the late) Prof. Hyslop had worked with people suffering from incipient possession and explained his procedure of bringing these unfortunate people to psychics to contact their possessors. He emphasized that he didn't necessarily endorse Hyslop's conclusions but that he was willing to concede that his predecessor's procedures could be efficacious in some cases. He went on to explain that a visit to a psychic probably wasn't necessary, for perhaps the possessing entity could be contacted directly through the patient. Dr. Prince concluded by informing Mrs. Latimer that, by formal psychiatric criteria, her problem existed solely within her psyche or brain; but he was personally willing to treat her problem spiritually if she would consent to a makeshift exorcism.

Mrs. Latimer didn't object to the plan, and the exorcism followed in short order. Speaking in a bold and powerful voice, the former Episcopal clergyman cajoled his patient's possessor to depart from her. Luckily for posterity, the fastidious Dr. Prince kept a record of his improvised speech.

> You probably think that you are justified in your treatment of the lady, and I shall not deny that you may have had provocation. You think that you are warranted in getting satisfaction out of your present course, and that you are actually experiencing it—that is, getting some sort of pleasure. I think that you are making a great mistake in regard to your own interests, just such a mistake as people often make on this side. They try to get even with persons who they think have injured them in the past, and increase the bitterness and discomfort of their own souls. I do not deny that you are getting a degree and kind of pleasure, but feel sure that you are depriving yourself of greater and a superior species of happiness, and that such pleasure as you get is mingled with bitterness. You are cheating yourself, for the balance is against you every time. You are also preventing your own development and progress. A hog gets pleasure wal-

lowing in the mire, but it is capable of no higher kind of pleasure. You are not so limited, and it seems a pity that you should keep yourself down on a low level.

Should you forgive this woman for any injury which you think she has done you or which she may in fact have done you, should your hatred turn to pity and friendliness, you would begin to experience a higher and far greater pleasure. You would come to find it a delight to help her and others by whatever means are within your grasp, and you would come to wonder at your former course.

Your habit of ill will against this woman results in what is called her obsession. In fact, you yourself are obsessed by the habit. We know that some habits or tendencies of disposition on the part of persons living here come from accidents to their mentality, emotional shocks, events which have made a twist in their inmost constitution. I understand that you had an emotional shock resulting from something your cousin did shortly before your death. You probably brooded upon it in your last hours. That may be the reason that the matter seems so important to you since your death. I don't know, but am only suggesting that the accident of your dying while this matter was troubling you may give it a seeming importance far exceeding its real value.

I have had persons come to me similarly affected by some experience which acted like a concealed ulcer upon their emotional life. Sometimes I have succeeded in getting the person to inspect the matter which caused the trouble throughout and on all sides, he has seen how trivial it was, and the ulcer has disappeared. Sometimes, falling short of this he has agreed to try some experiment in a new way of thinking and living, and the experiment has worked and he has since been much happier.

I do not expect you to accept what I say as the truth, on the moment. But I think you will admit the truth of what I now confidently assert. You are not happy. Even if tormenting this woman gives you pleasure, the pleasure is poisoned, and is brief. It is followed by deeper bitterness and pain. That means that something is radically wrong. I think I have correctly stated what is wrong. You would like to be happy, as all beings do.

Dr. Prince ended the speech by suggesting that the possessing spirit conduct a personal experiment. He instructed the discarnate to look upon Mrs. Latimer with his former compassion, appreciate their previously close relationship, and glimpse the contentment of that prior happiness. He promised the spirit that if he succeeded, a spiritual power could be invoked capable of helping his evolution into the great beyond.

It was a long-winded but powerful speech which took fifteen minutes to deliver. Dr. Prince's earlier career in the ministry served him well, even though he didn't know whether he was really talking to a spirit or treating Mrs. Latimer with psychological suggestion. He only knew that his performance had to be sincere and powerful.

> Whether what was to be said should act in the way of suggestion upon the patient or in the way of argument and persuasion upon the obsessor, I was bound to speak with an appearance of sincerity. Any words or tones indicating that I thought the performance a farce could not reasonably be expected either to impress the patient's subconsciousness or to win the respect and confidence of a spirit.

Upon completing the session, Dr. Prince instructed Mrs. Latimer to ignore the entity if his voice tormented her further. She was to refuse any further interaction with the possessor. She might try for psychic writing in the future, he suggested, but not for the present. It would be too dangerous.

The first evidence that Mrs. Latimer was responding to the exorcism came that same night. She dreamed of struggling through enshrouding cobwebs—a vision that Dr. Prince believed symbolized her fight to overcome her psychological problems. During the second night after receiving Dr. Prince's treatment, her deceased mother came to her in a dream and promised to help the cousin's plight. Mrs. Latimer awoke the following morning refreshed for the first time in weeks, and she returned to Dr. Prince to report on her progress on May 9. For the first time she felt no inner resistance against keeping the appointment. She told Dr. Prince that the voice had been keeping silent but she could still sense a presence within her that was mutely pleading for expression. Dr. Prince responded by telling her that her possessor was following his suggestions of May 5. Then he spoke openly to the possessor and congratulated him on his success.

Whatever had been incubating within Mrs. Latimer's mind broke forth on May 12, 1921, which was the date of her next meeting with Dr. Prince. She now explained that the presence within her wanted to write. Dr. Prince believed this remark stemmed from his own previous suggestion that such an experiment might be possible. Mrs. Latimer was, however, reluctant to offer her tormenter any opportunity to communicate. She had resisted the impulse to write, she explained, but as a result she had received strange nocturnal visitations. Both her deceased mother and her cousin would appear in her room late at night, sometimes in dreams and sometimes as spectres. Her cousin's shadow would especially stand by her bed silently and sorrowfully.

When they next spoke at the ASPR, Dr. Prince began treating his client with a different strategy. "I varied my method of treatment by putting the patient in a cushioned chair and inducing light sleep," he later wrote. "I asked the mother to help—a sensible thing to do whether as suggestion or on the theory that the phenomena were what they purported to be—and again addressed the supposed obsessing spirit. The lady was allowed to sleep awhile after the treatment was ended, and woke spontaneously. She was instructed to hold no conversation with the voices before the next interview."

Mrs. Latimer's next meeting with Dr. Prince was scheduled for later that week. The entity's voice refrained from bothering her during these critical days, and her problems began to clear up further. Her late mother kept appearing in her dreams, urging her to feel compassion toward her cousin. Mrs. Latimer was impressed by these visitations, and Dr. Prince was gratified by the way the case was progressing. He later wrote,

> The lady reiterated in my presence that her cousin had been an upright man, although with temperamental defects. Her whole aspect now was of one troubled by sympathy with suffering. I reminded her that from the first I had intimated that if there came indications of a change in his disposition it might be allowable to talk to him, although it might be advisable never to do so much. I stated that her present distress was quite different from her former distress. She had now demonstrated her power to control the voice and to be the mistress of her own soul (or else the disposition of the obsessing agent was changing and ceasing to be an object to fear), but I did not expect or desire that she should become so changed as to be incapable of suffering from compassion on the unhappiness of another. I therefore instructed her to talk some with the suppositious spirit before our next meeting with the object of extending to him sympathy and aid in the matter of completing his reformation, giving him the comfort of knowing that he was not deserted by his friend, even though his conduct had been injurious toward her. I gave her no special treatment, but assured her that the signs were favorable and pointed toward cure of her troubles.

Mrs. Latimer did not show up for her next appointment, and Dr. Prince heard nothing from her for two weeks. When she finally came to his office, she explained that a family emergency had caused her absence.

She also told the researcher about the current status of her problem. When the family crisis first struck, she became worried that the stress would reenergize her deceased cousin's power. She was very relieved when he failed to take advantage of the situation, and since she finally felt totally in control of herself, she decided to conduct an experiment. She settled down in her home, opened her mind to her cousin's spirit, and encouraged him to express himself. The entity took advantage of the offer and for the first time explained why he originally became so pathologically linked to her.

The entity explained that he died still resenting Mrs. Latimer. The slights she had incurred were fresh in his mind and his resentment seathed and finally took control of his psyche. He wanted revenge and so tormented her mercilessly. But then other discarnates were drawn into the fray. They linked with him and were partially and vicariously possessing her. Now, though, he was spiritually free and wanted to depart forever.

Mrs. Latimer's cure was entering its final stage.

Dr. Prince heard nothing more from his patient for several months. He finally wrote to her in January 1923 and asked for a report on her progress. Mrs. Latimer responded by paying a visit to the researcher later that same month, whereupon Dr. Prince learned that his exorcism had been only partially successful. The feelings of persecution and the voice had departed, but his patient felt herself only generally free from the obsession. Some of her previous problems were still lingering, and she felt internal presences fighting to control her mind. She was psychologically exhausted.

"I am all right now," she told him, "except that I am completely played out; I do not feel as though I had an ounce of energy left."

Dr. Prince decided to renew his psychological treatment and immediately placed Mrs. Latimer in a state of borderline hypnosis. He next exhorted the surviving spirit of the woman's mother to rid her daughter of her remaining problems.

"I was acting both from altruistic motives and as an investigator of psychic claims," wrote Dr. Prince in his final report. "Therapeutically, considering the nature of the case and what had gone before, such a suggestion might be helpful, regardless whether or not it was based on objective fact. And if there were spirits concerned, they had already acted as though they existed, and one of them had presented the appearance of responding to my advice and ceasing to persecute the lady. The game with them had thus far been played fairly, but it would be unfair to sweep the pieces from the board at this stage."

Mrs. Latimer improved steadily after receiving these suggestions. She visited the ASPR the following February, by which time Dr. Prince felt that sitting for automatic writing would be safe. Mrs. Latimer was an exemplary subject and discovered that she could produce these scripts with ease, though during her first experiment under Dr. Prince's direction she produced only isolated words and scrawls.

Dr. Prince continued with the sittings throughout February, conducted several more the following summer, and took part in a final experiment in April 1924. He later wrote in 1927 that "there developed considerable evidentiality of the supernormal, in that some of the scripts displayed knowledge of facts of which I was cognisant but which, for the most part, could not have been acquired normally by the medium." Dr. Prince considered publishing the scripts but to the best of my knowledge never followed through with this project.* Her mental health continued to improve and her earlier problems never returned.

So was she cured by an exorcism or wasn't she? This is a complicated question to answer properly. Conventional psychiatrists would probably say that the power of suggestion had been the key to the cure, while Spiritualists would most likely object to this facile solution. W. Franklin Prince realized that the case could be explained either from a psychological *or* parapsychological framework. Neither theory had a particular edge, and interpreting the case resolves to a matter of personal bias.

The critical point in understanding this case rests, in my opinion, with its proper diagnosis. From just what disorder was Phyllis Latimer really suffering? While her auditory hallucinations would point to paranoid schizophrenia, the lady never lost contact with reality. Her emotions never became flattened or inappropriate, and her communication skills remained perfectly intact during her meetings with Dr. Prince. These latter symptoms would point more properly to schizophrenia, and their absence is conspicuous and revealing. It would seem that she suffered more from a symptom than from a syndrome.

Looking at the case today, it is unlikely that Mrs. Latimer suffered from full-blown paranoid schizophrenia. It was probably a related disorder called classic paranoia, and it is important to realize that these disorders represent somewhat separate syndromes. For example, writing in his authoritative textbook *Foundations of Abnormal Psychology*, Dr.

---

* Dr. Prince placed these records in the archives of the ASPR for posterity. He tried to buy them back in 1925 along with his extensive diaries on the Doris case, but the files couldn't be found. They have not been found to this day.

Perry London—formerly a professor at the University of Southern California—points out that the classic paranoid is not genuinely insane. "In its purest, and rarest, form there is evidently nothing at all wrong with the paranoid person," writes the psychologist, "except that he has inflated a *single insane idea* until there is space for nothing else in consciousness." The paranoid person, in other words, remains intellectually intact, his or her social behavior is constantly appropriate, and they function well in their jobs.

Now this description fits Phyllis Latimer and her problems very well. But since she suffered from her symptoms for two years, can psychological suggestion explain her cure?

There are two mutually exclusive ways of dealing with this issue. It was Dr. Prince's feeling that the case would probably not respond to suggestion or psychology. He based this prognosis on the prolonged length of her symptoms and on his prior therapeutic experience. My own feeling is that in this respect Dr. Prince's opinion was probably faulty for a very basic reason. Psychiatrists have learned that the successful treatment of a psychological disorder can usually be correlated to the length of time the patient took to become sick. Patients who gradually develop their symptoms respond poorly to treatment, while patients who suddenly break down usually recover speedily. The ultimate duration of the symptoms may be only a secondary factor. Now Mrs. Latimer's voices were a sudden development in her day-to-day life; they seemed to be a borderline psychotic reaction to her cousin's death. So her prognosis for recovery was probably reasonably good from the very start of her disorder.

But would this same principle apply to a long-term case of classic paranoia? Dr. London addresses this issue in his textbook when he writes that "the prognosis for recovery with any kind of treatment is very poor compared to paranoid schizophrenia (and most other disorders)." The reason, he explains further, is that the patient's psychological intactness "may be so great that it permits effective maintenance of a singular delusion in spite of outside influence or persuasion."

Most psychiatrists today would probably endorse these sentiments, but perhaps Dr. London should have written "any kind of *conventional* treatment" and not merely *any* treatment protocol. For the procedures implemented by W. Franklin Prince were hardly psychologically or medically conventional. During the era when Dr. Prince practiced his therapy, most conventional forms of psychotherapy with schizophrenics or paranoids were oriented toward understanding their language and helping them improve their communication skills, but also toward denying the reality of their delusions. Psychoanalytically oriented psychotherapists usually searched for some root psychological cause for the syndrome, but the patient's inner reality was denied in this psychodynamic therapy, too. Dr. Prince differed in his approach to Mrs. Latimer's problem by never denying the ontological reality of his patient's private experiences. So by pursuing this course of treatment could he have stumbled upon some powerful form of purely psychological cure?

This would certainly be a valid interpretation of Phyllis Latimer's experiences and cure. She probably felt unresolved guilt when her cousin died. The guilt could have grown into a delusionary system within her mind which Dr. Prince successfully cured. Exorcism might have been the ultimate suggestion—i.e., the use of religious power to grant her absolution from her self-perceived sins.*

Or perhaps he simply *did* successfully exorcise spirit beings from Phyllis Latimer's mind and body.

Dr. Prince constantly vacillated between these possibilities, and he never really resolved the dilemma to his own satisfaction. But the former clergyman didn't have long to wait before experimenting with exorcism further, for just when he was grappling with Mrs. Latimer's problems, Leonard Tyrrell came back into his life.

Sometime in the early part of 1922, Mr. Tyrrell paid a return visit to Dr. Prince's office at the ASPR. Some of his previous problems had returned. He was suffering nightmares, once awoke to feel phantom hands choking him, and again feared for his sanity.

With the successful treatment of Phyllis Latimer still fresh in his mind, Dr. Prince decided to deal with Tyrrell's problems in a similar manner. He explained the concept of spirit possession and exorcism to the distraught gentleman and suggested that similar possibilities might exist in his case.

His client's response to this suggestion was guardedly enthusiastic. He didn't know what to think of the strange suggestion, but he was certainly willing to cooperate with Dr. Prince.

Dr. Prince first seated the patient in a comfortable easy chair and placed some paper on the chair's lapboard. The patient entered a self-

---

*There is even some psychiatric evidence that such an explanation is viable. Before the turn of the century Dr. Pierre Janet, a pioneering psychologist in France, discovered that guilt complexes could give rise to similar delusions. Makeshift exorcism or mock religious ceremonies sometimes worked to relieve this form of hysteria. He reported on his work in his classic book, *L'Automatism Psychologique*.

induced trance within moments, whereupon Dr. Prince planted a pencil between his fingers. Psychic writings were immediately produced and the messages seemed to come from his departed niece. She again warned that his discarnate enemy was in a rage, but there were some surprises in store for Dr. Prince, too. The calligraphy of the scripts suddenly changed and the patient's mother proceeded to write. She, too, warned Dr. Prince that her son was facing great danger. The penmanship then changed for a third time and Mr. Tyrrell's psychic persecutor began communicating directly!

"Here I am, damn you, what do you want?" the unseen communicator wrote.

"I am glad you are here," replied Dr. Prince. "I want to talk to you, as one gentleman to another."

"Well, I am waiting," came the reply.

The controlling personality placed the pencil on the lapboard, folded Tyrrell's arms, and scowled at the researcher. Dr. Prince wasn't in the least intimidated and recited a facsimile of the speech he had used to exorcise Phyllis Latimer. While he was speaking, the scowl on his patient's face began to soften. Dr. Prince continued by warning the communicator that he was hurting himself more than injuring his victim, and he concluded by beseeching the entity to seek contentment—not vengeance—within the spirit world.

After Dr. Prince finished making his speech, the entity resumed his communications through Tyrrell's pencil.

"Well, there may be something in what you say," he conceded. "I had never thought of it in that light before."

Dr. Prince and the entity spoke further, and finally the purported discarnate agreed to respect the former clergyman's counseling.

"Well, I'll think on it," wrote the communicator. "You may tell him that I won't trouble him this week."

Mr. Tyrrell then emerged from his trance and Dr. Prince explained what had transpired. He also booked an appointment to see his client back at the ASPR in a week.

When Leonard Tyrrell returned he was obviously enjoying a better state of mind. He reported no return of his previous symptoms and seemed to be recovering, but despite these fortunate developments Dr. Prince decided to conduct a second experiment. Once again he asked Tyrrell to enter into trance and the gentleman willingly complied. It didn't take long for the patient's obsessing spirit to begin communicating through his victim's pencil. This time he explained that Tyrrell's deceased sister was helping him progress into the beyond, but little more was said. Dr. Prince's makeshift séance was relatively short and the entity promised not to bother Tyrrell again. Dr. Prince stayed in touch with Tyrrell for five months to make sure the exorcism was permanent. The communicator apparently kept his word, and Tyrrell never relapsed.

Dr. Prince refrained from publishing a report on these two cases until 1927. By then he had severed his connection with the ASPR and was living in Boston. (The story behind this move will be told in the next chapter). Not only did he report on the cases in detail, but he also wrote a lengthy commentary on them.

He pointed out in this commentary that, in his opinion, the cures were psychologically inexplicable. Through his practice as a psychologist and pastoral counselor, the researcher knew that such cases were difficult to treat. He had seen several related cases of insanity during his therapeutic work, and he explained in his report that "I had never cured or permanently helped a single patient whose voices or other symptoms of persecution were so firmly established that he could not be persuaded, during the first hour of consultation, to admit that possibly he might be the victim of delusions." But the case of Phyllis Latimer was certainly an exception to this principle. Her symptoms had been severe and prolonged, and after two years of constant suffering Dr. Prince didn't believe she would ever reject the reality of the voices. The researcher also believed that Leonard Tyrrell's unconscious was "expressing convictions so long and firmly rooted that it would have scouted any such attempted persuasion." Because these two cases *were* so hopeless was the reason Dr. Prince pursued his radical therapeutic intervention. He had no viable alternative to consider.

The implications offered by these cases were revolutionary, so far as Dr. Prince was concerned. He personally believed that, in the long run, his patients genuinely suffered from spirit possession . . . even though he refrained from endorsing this theory officially or wholeheartedly. But it is obvious from his commentary that he favored this explanation. Dr. Prince believed that from a purely psychological perspective, his procedures should have reinforced his subjects' delusions and shouldn't have cured them.

Dr. Prince didn't suggest, though, that most cases of classic paranoia are due to preternatural causes. He specifically pointed out in his report that the Latimer and Tyrrell cases represented a specific and perhaps unrelated phenomenological syndrome—a syndrome distinct from paranoid psychosis or multiple personality which pointed directly to the reality of spirit return. He reminded his readers that his patients' delusions were not general feelings of persecution but focused on specific deceased relatives or enemies, people who had really lived and died. Perhaps this is why, he suggested, they responded to spiritualistic treatment. Perhaps the symptoms only masqueraded as psychiatric disorders while the root cause remained clandestine.

Later during his career Dr. Prince was able to reconfirm this fascinating theory. Several times people suffering from delusions of persecution came to his office in Boston where he worked with the Boston Society for Psychic Research between 1925 and 1934. These people invariably believed they were possessed, but in each case the client's delusions were unfocused. They didn't know *who* was purportedly possessing them. Dr. Prince experimented with exorcism when treating these unfortunate cases but always failed. His feeling was that these people were psychotic and therefore beyond spiritual intervention. He couldn't cure them because no spirit entities were present to hear his exhortations.

CHAPTER 11

THE MINISTRY OF
DR. ELWOOD WORCESTER

Dr. Prince's work was hardly a voice calling from the wilderness. While the former Episcopalian clergyman was grappling with the problem of possession in New York, similar work was being undertaken in Boston.

While experimenting weekly in Boston with Minnie Soule, James Hyslop successfully converted another minister to his important work. The professor usually spent a day or so visiting Emmanuel Church in Back Bay, whose rector was a great friend of his. Dr. Elwood Worcester combined his training in psychology with a call to the ministry, and between 1905 and 1940 he was engaged in blending the powers of religion and psychiatry to cure the sick. Dr. Worcester was a social pioneer in several respects, and his psychic work was an outgrowth of this ministry. His experiences with the paranormal represent part of the continuing chapter in the search for the byways of the infinite boundary.

Elwood Worcester was born in 1862 in the small community of Massillon, Ohio. He could boast of an unusually satisfying childhood, since his parents were loving, educated, and relatively wealthy. His father taught the future clergyman both Latin and Greek, and young Elwood was ready to matriculate at Rochester University in 1875 at the ripe old age of thirteen. He never studied there, however, due to some unfortunate and unforeseen circumstances. His father's finances suddenly reversed, and the man died psychologically broken five years later. Elwood Worcester subsequently moved to the east coast. He worked in

Rochester in the freight office of the New York Central Railway, where he served as an exemplary employee. But he never felt fulfilled and constantly yearned for a scholarly career. It was during this period in his life that Worcester received his first religious revelation. While working in the dreary freight office one day, the wall before him suddenly radiated a bright yellow light. Then a voice spoke to him and requested that he make a commitment of faith to God. The young man didn't know what to make of the experience, so right after receiving this message he rushed off to speak with a local minister, who urged him to trust in the revelation.

From that day forward the young Worcester engaged in a strict course of self-education, and when his family's fortunes finally improved, he was prepared to enter Columbia University. He graduated with a baccalaureate degree in 1886. From there he studied theology at General Theological Seminary in New York, but he still wasn't intellectually satisfied. He believed that to finish his education he should explore the related fields of philosophy and psychology. This challenge took him to the University of Leipzig, where—like Prof. Hyslop—he studied with both Wilhelm Wundt and Gustav Fechner, who were both pioneering research in the behavioral sciences. He received his doctorate in 1889 and returned to the United States where he was ordained an Episcopal priest in 1891. His first pastoral appointment was at St. Anne's Church in Brooklyn.

His true calling came, however, when he moved to Pennsylvania. His first position was at Lehigh University in the steel manufacturing city of Bethlehem, where he served as chaplain while teaching psychology, religion, and philosophy. During his stay in the city, Dr. Worcester's life's work became increasingly clear, for he soon realized that some bodily sicknesses were really sicknesses of the soul. This discovery led him to propose that some bodily symptoms could be treated by suggestion, prayer, spiritual guidance, and psychological reeducation. He also believed that research and therapy could prove the reality of the soul. "It seemed certain to me," he would later write, "that a non-existing thing could not suffer or be sick."

These were possibilities rather than probabilities in Dr. Worcester's emerging worldview, but their status soon changed. The young clergyman departed from Lehigh University in 1896 to take up ministerial work at St. Stephen's Church in Philadelphia. There he became close friends with Dr. S. Weir Mitchell (1829–1914), an expert on ner-

vous disorders and a famous writer and poet. Dr. Mitchell was a parishioner at St. Stephen's and he shared his minister's suspicions concerning the soul. They often spoke of combining religious practices with
sound medical treatment, but nothing came of it initially.

This revolutionary project wasn't realized until 1904 when Dr.
Worcester became the rector of Emmanuel Church in Boston. With
the help of his associate pastor, Dr. Samuel McComb, he launched the
now-famous and socially progressive Emmanuel Movement. (This ap-
pellation was coined by the Boston press and never enjoyed the endorse-
ment of either Dr. Worcester or Reverend McComb.) The ideal behind
the movement was to minister to the general public with both religion
and science. Their first enterprise was the formation of a tuberculosis
class in 1905, which was devoted to public health education (and which
was eventually taken over by the commonwealth of Massachusetts). They
later expanded their work to people suffering from nervous, psychological, and what were then called "moral" diseases—conditions in which
people felt compelled to practice moral or social evils. The medical
establishment initially welcomed their outreach program, and several
noted physicians provided educational services for the church's clien-
tele. Treatment under the auspices of the church consisted of education
in personal hygiene, medical intervention when necessary, pastoral
counseling, and prayer. Soon the movement was sponsoring wide-ranging health conferences and deeply embroiled itself into Boston's medical
community. Their radical encroachment into the medical and psychiatric fields caused something of an uproar, since it was unusual for a
religious establishment to become so socially and scientifically prominent. But the church survived the publicity and controversy to become
a vital force in the Boston area.

Dr. Worcester was, of course, deeply committed to this work. What
was his secret of success? Develop your intellectual faculties, develop
your spiritual faculties, and then you will increase your ability to
heal—these were the instructions he always offered to his volunteer
workers.

The work and influence of the Emmanuel Movement survived
Dr. Worcester's pastorship and earthly life. Popular appreciation of the
church's work was rife in Boston, and the commonwealth's civic organizations also became increasingly concerned with the benefits of public
health education. One immediate result was that the institutional treatment of the insane improved markedly. The Emmanuel Movement was

an important part of this country's religious and psychological heritage, and it was Dr. Worcester's everlasting gift to Boston.*

Dr. Worcester summed up his life's work best in his final book and autobiography, *Life's Adventure:* "The more good religion does," he stated, "the more men believe in it, and the less good it does, the less faith it is able to inspire."

James Hyslop first met Dr. Worcester during these exciting and busy years. He often stopped by the rectory of Emmanuel Church and eagerly attended their frequent health conferences, and a close friendship soon developed between the two men. Given their similar intellectual and educational backgrounds, this friendship was probably predictable. Of course there was some contention between them, since Hyslop wasn't totally taken with the Emmanuel Movement's theoretical premises. He even criticized them severely in a long (and frankly dull) paper he wrote in 1911. (This paper was published in the June 1911 issue of the *Journal of the American Society for Psychical Research*.) But these objections were more theoretical than empirical, and Hyslop's personal regard for his colleague never waivered.

It was also Hyslop who first introduced Dr. Worcester to the field of psychical research. Working with the spiritually and mentally ill would bring his colleague into contact with psychic phenomena, he warned, and this included spirit possession. Dr. Worcester was open to this possibility since he was a devout Christian practitioner. But his immediate focus was more on treating people suffering from phobias, nervous disorders, sleep problems, and depression. The conceivable reality of possession existed solely as a theoretical possibility, and he couldn't initially fathom his friend's messianic devotion to the study of psychic phemomena. Eventually though, the clergyman did come to appreciate Hyslop's wisdom. When he co-authored his famous book *Mind, Body and Spirit* with Samuel McComb (see below) in the early 1930s, Dr. Worcester openly affirmed the existence of the possession syndrome. He also admitted that with the assistance of both Hyslop and Dr. Titus Bull, he had successfully treated several such cases.

"I have treated successfully ten patients who had been diagnosed by competent alienists as suffering from what is vaguely designated, paranoia," wrote Dr. Worcester. "These cases were not taken at random.

---

*Dr. Worcester resigned from Emmanuel Church in 1929, and along with Courtenay Baylor reincorporated their work under the laws of Massachusetts. They founded the Craigie Foundation to carry on their work and operated from a private home in Boston.

In each of them we had at the outset evidence which pointed toward the probability of Spirit Possession."

Such a statement shouldn't be surprising, since close ties existed between Emmanuel Church in Boston and Dr. Bull in New York. Dr. Worcester never worked directly with Mrs. Duke, but his associate pastor, Samuel McComb, served on the board of Dr. Bull's foundation. Dr. Worcester consulted regularly with Dr. Bull and sometimes employed his procedures in his own pastoral counseling.

Who were these ten fortunate patients? We don't have the records of their provocative cases, but we do know something about them. Most of them were ordinary people who liked to dabble in the occult—operating ouija boards, practicing automatic writing, and/or participating in Spiritualist meetings. Spiritual emergencies and possession often resulted from these sometimes dangerous practices.

"It took me ten years to bring myself to entertain this hypothesis," Dr. Worcester wrote in 1932, "and I accepted it as possible only on evidence I could not resist."

Dr. Worcester left posterity with only two case summaries, since Hyslop's devotion to careful record-taking never inspired him. He was more interested in implementing cures than with conducting scientific research.

The first case involved a cure he executed with the help of Hyslop. We don't know the date of the events, but they probably occurred toward the end of Hyslop's life. The patient was a married woman whose problems evolved from her infatuation with Spiritualism, which had prompted her to attend several of the sect's services and meetings. Without any proper supervision she later tried sitting for automatic writing herself, but her husband disapproved of the practice. He ultimately confiscated her writing materials and commanded her to desist from the experiments. Soon the poor woman was hearing voices in her mind that her husband, unfortunately, couldn't similarly banish. The frustrated gentleman finally took his wife to a physician, whose opinion was that she was suffering from classic paranoia. His only advice was to institutionalize her.

The lady was devastated by the diagnosis and recommendation and begged to see Dr. Worcester even though she had never met him. She had heard of him through his spiritual and social work. The couple drove immediately to Emmanuel Church, where Dr. Worcester was confronted with her pressing case. When the woman's husband completed the story behind their visit, he challenged the clergyman. He was skeptical that Dr. Worcester could help remedy the situation but permitted him to work with his wife for two weeks.

Luckily for both the woman and Dr. Worcester, James Hyslop was paying a visit to the rectory that same day. Since he was in Boston to work with Minnie Soule, Dr. Worcester decided to recruit the professor's help. Hyslop complied by taking the possessed woman to Mrs. Soule's residence, where she was invited to participate in his own sitting.

The session probably saved the woman from being committed. Dr. Worcester recorded that,

> Dr. Hyslop was always most kind and generous in cases of suffering. He gladly laid aside his own important work and devoted himself to the case of this woman with the result that the obsessing personality was discovered during the first sitting [with Minnie Soule]. The case did not require two weeks. At the end of nine days the voices had ceased to trouble her and she was able to resume her usual occupations. Both Dr. Hyslop and I explained to her the danger to which she had exposed herself, and we strictly commanded her to indulge no more in automatic writing.

Dr. Worcester's second case was more severe and recalcitrant. It involved a fifty-two-year-old woman, the wife of a grocer. She was uneducated and had immigrated to the United States from Ireland. She was addicted to morphine, and when Dr. Worcester first met her, she was taking the drug intravenously every day. The clergyman was very pessimistic about curing her. He believed that drug addiction should be treated by both medical and moral education, and the only treatments then in vogue were purely somatic.

During their first meeting Dr. Worcester urged the woman to undergo treatment at the Towne-Lambert Institute in New York, which specialized in drug-detoxification programs. Unfortunately, the cost was prohibitive and the poor woman begged the clergyman to treat her personally. Dr. Worcester was moved by her situation and consented. His therapeutic tools were primarily psychological and included prayer, suggestion, encouragement, and friendship. He also outlined a program whereby his client progressively reduced her daily morphine intake, and by the end of the month Dr. Worcester had cured her physical dependence on the opiate. Her weight increased, her color improved, and her personality became chipper.

But then came the fall. The patient often experienced wild mor-
phine-related hallucinations while shooting the drug, and after the case
was seemingly cured, Dr. Worcester encouraged his patient to describe
them in writing. She was reluctant to act on this suggestion, but he
pressed her. This was a tragic mistake, and when he next saw the patient, she looked dreadful.

"She seemed dull and apathetic," recorded Dr. Worcester, "and
what puzzled me most was that her right arm was paralyzed and hung
as if attached by wires to her shoulders."

Dr. Worcester immediately concluded that she was again injecting
morphine, but the frightened woman denied the charge emphatically.
"She affirmed that she had not used morphine or any other drug," he
recounted, "but that the old hallucinations, for which during the latter
part of my treatment she had become practically free, had returned with
fearful intensity and that they tormented her night and day."

These experiences had returned while the woman was writing her
descriptions for the clergyman. The paralysis had resulted from the task,
too. Dr. Worcester was extremely disappointed by these complications
and began seeing his patient every day for further therapy. He treated
her principally with hypnosis, and during these sessions he began to
suspect that a spiritual factor was behind his patient's problems. It seems
that the woman kept seeing a malicious figure during her trances. The
phantom looked vaguely familiar to her and usually appeared carrying
a syringe. When this phantom appeared, it invariably exhorted the woman
to return to her former practice. Dr. Worcester immediately responded
to this crisis by combating the phantom's influence with everything from
hypnotic suggestion to prayer. But nothing seemed to work. He couldn't
exorcise the figure nor could he cure his patient's mysterious paralysis.
That she would be lost to spirit possession seemed ultimately likely, and
this prospect was reinforced when raps began breaking out in her presence. Dr. Worcester heard them in his own office, where they seemed
to emanate from his desk during a critical session in the woman's treatment.

This was a surprising development in the case, and it gave Dr.
Worcester the idea for his next experiment. He was to meet a young
psychic later that enlightening morning, and she was even then in his
waiting room. Since he was familiar with Hyslop's research on possession, Dr. Worcester decided to use the psychic for an impromptu experiment. He invited the young lady into his office but refrained from
introducing his patient to her. He then asked her to sit comfortably in

a chair and requested her to pass into trance. The psychic willingly complied and soon began speaking.

"Dr. Worcester, this is not your fault," the psychic (or her first communicator) stated. "You could not have anticipated what it would cost this poor woman to write these statements. When she tells you that she has not touched morphine, she is telling you the truth."

Dr. Worcester was grateful to know of the patient's good faith. It was also a brilliant display of the sensitive's psychic capabilities.

"If it is not my fault, whose fault is it?" he asked.

The psychic's reply was cryptic. "It is Harris's fault," she said.

When these words were spoken, Dr. Worcester's patient rose from her chair without provocation, lifted her unparalyzed left limb and screamed. Dr. Worcester tried to silence her, but the incident in all likelihood disturbed the delicate psychic conditions in his office. The psychic passed back from trance within moments and left the room.

Dr. Worcester could see that his patient was shaken and seemed prepared to enter into trance herself. It was a bizarre situation. The clergyman responded by seating her comfortably, and he instructed her to succumb to the inclination. But he probably wasn't prepared for the subsequent events. Even though his patient consistently spoke in a thick Irish brogue, her voice now changed radically, and she brought through a communicator who spoke crisply, with no accent whatsoever.

"This is Dr. Theodore Parker," the entity explained. "I have taken a great interest in your efforts to help this poor woman whom I knew years ago. For a time you succeeded well, but you have not been succeeding so well lately, have you?"

Dr. Worcester agreed with the communicator's evaluation. "No, Dr. Parker," he replied, "and I should like to have your help and advice."

The self-appointed communicator then explained the basis of the patient's problem in considerable detail.

"I have come to give them to you," the purported Dr. Parker began. "You did well in your treatment of the morphine habit because you knew what you were dealing with, but you have not known what you were doing since. This woman stopped taking morphine when she told you she had done so. All her life she has been a medium, although she has not known it. When you asked her to write our her visions and to relate the most painful experiences of her life, she became so affected that in that time she passed into trance. While in trance, the spirit of Dr. Harris entered into her and he has been raging within her like a wild bull ever since, and in order to prove his power over her he deprived her of the use of her right arm, *which I now restore."*

After he finished this speech, the patient was able to lift her previously paralyzed limb. Then Dr. Worcester resumed his conversation with the communicator.

"Who is this Harris about whom I am hearing so much?" he asked.

But the communicator was reluctant to answer, saying only that "I should prefer to have our patient tell you herself, later."

Dr. Worcester pressed the matter. "Will you tell me what is to become of this case and what I am to do further?"

The communicator assured him that the case was finally under control.

"You have already done all in your power," stated the entity. "Now it is my case. I have taken charge of Harris and he will trouble you no longer. You will find that this woman is well and needs no further treatment."

The patient emerged from her somnabulistic state as Dr. Parker faded from the scene. She was surprised to see that her paralysis was gone. Dr. Worcester was still fascinated by the role of the mysterious Dr. Harris in her problem, however, and asked if she recognized the name. The patient's reaction was almost violent. It seemed that Dr. Harris was her former physician. He used morphine recreationally and finally died from the practice. He took delight in sharing his drug-taking ways with his patients, and the woman's problems had originally resulted from her relationship with the doctor.

Whatever the truth behind this story, the strange events that took place in Dr. Worcester's office that day were curative. From that morning forward the patient's symptoms disappeared. She left his office completely cured.

In light of such encounters, it isn't surprising that Dr. Worcester came to respect the clinical work of Dr. Titus Bull and Dr. W. Franklin Prince. When the clergyman was writing his *Body, Mind and Spirit* toward the end of his career, he echoed the viewpoints previously expressed by his fellow Episcopalian in 1927. He acknowledged that his psychic encounters would be "regarded with skepticism and derision," but he prophesied that such cases "may be one of the foundation stones of a new therapy for the treatment of certain types of paranoia." Dr. Worcester eventually hoped to draw the medical community into this sort of work. His plan was to recruit physicians willing to supply Dr.

Bull in New York with some of their more recalcitrant patients, in hopes that religion could succeed where medicine was failing.

Since their sentiments were similar, it isn't surprising that Dr. Worcester and Dr. Prince became close friends and professional colleagues. Sometime in early 1920 Dr. Worcester and some of his friends decided to organize a society in Boston for the study of psychical phenomena. Such an organization was certainly needed since—as I pointed out previously—the standards of the American Society for Psychical Research were steadily declining, much to the dismay of its more critical members. Since this sad state of affairs relates directly to the work of Dr. Prince and Dr. Worcester's encounters with the world of spirit possession, let's digress for a moment from the study of possession. The story behind the founding of the Boston Society for Psychic Research will help the reader to understand why Dr. Prince was forced to leave the ASPR and ended up in Boston collaborating with Dr. Worcester.

Upon the death of James Hyslop in the summer of 1920, the society fell into the hands of his devoted and slightly eccentric secretary, Gertrude W. Tubby, Dr. Prince, and the Board of Trustees. It was imperative for the organization to find a new president, and they discovered an eminent successor in Prof. William McDougall, the great British psychologist then teaching in Cambridge, Massachusetts at Harvard. The psychologist accepted the post graciously and enthusiastically. Everything seemed to be going smoothly until he began restructuring the society's goals. He wanted to move the organization from survival research (which had been Hyslop's preeminent passion) toward more international cooperation with other organizations devoted to different research questions. For example, he wanted to create links between psychical research and the scientific and psychological establishments. He felt that only by placing psychical research within this context would the field ever gain academic recognition. So in order to implement this enviable plan, McDougall formed a "scientific advisory board" to encourage public recognition of the society's work. These were wise and far-reaching decisions, but they offended many of Hyslop's devoted followers, who were often more interested in promoting Spiritualism than in promoting science. McDougall was also more interested in experimental research than with searching for gifted psychics, which a few members also felt betrayed the goals set by the ASPR's late founder.

Despite his personal interest in the survival issue Dr. Prince was sympathetic to the new president's objectives. It was therefore a personal defeat for him when the Board of Trustees ousted McDougall and elected a new president in 1923 who was more to their liking and certainly less scientifically oriented. Rev. Frederick Edwards was more of a Spiritualist than a psychical researcher, and he was soon battling with his research officer over the society's future work. The confrontation was inevitable and perhaps was partially due to Dr. Prince's own personality flaws. Dr. Prince was not exactly easy to deal with. He tended to be pompous and stubborn, and he was often downright rude to people he didn't like. And he certainly didn't like Reverend Edwards's plans for the organization. The new president planned to popularize the society and its publications and wanted to set up branches of the ASPR throughout the country. His break with Dr. Prince ultimately came when he decided to edit the society's publications in order to make sure they accorded with the organization's new look.

Even though Dr. Prince had worked steadily with the ASPR since 1917, he couldn't sanction these new policies. Dissatisfaction was simultaneously growing in Boston, where members such as Dr. Worcester were looking toward New York with growing disenchantment. So finally the clergyman and some of his associates—including Dr. Prince— founded the Boston Society for Psychic Research in 1925. Their aim was to reimplement the unimpeachable standards for which the late Prof. Hyslop had stood. They soon made Dr. Prince their chief research officer, while Dr. Worcester served as the new society's president.

It was a mutually satisfactory situation. Not only did the Boston organization support Dr. Prince's field investigations and mediumistic studies, it also offered support to the young J. B. Rhine—who was then beginning his famous career researching extrasensory perception at Duke University in Durham, North Carolina.

Dr. Prince worked steadily with the Boston group until 1934. He wrote virtually nothing on the subject of possession after 1927, while Dr. Worcester reported briefly on his own encounters in 1931 and 1932. But upon the death of his colleague, Dr. Worcester found himself grappling with one final case of possible possession—the most difficult case of his distinguished career.

When Dr. Prince died near Boston in the summer of 1934, Dr. Worcester was in New Brunswick, where he operated a retreat for his mental patients. His work with them was critical, and he couldn't rush back to Boston nor offer his support and comfort to Prince's daughter, to whom he was very attached. Doris Fischer was still living with her foster father and taking care of his domestic life when his death finally came, and his passing was a considerable blow to her. Despite her cure, her mental health was far from perfect and—still stuck in Canada—Dr. Worcester was secretly worried for her sanity. He was concerned that the crisis would break Doris's fragile personality. Dr. Worcester wasn't able to return to Boston until the following October, and by this time his worst suspicions were bearing out. He found Doris distraught, and her sanity seemed to be gradually disintegrating. She refused any comfort for her loss and preferred to live, sunk in depression, with her cocker spaniel in her father's bungalow near the coast at Hingham Bay. Dr. Worcester visited her there frequently.

Dr. Worcester wanted to keep Doris under close supervision, so he usually invited her to spend part of each week with his family in Boston. Each time he visited her at Hingham Bay, though, he tried to place her in a light sleep in hopes of establishing contact with her psychological guardian, "Sleeping Margaret." He wanted to keep close tabs on the inner workings of Doris's mind in order to save her from a breakdown. But each time she passed into trance, she would produce copious written scripts. These messages purported to come from a band of discarnate entities devoted to destroying Doris's sanity.

Dr. Worcester was willing to take these claims at face value since he firmly believed in spirit obsession. He even recognized the identity of the fourth possessing entity, who "gave the name of an evilly-disposed man whose deportation from America for sexual crimes on young girls Dr. Prince had obtained many years [prior]." Dr. Worcester tried unsuccessfully to deliver Doris from her tormentors, but he later sadly reported:

> I was not interested in verifying the statements of these wretches who appeared regularly week after week. My concern was to banish them, if possible, before they overthrew the reason of my patient. Their nature was essentially evil, cruel, and perverse; and from my experience with such obsessing personalities I was convinced that they would soon reduce Doris' inner life to a condition worse than it was when Dr. Prince began his work with her. During this period which lasted nearly three months the progressive deterioration of Doris' mind was perceptible from week to week. To my suggestions, commands, and entreaties that they depart they replied with mockery and derision (all in automatic writing). Finding me unmoved by their threats they began to take more active measures to destroy what remained of Doris. For one week she had a series of ghastly nightmares of suicide through poison, hanging, stabbing, shooting, and drowning. The next week she dreamed of similar forms of death inflicted

on me. The third week with such revolting sexual visions that, after experiencing a few of them, Doris refused to go to bed and tried to keep herself awake for five nights. All these nocturnal horrors occurred while Doris was entirely alone in her bungalow by the sea.

In addition to all these assaults on Doris' sanity these personalities, presences, nonentities, what you will, made repeated attempts to keep her from me by the infliction of painful physical symptoms. As the time approached for her to come to me in Boston she would be incapacitated by headache, or by nausea, vertigo, and other afflictions of which I have kept a careful record.

The symtpoms were so severe that Dr. Worcester feared for Doris's life.

The ultimate crisis came on New Year's Day of 1935. Doris was expected to join the Worcester family for an early dinner, but she never came. They heard nothing from her for several days and frantically tried to reach her in Hingham. They finally discovered that her house was deserted and that she was missing. The solution to the mystery only came a week later when Dr. Worcester received a surprising letter from Doris. It was a puzzling and disturbing note. Doris obviously no longer remembered who Dr. Worcester was, but she had uttered his name while recovering from an episode of delirium in a local hospital. She couldn't recall any of the events leading to her breakdown, and her physician had suggested she make contact with Dr. Worcester.

Upon receiving this letter, Dr. Worcester made arrangements to bring Doris to his rectory. She was dropped off by cab later that day, and it soon became clear that she was severely disoriented. She didn't recognize the Worcesters, her cocker spaniel, nor her surroundings. She even failed to recognize her foster father when Dr. Worcester produced a photograph of him. Dr. Worcester was nonplussed but finally figured out a strategy to cure Doris, for he realized that if she could be convinced to enter trance, he could make contact with her unconscious by way of "Sleeping Margaret." This personality would know what to do, he thought.

The plan made perfect sense, but Doris was reluctant to follow such strange advice—especially from a (to her) complete stranger! But after endless pleas Doris finally consented to try the experiment. She simply laid down, relaxed her mind and body, and soon seemed to become unconscious. "Sleeping Margaret" quickly emerged from her unconscious mind and explained the problem in considerable detail.

The personality told Dr. Worcester that Doris had been looking forward to her New Year's dinner with his family, but since the weather was so poor that day, she had called a friend in Brookline (a Boston suburb) to chauffeur her. The young man was more than willing but was unavoidably delayed. Doris's sense of outrage over the incident exacerbated her chronic depression, and she responded by trying to poison herself with a combination of strychnine and morphine.

Doris's fragmented life could have ended right there, explained "Sleeping Margaret," but her friend fortunately arrived in the nick of time. He found the woman unconscious and writhing on the floor, placed her in his car, and drove speedily to a Boston hospital.

It was clear to Dr. Worcester that while Doris had survived the ordeal physically, her psychological condition was grave. During the following weeks he tried to help her in every possible way. His basic method was to use hypnosis and gradually—through constant suggestion—Doris's memories returned. During these critical weeks Dr. Worcester also tried to treat her severe depression. These therapeutic interventions worked additional wonders.

> In the course of a week both these suggestions were fulfilled to the letter. On the following Saturday morning Doris came down stairs with shining face, a transformed being, and informed me that during the night she had not slept but that the memories of her past life, beginning with recent events, kept pouring in like a flood, that she now recalled every incident of her life with Dr. Prince and of her childhood, but that strangely she felt no grief whatever in recalling him, and that her love for Fifi [her dog] had returned. I have seen too many examples of amazing spiritual changes which have not proved permanent to dare to express the opinion that this new cheerfulness, serenity, and freedom will continue indefinitely. Nevertheless, nearly eight weeks have passed without any change for the worse. I have known Doris for more than twenty years, and at no time has she seemed so completely normal mentally and physically as during this period. Deeming her weight excessive I consulted a good internist as to a diet and by her willing cooperation she has already lost more than ten pounds.

Except for a few more paragraphs Dr. Worcester's report ends with these optimistic comments.

The rest of the story subsequent to 1935 isn't so uplifting, though. Doris's recovery proved temporary after all, and her previous problems and dissociative episodes returned. Her mental state became so bad that she was finally institutionalized. Though the date of her death isn't known,

Doris apparently spent her remaining life confined to a mental hospital. Dr. Worcester died in 1940.

Did Doris undergo a psychological breakdown or did the spirits drive her crazy? Dr. Worcester probably believed that both realities interacted to destroy her, but whatever the case, it was a pathetic denouement to one of psychical research's greatest cases.

With Dr. Worcester's death in 1940 came the demise of the Boston Society for Psychic Research. Without the leadership of people such as Dr. Worcester and Dr. Prince, the organization had little chance of surviving.

Luckily, however, important changes were revising the policies of the ASPR in New York. The following year saw a "palace revolution" that promised to place it back into the forefront of psychical research. The organization's critical standards were reimposed by some newly elected board members, and the Boston group merged with it.

The death of Dr. Worcester also heralded the end of a great tradition in psychical research. During the previous decade, psychical research increasingly became an experimental science concerned more with the study of extrasensory perception than with survival research. The days when it was merely the scientific face of Spiritualism were dead, and such subjects as spirit possession and trance mediumship fell from grace. Few researchers were willing to continue with the important research begun by James Hyslop and his successors. This change in emphasis was in some sense predictable, for despite their diligent work, neither Hyslop nor his disciples ever succeeded in proving the reality of the soul's survival. So the next generation of parapsychologists simply lost interest in the subject. There were more practical research projects on the psychic horizon, and most of them were modeled on the laboratory research emanating from Duke University, where Dr. J. B. Rhine was proving that psychic phenomena could be explored experimentally and systematically.

But research into the possible reality of spirit possession didn't come to a complete end. Although the subject did not appeal to the psychical researchers of the 1950s and 1960s, it began slowly creeping into the domain of conventional psychiatry. It underwent a surprising renaissance in the 1970s and 1980s, when psychiatrists working with cases of multiple personality confronted the same dilemma Dr. Titus Bull, Dr. W. Franklin Prince, and Dr. Elwood Worcester faced in the 1920s. Could some cases of this complex syndrome represent spiritual rather than psychiatric problems?

PART III

RESCUE WORK TODAY

CHAPTER 12

RESCUING THE DARK SPIRITS

Depossessing people who are suffering from psychological disturbances has never been popular in conventional psychiatry, to say the least. But the situation is very different south of the United States' border.

Brazil is probably the most Spiritualist country in the world. Three different versions of the sect popularly flourish there. The range of these beliefs combine elements taken from folk practices, superstition, vegetarianism, black magic, European Spiritualism, and even Catholicism.

The origins of these practices date back to the sixteenth century, when the first black slaves were sold to unscrupulous European traders by rival tribes in Africa and were imported into the country. The slaves brought their own culture with its pantheon of gods, spirits, and other supernatural beings to the Western Hemisphere. The New World was being rapidly converted by the Catholic Church and its missionaries during these years, and the blacks were soon indoctrinated into the new religion. But although the continent's new residents conformed to this monotheistic religion of salvation, they never relinquished their own cultural traditions but simply incorporated them into Catholicism. The religious figures of early Christianity became identified with the many colorful figures of African folklore, and a curious hybrid religion eventually evolved. The basic tenets of Christian belief were not rejected, but the slaves kept their cultural integrity by retaining their rituals, their belief in the supernatural powers of departed spirits, and their folklore.

With such a colorful and complicated history behind its popular religious practices, Brazil was ripe for the taking when Spiritualism became popular in Europe during the 1850s. The impetus behind the development of the sect in the country was the writings of Hippolyte

219

Léon Denizard Rivail (1804–1869), a Spiritualist convert who lived in France during the heyday of the movement. Rivail (who wrote under the *nom de plume* of Allan Kardec) was an intelligent and inquisitive gentleman who spoke both Latin and Greek and whose educational background was in medicine. He studied the new religion when table-turning was the rage in France, and his experiences with the talking tables and with several trance psychics was personally convincing. He wrote of his research in 1857 in his celebrated book *Le Livre des Ésprits.* Rivail's popular brand of Spiritualism differed from its progenitor's simple theology, though. Spiritualism had been born and nurtured in the United States the previous decade and had later spread to England and to the Continent. The chief tenets of the creed were that personal survival and communication with the dead were scientific facts. Rivail contributed a new doctrine to these beliefs, for his psychics convinced him that the soul is continually reborn through a succession of earthly lives.

These views were presented by Rivail in a series of books that became the bibles of his movement, which was soon called Spiritism to differentiate it from Spiritualism—which didn't incorporate the reincarnation doctrine and never would. In fact, while Rivail's movement-within-a-movement became very popular in France, it never became fashionable elsewhere in Europe. It did, however, find fertile soil in the Western Hemisphere. His writings were translated into Portuguese (even though the upper classes in Brazil were conversant in French), and the sect became extremely popular there. The more educated classes saw in "Kardecismo" a metaphysical way of looking at the world that was more sophisticated than the folkloric Spiritualist beliefs of the blacks. The folkloric elements did not die completely, though, nor were they totally replaced by Kardecian religion. Both traditions survived this cultural crisis, and three different forms of Spiritualist belief are still practiced in today's Brazil.

Candomblé is primarily a folk religion that combines basic Spiritualist philosophy with rituals in which the followers psychically merge with folk deities.

Umbanda is more formally a Spiritualist cult, since it practices a rudimentary form of the religion. It teaches belief in reincarnation, and its psychics bring through popular spiritual "mentors" and entities during special public shamanic-style rituals.

Kardecismo is a philosophically oriented Spiritualism that teaches the doctrine of reincarnation. Its mediums bring through spirits of the dead and so-called spirit guides, who usually offer commentaries on metaphysical issues and social doctrines.

Although all three of these sects believe in the reality of spirit obsession and possession, only Kardecismo evolved specific doctrines linking the phenomenon to several forms of psychopathology. Some physicians and psychiatrists living in Brazil have even merged conventional psychiatric practices with Kardecismo philosophy. Today they openly practice the same kind of therapeutic work that Dr. Titus Bull, Dr. Elwood Worcester, and Dr. Carl Wickland once conducted in our own country.

Kardecismo philosophy teaches that three psychological disorders can sometimes be caused by interference from spirits of the dead: these would include epilepsy, schizophrenia, and (most commonly) the strange disorder of multiple personality. The popular belief is that spirit obsession and possession sometimes play a complicating factor in seizure disorders and insanity, but they play an even more complex role in multiple personality. Kardecismo theorists posit that people suffering from these bothersome secondary personalities can either be (a) possessed by spirits of the dead, who "become" their secondary egos or (b) possessed by their own previous lives. This second possibility entails the belief that within our personalities we carry subsystems that come (i.e., we inherit) from our previous earthly existences. Sometimes these secondary systems will become powerful and control our present lives. This unfortunate situation can result in dissociative episodes during which our past lives emerge into consciousness, usurp our present sense of identity, and control the body for extended periods of time.

To make this convoluted theory a bit simpler: Kardecismo teaches that sometimes we can be possessed by elements emerging from our own minds, but inherited from our past existences.

This doctrine may seem strange, but it is the cornerstone upon which many Kardecismo psychiatric practices are based. Its strangeness may rest in the fact that no similar Western researchers in the United States ever reported such a strange phenomenon. Such an unusual past-life syndrome certainly played no role in the cases reported by James Hyslop and his diligent successors.

This doesn't mean, however, that such a phenomenon doesn't or couldn't exist. People suffering from multiple personality in our culture do, in fact, sometimes intuitively link their secondary personalities to their possible previous lives—even if they previously entertained no prior belief in the rebirth principle before becoming ill. Kathy Roth, for example, was a young wife and mother living in the bustling city of New York when she discovered she suffered from the multiple personality syndrome. She later wrote her memoirs (in collaboration with Nancy

Hughes Clark) in which she talks openly about her therapy and reintegration. She also discussed the psychic side of her problem in her book *Shatter*. During one phase of her life, she experienced dramatic déjà-vu experiences that reluctantly forced her to believe in reincarnation. She eventually linked one of her secondary personalities to a past-life existence she had once led in New England.

Kathy Roth's experience may seem unique, but other people victimized by this strange disorder entertain similar sentiments.

But now back to Brazil.

The Brazilian followers of Kardecismo combine their religious beliefs with a commendable social conscience, and they are pioneers in the promotion of wide-ranging social programs. By the turn of the century, several Kardecismo leaders had contemplated establishing treatment centers for the psychologically disturbed where both psychiatric and spiritistic therapies could be strategically combined. It saddened them to think that the insane were serving life sentences in their country's mental institutions. Since it was their belief that Spiritism might succeed where psychiatry was failing, in 1912 Dr. Oscar Pittham, an eminent Brazilian physician, began collecting funds to back a "spirit" hospital. This commendable plan finally became a reality, even though it took several years of negotiation and several sizable donations to complete it. This unusual hospital was fully operational by 1934 and was established in the city of Porto Allegre, a port city located near the southern tip of Brazil. It has been functional ever since and expanded its operations with a second wing in 1951. By the mid-1960s the hospital was servicing some five hundred patients and receiving patient referrals from fifteen Brazilian psychiatrists. Not only is it a modern medical facility, but it is also a charitable institution since its directors do not receive salaries.

The goals and principles of the hospital are set forth in its four statutory rules.

1. The center is not to focus on profits but should offer services to the spiritually unwell for the lowest possible cost.
2. The personnel who maintain the center have no rights beyond their specially prescribed duties.
3. The staff is to receive and treat neuropsychiatric patients without regard to their race, religion, or social position.
4. The hospital must retain its own staff, but it should cooperate with any specialist competent to serve its patients' needs.

The specific procedures employed by the hospital follow a standard protocol. Treatment is offered to people suffering from any form of psychological dysfunction, which would include disorders ranging from insanity to drug dependence. When a patient is first admitted to the center, he or she receives both a psychiatric and a physical examination. The patient is then interviewed by a second psychiatrist, who issues a follow-up report to the hospital's director. This double-check procedure is employed to reduce errors in diagnosis—which is a constant problem since psychological dysfunctions can often be difficult to classify. When the patient is finally correctly diagnosed, he or she is subjected to a program of medical and psychiatric treatment, which might include such physical therapy as electroconvulsive shock. (ECT is a common procedure for dealing with chronic depression.) Simultaneously, though, each patient receives a form of psychic treatment. The hospital keeps several teams of psychics on staff, and they care for the patients by making healing "passes" over their bodies at regular intervals during their stay. These so-called magnetic passes are executed like the way "therapeutic touch," which is believed to restore and balance the body's energy system, is administered by some nurses in our own country.

(This procedure was first formally developed in the United States by Dr. Dolores Krieger, a professor of nursing in New York while working in collaboration with a psychic she knew. This psychic claimed that she could see energy forces surrounding medical patients that needed manipulating. The procedure Dr. Krieger effected is surreptitiously based on nineteenth-century mesmerism, and seems to relax hospitalized patients and sometimes helps to cure them. Brazil's psychic practitioners have employed the same system for years, since mesmeric practices were part and parcel of nineteenth-century Spiritualism and Spiritism both in the United States and France.)

Sometimes a psychiatrist in charge of a particular case will come to believe that a patient's problem stems from obsession or full-scale possession. When such a situation arises, the hospital staff will conduct special séances on the patient's behalf twice weekly in private. The psychics will meet together and will enter trance to contact the patient's tormentors and exorcise them à la Dr. Carl Wickland. They work together without seeing the patient, since they only receive the name and location of the client. He or she is never present during these special meetings but remains elsewhere in the hospital, at home, or possibly even in a neighboring community.

The work of the Porto Allegre hospital is not well known in this country, and certainly not to the psychiatric community! Very few of its reports have been translated into English, but during the 1970s information concerning the hospital became better known outside Brazil.

Mrs. Ann Dooley is a British writer and former industrial correspondent who traveled widely in Brazil in the 1960s to explore the country's psychic heritage. As part of her extensive travels she visited the hospital and became friends with Conrado Ferrari, who was then the elderly president of the center. She published an interview with him in 1972 in which he presented the hospital's views on the obsession/possession syndrome. It was Kardecismo philosophy in its purest and most fascinating form. Senhor Ferrari explained to the correspondent that possession can result from a number of disparate circumstances. It can evolve from a shock to the patient's nervous system, but it can also result when black magic is projected at the patient.* Whatever the facts of a given case, psychic treatment usually works when coupled with more conventional medical therapy. The results of spiritistic treatment usually become evident immediately, though.

"In obsession treatment the difference in the patient can be seen by the following day," Ferrari explained to his guest. "As Spiritists we are convinced that our high percentage of successful treatments at this hospital is due to this work, though the doctors, of course, naturally attribute such cures to their own medical treatment!"

There are some exceptions to this rule, however. The patient must be responsible for maintaining the cure, since it is Kardecismo belief that people suffering from possession are probably psychic to begin with.

"We regard many of the patients classified by doctors as 'schizophrenic' as being obsession cases," Ferrari continued. "These are treated mediumistically by removing the obsessors as I have already described. It must be said, however, that if the patient does not then play *his* part in consolidating the healing carried out, i.e., by developing his psychic powers if he is a budding medium or by mending his ways if the obsession has been caused by bad habits, or learning to forgive his enemies, then he may again relapse, for the healing of obsession depends ultimately *more* upon the patient himself than those who seek to help him. We only carry out emergency treatment."

What is perhaps even more interesting is the lack of public preju-

---

*This position may sound like rank superstition, but the Roman Catholic Church entertains the same position concerning curses, black magic, and possession. For more information, the reader should consult *Evidence of Satan in the Modern World* by Leon Cristiani.

dice against the hospital's therapeutic work. Such bias existed when the institution first began its work but was rapidly overcome. "With the passing of time and because of the good treatment patients receive at the hospital," claimed the elderly spokesman, "the situation has improved. Today there are many [people] who *prefer* the treatment received at this hospital and a considerable number seek us out just because of our healer-mediums. To sum up I would say that prejudice is exceptional, mainly confined to people who don't think for themselves."

Probably the most surprising aspect of the hospital's work relates to its staff physicians, who do not necessarily sympathize with Kardecismo philosophy. (This shouldn't be considered strange, since many Jewish and Protestant doctors in the United States work in Catholic hospitals.)

"Our doctors do not interfere with the mediumistic service, and the mediums don't interfere with the medical area," commented Ferrari.

While collecting material on Brazil and its psychic practices, Ann Dooley conducted a poll of several psychiatrists practicing in the south of Brazil. They were all sympathetic to the hospital and considered its patient care and psychiatric programs excellent.

Psychotherapy based specifically on psychic and mediumistic treatment is not restricted to Brazil's spirit hospitals, of which the institute in Porto Allegre is representative. Some psychiatrists conduct depossession work in private practice or maintain clinics for this same purpose. Probably the two best-known practitioners of spirit psychiatry in South America are both (predictably enough) Kardecismo followers. The first is Dr. Eliezer C. Mendes, a retired surgeon currently operating a therapeutic community in the outskirts of São Paolo. He also treats patients privately in his office within the city. The other therapist is the kindly Dr. Inacio Ferreira, who is somewhat of an elder spokesman for Kardecismo philosophy and psychiatry. He practices in the small town of Uberaba, which is a five-hour flight from Rio de Janeiro. He has worked steadily with patients suffering from spirit possession since 1959, and in his several books he claims that 80 percent of all mental illness is due to this cause. Dr. Ferreira originally offered his services free of charge, but he was forced for financial reasons to institute fees in 1969.

Dr. Ferreira has published several startling cases of spirit possession in his books, which unfortunately have never been translated into English. Because both he and Dr. Mendes are followers of Kardecismo spiritism, they believe that reincarnation memories can contribute to the possession syndrome.

To explain this concept in a little more depth, let's take a detailed look at Dr. Mendes's work.

Dr. Mendes currently operates therapeutic communities in four Brazilian cities, where he specializes in the treatment of epilepsy and schizophrenia. He especially likes to work with people suffering from multiple personality. His work has been summarized in a privately printed book, whose title translates from the Portuguese as *Psychological Synthesis in Clinical Parapsychology*. It is important to remember, though, that Dr. Mendes's use of the term *psychosynthesis* has little relationship to other psychological systems that use the same title. Dr. Mendes believes, like most of his Kardecismo colleagues, that spirit obsession and possession primarily affect psychically gifted people. When he deals with particularly recalcitrant cases of multiple personality, it is his opinion that these personalities often constitute the patient's former lives still existing within their psyches. They represent karmic remnants that can be triggered into emergence when the patient suffers a physical or psychological trauma.

The way this process—and its cure—works has been described by Dr. Stanley Krippner, who visited Dr. Mendes in Brazil and reported on his work in 1985. Dr. Krippner, a professor of psychology at the Saybrook Institute in San Francisco, made this report to the Second International Conference on Multiple Personality/Dissociative States, which convened in Chicago. The following excerpt from his report summarizes a typical case from the Brazilian therapist's files.

> In an interview with me, he described one case he had treated that involved a 12-year-old girl who, at the onset of puberty, began to play boys' games in the street. At the same time, she started to exhibit a critical attitude toward her rapidly-developing female physiology. Mendes consulted a group of mediums he refers to as a "superteam" because of their alleged proficiency in diagnosis. This superteam reported that the client had been a male in a previous life and that this former personality had been evoked by the biological changes accompanying puberty. After about three months of psychotherapy, the alleged alternate (or alter) male personality was merged with the host female personality. The girl's gender was accepted by what Mendes referred to as the client's "psychological center," a deep-seated aspect of the psyche underlying all personalities, both host and alter.

During the treatment of this case, no formal depossession was undertaken or really even required. Dr. Mendes used his team of psychics to properly diagnose the client's problem and then relied on this information to develop a program of psychotherapy for her. Sometimes his cases involve more serious problems, however, and formal depossession must be implemented—even if the possessor is an element drawn from the patient's own psyche! This is especially true of people suffering from multiple personality; for these patients Dr. Mendes employs a four-stage program of psychological treatment.

1. **Diagnostic stage of evaluation.** In order to properly diagnose a patient's spiritual problems, Dr. Mendes relies upon a group of three psychics who meet directly with the client. During this preliminary meeting, the patient is encouraged to enter into a trance or other change of consciousness, which is implemented through special music and dance. When the patient begins to respond to the music and body exercises, the psychics make contact with his obsessors (whether they be discarnate entities, the sufferer's previous lives, or simply aspects of the client's present personality).

2. **Early treatment program.** Each of the patient's secondary personalities is given a chance to express him- or herself through the patient so that the emotional life of the personality can be examined and explored. This exploration is undertaken by the client with the help of the psychics and the therapist.

   The therapist then begins to synthesize the personalities by creating common linkages between them and by teaching them to cooperate by forming a single personality.

   It is Dr. Mendes's feeling that a patient's secondary personalities must be encouraged to reveal themselves before they can be synthesized. He strongly criticizes those forms of therapy that seek to repress their emergence, feeling that such procedures can be detrimental to a patient's well-being.

   Sometimes, however, secondary personalities represent either spirits of the dead or particularly destructive karmic carryovers from a past life. The proper therapy for this condition is formal exorcism and no synthesis is considered.

3. **Later treatment strategies.** This stage of Dr. Mendes's program evolves naturally from the second, in which each of the patient's secondary personalities is merged back into the primary personality. The weaker personalities usually disappear first, and then the

stronger personality must be dealt with psychologically. Serious questions may develop at this point depending on the patient's problem. If the patient's strongest secondary personality is merely part of the existing personality, it usually merges through proper synthesis, in the same way Dr. W. Franklin Prince cured his foster daughter, Doris Fischer. Carryovers from the patient's previous lives usually become expunged, while exorcism is employed for discarnate entities or entities sent by a sorcerer or other practitioner of black magic.

4. **Group ritual therapy.** Dr. Mendes also believes that it is therapeutic to conduct group sessions with his patients. These ritualistic sessions include dancing, movement exercises, and psychodrama-like procedures (in which the patients are encouraged to dramatize their problems). Friends of the patients and even casual visitors to the center are prompted to join in the sessions. Sometimes folk healers from the local community will participate and will give laying-on-of-hands during the rituals.

Some patients respond successfully to this form of therapeutic intervention. Like most unorthodox psychiatric practitioners, Dr. Mendes can claim a fair share of clinical successes with multiple personality patients. The story of his patient Sonia is probably a typical success story, and her case's main features were also presented by Dr. Krippner at the Chicago convention.

Sonia was an eighteen-year-old woman who resided in the city of Salvador. Her problem stemmed from her inability to establish lasting relationships with members of the opposite sex. She was prone to brief and frequent sexual encounters that never resulted in orgastic fulfillment (which, though not pointed out by Dr. Krippner, is typical of people prone to rampant anonymous sexual involvements). The unfortunate girl finally realized that something was wrong when she began experiencing memory lapses. Sometimes she physically fought with her escorts but could never remember the incidents. At other times she would book several dates for the same evening, only to be shocked when her callers arrived simultaneously! These troubling circumstances led her to seek hospital treatment, where she received drug therapy and electroconvulsive shock.

It was fortunate that Sonia was finally directed to Dr. Mendes, who scheduled several sessions with her during which she met with his group of psychics. At the first of these sessions, the girl was encouraged to pass into trance. This request posed little problem for Sonia, but to the surprise of everybody present, she became controlled by a personality who spoke fluent French. Sonia had never formally studied the language and the controlling persona called herself "Violetta." She was apparently a past life of the girl's and had purportedly lived in eighteenth-century France. She wanted to kill Sonia to take complete control of her body. This personality was extremely promiscuous and was the source of Sonia's poor sexual adjustment and dissociative episodes.

Dr. Mendes treated his troubled client in his São Paolo office. Over the course of six sessions he merged her secondary personality's strong aspects back into Sonia's own poorly developed personality. This synthesis was partially accomplished by limiting "Violetta's" power to control the girl, who suddenly began to experience full orgasm for the first time.

Even though the synthesis between Sonia and her eighteenth-century past life was successful, there were complications disrupting the therapy. Another secondary personality emerged during Dr. Mendes's treatment program. This personality claimed to be a Jewish housewife from the sixteenth century and another of Sonia's past lives. She was extremely mature and was apparently beneficial to the patient, so Dr. Mendes didn't immediately synthesize her with Sonia.

Sonia responded so well to the therapy that she eventually married. But then secondary personality number three emerged from her mind. This male personality claimed to be a former Chinese spiritual initiate. The emergence of this secondary personality also seemed beneficial to the patient, even though the entity seemed to be a genuine discarnate.

"Sonia claimed to recall seeing all three of the alter personalities when she was a child," reported Dr. Krippner to the conference on multiple personality, "and considered them to be her spirit playmates. When she told her mother about them, she was scolded, told that she was 'crazy,' and warned never to talk about them again. The recall of childhood experiences appeared to accelerate Sonia's therapy. A merging took place after 18 months of work with [Dr.] Mendes, and the psychological synthesis reportedly was still intact three years later."

Dr. Mendes's work is tolerated in Brazil, but it certainly doesn't possess an imprimatur from the country's psychiatric establishment. Despite his sometimes striking clinical successes, Dr. Mendes isn't allowed to present his work before medical meetings, and he receives little support from the psychiatric community. Most Brazilian psychologists are skeptical of his procedures, and he is not allowed to call himself a clinical psychologist.

It is, of course, difficult to determine whether the surgeon's successes result from simple suggestion or from genuinely psychic (i.e., reincarnation or possession) factors. But whatever the reason, Dr. Mendes claims a remarkable cure rate. He claims to have rehabilitated some 70 percent of his multiple personality patients and a whopping 85 percent of his epileptic clients by using past-life or depossession procedures. He only claims a 15 percent success rate, however, when dealing with schizophrenics.

Despite the fact that both Dr. Ferreira and Dr. Mendes conduct their work without official psychiatric sanction, they are not Brazil's only explorers of the infinite boundary. Similar work is currently being undertaken by Hernani G. Andrade, who is probably Brazil's most respected, most scholarly, and most widely published parapsychologist. He is also a Kardecian Spiritist and is devoting considerable time to depossession work and reincarnation research, even though his educational background is in the field of engineering. He has reported on his work in a series of pamphlets and papers issued by his own organization, the Brazilian Institute for Psychobiophysical Research in São Paolo.* Andrade estimates that he has encountered and treated over a thousand cases of spirit obsession and possession. The procedures he uses for his treatment are based on Kardecismo. He uses the services of several psychics who circle themselves around the patient during special séances in order to establish contact with the possessing entity. Some of the members of the group (who don't become entranced) then reason with the offending spirit and convince it to depart.

Repossession is always a serious possibility in such cases, so after the conclusion of the treatment considerable follow-up is required to protect the client. Special diets and foods may be used in conjunction with psychologically oriented procedures such as prayer, imagery exercises (so the client can "shield" himself from any further possessing entities), and spiritual rituals.

Hernani Andrade is not merely a follower of Kardecismo, though. He is also an extremely well-informed and critical parapsychologist keenly

*Some of the work of this indefatigable researcher is reported by Guy Lyon Playfair in his books *The Unknown Power* and *The Indefinite Boundary*. Playfair lived in Brazil for several years and is personally familiar with the researcher's work.

aware of the traditions both of the Society for Psychical Research and of the American Society for Psychical Research. His critical and skeptical approach to his research has even caused occasional problems between his institute and the Kardecismo establishment.

The contents of this chapter may strike the reader as especially strange. The work of such Kardecismo practitioners as Dr. Ferreira, Dr. Mendes, and Hernani Andrade seems to be a hodge-podge of psychodrama, Spiritualism, and superstition presented in the form of a makeshift psychology. Their work stands in striking contrast to the pristine simplicity of the similar research pioneered by Dr. Titus Bull, Dr. W. Franklin Prince, Dr. Elwood Worcester, and others in our country— researchers who didn't complicate their work with reincarnation claims, black magic, or ritualized shamanic practices.

It is suspicious, in fact, that these American researchers never confronted the specific types of "reincarnation" cases reported by their South American confrères. It looks as if cases of past-life possession occur *only* in those countries where reincarnation is a popular religious or folk belief! This would suggest that Brazilian cases of spirit possession are a cultural and psychological phenomenon rather than anything genuinely paranormal. I am especially skeptical of cases such as Dr. Mendes's, since Sonia's past life as the sexually liberated "Violetta" in France is surprisingly similar to the fictitious "Violetta" who serves as the heroine of Giuseppe Verdi's opera *La Traviata*. (This opera is very popular in Brazil.)

If we may extrapolate from this simple but important principle, it seems logical to conclude that the spirit possession syndrome in general is purely the result of psychological conflicts.

I am pointing this out only as a possibility, however. For the suggestion that cases of spirit obsession and possession may be purely psychological must be considered in light of the Thompson/Gifford case, which directly points to the literal reality of the syndrome.

Despite cultural dissimilarities between those possession cases reported from the United States and those reported from Brazil, some of the practices of the Kardecismo rescue circles have begun to gain a foothold in our country. The cases summarized in this chapter may seem strange only because they were reported from a strange and unfamiliar culture. Not only are similar Kardecismo-based depossession groups operating in this country, but a few are even being conducted by psychologists and psychiatrists!

I first made this discovery by way of some rather unusual circumstances, so I'm going to digress from our main subject momentarily.

Like most researchers professionally involved in the field of parapsychology, I retain a membership in the Parapsychological Association, whose membership consists of an international body of researchers interested in the scientific study of psychic phenomena. It is a professional organization for parapsychologists, just as the American Medical Association is this country's leading society of physicians. The organization was first formed in 1957 by the late J. B. Rhine, who felt that the field deserved its own peer-reviewed and elected professional society. Most of its full members possess their doctorates and maintain research positions or college teaching posts.

Toward the end of each summer, the Parapsychological Association organizes an international convention so that everybody working in the field can meet and share their latest research findings and progress. These conferences can become boring and tedious, though, since the focus of the convention is usually devoted to experimental research on ESP and psychokinesis that is being conducted in labs all around the United States and Europe. That means that those attending end up sitting through endless debates over experimental designs, statistics, and so forth, for four days straight! Most of the research chosen for presentation by the program committee is mainstream and unexceptional. Most of the papers and research briefs concern such issues as whether the mind can influence subatomic particles, whether people who believe in psychic phenomena score better on ESP tests than skeptics, and so forth. The triviality of many of the presentations would be shocking if it weren't so sleep-inducing.

I've been going to these conferences for many years, probably more out of a sense of professional responsibility than from keen interest. Despite the chronic boredom, though, these conventions have their fair share of benefits. It is a genuine pleasure to see your colleagues in person, to socialize with them, and to share future research plans together. Some of the field's most important breakthroughs are first presented there, too. These conventions also usually present informal programs in the evenings. These meetings often consist of round-table discussions and workshops devoted to more off-beat and speculative subjects than the earlier more formal contributions. They are not an official part of the conference but are sometimes more enlightening than the scientific experimental papers! It was during such a round table that I learned that depossessing work is still being practiced in the United States.

My discovery came during the 1986 convention, which convened on the sparkling campus of California State University at Sonoma in Rohnert Park. This modern and picturesque community is situated some sixty miles north of the Bay area, sitting in dramatic contrast to the European formalism of San Francisco and Oakland. The weather there is wonderful during the summer, and it was a pleasure to stroll down to the meeting rooms from the dormitories every morning. Each evening, though, I had to decide whether to sit through a workshop or drive into town for some dinner and light entertainment. This was especially hard when one postsession workshop was being devoted to "channeling"—the psychic practice of "bringing through" foreign intelligences, who like to pontificate endlessly on metaphysical issues and social concerns. The skill seems to be a contemporary mixture of voluntary dissociation and old-fashioned trance mediumship, but my opinion is that most channeling is a psychological rather than a paranormal phenomenon. Channeling is the current rage in my home state of California. It seems to be partially a learned skill. Channeling became popular in the 1970s in part due to the work of the late Jane Roberts of Elmira, New York, whose trance personality "Seth" dictated a series of best-selling books. Since the death of Mrs. Roberts a few years ago, several new channelers have been riding the metaphysical bandwagon, and everyone seems to be practicing the skill.

Frankly, I wasn't too keen when it came to this round table. I tried reading the Seth books when they were first published, but I eventually found raking up the leaves from my mulberry tree more interesting and spiritually enhancing. (I find that most channeled discourses possess the spiritual and philosophical sophistication of a Dick-and-Jane book.) So when I saw the program listed for that night, it struck me that eating a pizza in town would be more enjoyable and certainly more philosophically satisfying.

Despite these reservations, I ended up sitting through the meeting because my ex–research assistant from New York was bugging me to keep him company. I was glad that I went, and much to my surprise, most of the presentations were genuinely fascinating. I was amazed at the sophistication of the talks, and most of the reports concerned psychological and linguistic strategies for examining channeled information.

During the presentations I kept watching a young gentleman sitting up on the rostrum with the other speakers. Most of the speakers were professional colleagues of mine, but this presenter was a stranger.

He was rather boyish and looked in his late twenties, was nicely but not elegantly dressed, and walked with a delightful bounce. His hair was short, which contributed to his pixyish and cheerful demeanor. When it was his turn to speak, I learned that his name was Matthew Bronson and that his background was in the field of linguistics. He was currently working in the hard business world with a computer company in Oakland, but he had recently developed channeling skills and was eager to explore his evolving psychic capabilities. Bronson spoke for twenty minutes about his sudden development as a channel—and about his recent work with a Kardecismo group performing depossessions right nearby the Bay area.

Bronson was an engaging speaker, and I resolved to meet him when the workshop concluded. What resulted was an immediate friendship, during which I received some fascinating insights into the experiential side of spirit rescue work. (It was an educationally symbiotic relationship, too, since Matthew was surprised to learn of the work of Dr. Carl Wickland and others.)

I was able to meet with Matthew several times between the summer and end of 1986, and I tape-recorded the story behind his work during a short trip I took to the Bay area that November.

Matthew Bronson's spiritual odyssey began innocuously enough while he was vacationing in Brazil in the spring of 1984. (He spoke fluent Spanish and was partly using the trip to learn Portuguese.) He wasn't exactly callow to the strange world of popular metaphysics, having been born and raised in California, where off-beat religion and philosophy are rife. His interest in metaphysics had been sparked in his early life by his interest in holistic health practices and their philosophical underpinnings. But in 1984 he was visiting Brazil simply as a tourist. So one evening after being in the country for several days, he and his traveling companions decided to visit an Umbanda ritual. It was being conducted at an Umbanda center outside São Paolo. The usual public Umbanda ritual incorporates elements both from shamanic folklore and from Spiritualism. The ceremony is extremely colorful and noisy since drum beatings, chanting, and dancing are incorporated into it. These practices help the Umbanda followers pass into trance and bring through deities, guardian spirits, and other supernatural beings.

Matthew and his friends were observing just such a ritual, which was being attended by followers drawn from Brazil's disparate social classes. He was particularly fascinated when one of the Umbanda worshippers, who were sitting in a circle in front of an altar, became entranced and began dancing spontaneously in response to the rhythmic drumming. She then began shivering, and when a spirit entity incorporated into her body, she started to speak in the entity's curious style of punctuated speech. The spirit being must have been pretty earthy, since it forced the woman to stick a huge cigar in her mouth! The woman (or her controller) then promenaded around the circle of followers, strategically touching specific points on each of their bodies. This ritual was meant to enable each of them to enter into trance. She was successful, too, since each of the followers shook and routinely passed into trance as the ritual frantically progressed.

Soon everybody in the Umbanda circle was incorporating spirits into their beings, and the visitors to the center were invited to join the ritual and receive the group leader's healing power.

"My turn came and I walked up there [into the group]," Matthew told me. "The lady touched me on a couple of places on my arm, kind of like pressure points."

The young, unsuspecting tourist was nothing if not surprised by what happened next. "I felt this tremendous warmth and kind of a whitish light that sort of filled up my entire being," he explained. "My whole head filled up and the music, at the same time, was in exact cadence with the internal changes I was going with. It began to beat and go faster and faster. I was suddenly aware that I was on the brink of a very profound spiritual experience, and then there was a moment of hesitation almost as though I could feel—up to the left and behind me—this presence, this sort of ball of light or energy that was waiting to come in and occupy my body if I would but stand aside."

Matthew realized that this critical point in his spiritual initiation was a "moment of truth" and that his responsibility was either to reject or to incorporate the presence. He instantly sized up the situation and decided to flow with the experience, since he trusted the Umbandist circle and the sense of love and community emanating from it.

"When I made that decision I felt these bands of warm energy and color coming all at once," he explained to me. "It was as if the Matthew you're speaking to now stepped aside and became a fair witness looking through thick glasses, witnessing what next took place. I found that I was beginning to hoot, holler and dance and the drumming was going right along with it."

The young linguistics student was coming to a critical phase in his Umbanda shamanism, but then the circle's leader motioned for the music to stop. Matthew knew that he was fully entranced, but he didn't lose consciousness. Instead he found himself dancing and twirling like a whirling Dervish, and he finally proceeded to speak involuntarily in Portuguese. What he said wasn't particularly enlightening and consisted of a single phrase repeated several times. He stopped spinning and only emerged from trance when the leader began touching specific points on his body.

"I felt all cleaned out inside," he told me, "like I'd been scrubbed out with steel wool or something." Later that night, the leader told Matthew that he possessed a powerful spirit protector.

Matthew didn't pursue his burgeoning mediumship even after this experience but simply returned to the Untied States and to his white-collar desk. But fate seemed to be planning a different course for his future, for he was reinitiated into the world of the paranormal some months later, under circumstances equally puzzling and spontaneous.

Sometime toward the end of 1985, some people in the Bay area decided to bring an eminent Brazilian psychic healer to California. Edson Queiroz lives in the city of Recife on the coast of Brazil. It is claimed that he can remove tumors with his psychic powers, that his spirit control is a deceased German physician, and that he can create painless and miraculous incisions on his patients' bodies with common knives. Many of these claims seem based on Brazilian folk medicine (or "psychic surgery"), and Edson is merely the most famous of several such practitioners in Brazil. Despite what may seem like folkloric elements in his work, Edson Queiroz is a committed follower of Kardecismo. He doesn't blend his philosophy with elements derived from Brazil's other psychic sects.

The reason for his visit to California was simple: Some of his contacts in this country wanted to know more about psychic healing and how it could be implemented.

As I explained earlier, the existence of spirit possession is doctrinal in all forms of Brazilian Spiritism, the same way it is in our indigenous Spiritualism. Brazilian Spiritism also teaches, however, that some physical conditions may result from this form of spiritual influence.

Edson Queiroz was explaining these principles to a group of people meeting with him in Palo Alto, a beautiful community several miles south of San Francisco. It was January 1986, and the workshop was being conducted in a suite of rooms at a local hotel.* Matthew was

---

*In order to insure the privacy of the people involved in the following story, a few identifying features of the people and their meeting have been changed.

attending the meeting since his Portuguese was now fairly fluent and the psychic couldn't speak English. He had been recruited to interpret by a contact within the group. Later during the ten-day workshop, the whole group visited a local healing center where holistic health practices such as visualization exercises were being used to help cancer patients. This visit was crucial for Matthew. It turned out that a person who worked with the center was disfigured by a lesion or tumor bulging from her face, the result of a complication from a patch of skin cancer. She wasn't responding to conventional therapy. The Brazilian healer noticed the woman but didn't treat her or clairvoyantly diagnose her problem for the group. But when he returned to Palo Alto with his students, Edson Queiroz started talking about this particularly unfortunate patient.

The story becomes wild from this point, so perhaps Matthew should explain the rest of the proceedings in his own words.

This particular evening Edson related to us that he noticed with his clairvoyance that there was a "vampiric" spirit that was stuck to this woman, who was completely fascinated by her. The spirit was literally sucking the life energy from her, he said, and especially from the large lesion or cancerous tumor that was present on her face. It was a grizzly entity with bulbous eyes and it was skeletal and followed her wherever she went. Edson then explained that, in a case where you have a spirit which is obsessing some one and stuck and fixated on them, this will hold in place any illnesses which are spiritually or karmically derived. He felt that this was the case, that this spirit was preventing this woman's recovery and presented a real block in her evolution as a person. He also felt that it could be dealt with and would be an ideal case for disobsession therapy.

So we were very curious about it, and he said we should go ahead and do some disobsession! He had turned to me earlier and said (in Portuguese), "Matthew, would you mind serving as the intermediary this evening?" I wasn't sure what he meant since I was already serving as the intermediary since I was his interpreter. It sounded like an interesting suggestion, though, so I said sure.

We proceeded to darken the room and put on a red light. We had a group of about fourteen people and soon we were asked to pray and put ourselves in a trance state by imagining ourselves in a comfortable and beautiful place. We understand that we were to be invoking this vampiric spirit obsessing the lady with the tumor [who wasn't present but back at the center]. Edson came over to me and the energy was right, I suppose, and he began to press his hands over my head and chest area. I felt some energy coming from his hands, and he set it up so that once I incorporated the spirit [another member of the group] would help the spirit along to recognize it was dead and needed to take its place of progression, was causing a lot of ill and harm, and that his presence wasn't welcome or requested. So at a certain point Edson said, "I ask that the spirit associated with this woman now come and incorporate into our brother Matthew."

What resulted was a replay of Matthew's experience with the Umbanda circle outside São Paolo in 1984. But this time the sensations were more frightening.

I became aware of kind of a coldness rather than energy—which was the case with my experience with Umbanda. It was like a lack of energy in a space that was up to the left behind me, and I knew or had the feeling that this was the spirit that had been invoked by Edson. The only other experience I had with anything like "channeling" was my prior experience with Umbanda, so I didn't have a lot of experience to relate my feelings to. But once again I had that same sort of moment of truth where I felt like this wasn't the sort of spirit I wanted to deal with, and I didn't want to let this spirit enter my body. I was having a lot of second thoughts. So I thought, "What the hell, I might as well go for it."

The coming of the spirit was like a coldness and hunger which came over me. There was this tightness in my throat, which I've always felt ever since when I incorporate a spirit entity. Then [the other member of the group] invited the spirit to speak and come into the group and share his story and let us know what was going on with him. At first there was this low sort of howling that I produced. What was going on was that, once again, it was as though I was just a witness kind of in the background listening to my own voice, just having these pictures, images, or half-formed sensations coming up as well. It was like having a split awareness and part of me was with my normal self and the other was undergoing these other experiences.

My interviewer kept talking to the spirit, telling it to come and speak to us. So the spirit began to speak, and in a very high kind of whining voice alien to my own related its story.

What followed was a typical Brazilian-style obsession story, in which reincarnation elements were conspicuously present.

Matthew (or the entity controlling his speech) explained that "she" was a mother who lived with her small daughter in the high, plains region of some country. The village where she lived was undergoing a severe famine, and she had deserted her daughter in their hut in order to search for food. Since a blizzard was occurring outside, her sojourn was doomed to failure, and she became lost in the snow. She eventually found her way back to the village, but to her shock her daughter was dead. She had expired from exposure and starvation.

"I had this clear image of holding the child and looking at these wide and vacant eyes," Matthew tried to explain. "She was a two-year-old child and feelings of terrible grief and anguish came over me. And tremendous anger in which I said I'd never leave the girl again."

The rest of the story contained the reincarnation element. It turned out that the cancer patient was the alleged reincarnation of the dead child. The woman had died of exposure soon after her daughter's death, but her grief had prevented her from progressing into the world beyond. She had wandered in some kind of earthbound condition for centuries and was currently possessing the daughter's present incarnation. The entity wasn't really evil but was merely fulfilling her promise to stay with her daughter.

Luckily for the cancer patient and the presumed entity, the little group in Palo Alto convinced the obsessing entity to depart and seek enlightenment in the world of spirits.

"It was a pretty good first deobsession, so far as we could tell," said Matthew in a disarming, matter-of-fact way.

Little more was undertaken that evening, but the group met for another workshop the following evening. It was then that the result of the previous night's work came to light. While visiting the cancer center earlier in the day, a person working with the group had run into the cancer patient. She was awed by the woman's stunning appearance, since it appeared that her tumor had shrunk! The patient, of course, still knew nothing of the work implemented by the group in Palo Alto on her case. But when she was told of the previous meeting, she willingly made a curious concession. She explained that she had always felt a presence connected to her. This sensation dated back to her childhood.

From what I gathered from my talks with Matthew, the patient continued to improve physically though she suffered a momentary relapse. Unfortunately, neither Matthew nor his original group followed up the case to a proper extent. They knew only that she continued to improve after she openly confronted the possible past-life cause of her problem.

It is, of course, difficult to evaluate this sort of story. Although I received it directly from Matthew, whose good faith and honesty I have no reason to question, it is neither more nor less impressive than many "psychic" tales that find their way into print. Before passing judgment on this series of events, we would need to carefully document the clinical history of the patient's cancer. We'd need to know what kind of therapy had been previously used to relieve the lesion. Why had it failed? What sort of current treatment was she undergoing? We would also want to explore what positive events were occurring in her personal life at the time the healing took place. Cancers and tumors can spontaneously remit when a patient's psychological outlook improves, so perhaps the shrinkage of the tumor was purely coincidental to the group's effort.

I find this possibility feasible in this particular case. Matthew explained to me that Edson Queiroz had been fascinated by this patient when he first saw her. Perhaps she noticed the famous healer's interest and unconsciously deduced that he would be willing to help her condition. Some sort of placebo effect could have resulted; since psychologists know that people suffering emotionally linked problems often improve if they think they'll soon be receiving help.

I'm not trying to explain away this report or present these theoretical possibilities as certainties. I'm only trying to demonstrate the difficulties involved in researching a case of psychic healing—or even conventional healing, for that matter!

What is interesting, though, is that the experiences of Matthew and his friends coincide with those of others involved in similar work. While collecting information regarding spirit rescue work, I reread Dr. Carl Wickland's *Thirty Years Among the Dead* for the first time in twenty years. I noticed that he and his wife also reported the cure of physical conditions; they didn't limit their work specifically to psychological disturbances. Dr. Wickland reported that some of his patients were cured of brain tumors, paralysis, chronic invalidism, and so forth—even though his spirit contacts specifically refuted the reincarnation doctrine when requested to comment on it! I've collected no evidence that Dr. Titus Bull worked with similar patients, but there are hints in his writings that he experimented with the possibility.

But is spirit possession merely a psychological disturbance that responds to suggestion or to psychic healing? Or is it a genuine reality? This complicated riddle will be discussed in Chapter 14.

Suffice it to say that Kardecismo groups and those following Dr. Wickland's works still exist in this country. Matthew Bronson is currently working with such a rescue circle in northern California that treats people suffering both from cancer and from psychological disorders. Similar work is being conducted in Nevada, where a group exists that is devoted to the psychic and spiritual deliverance of people suffering from multiple personality. Remember, too, that Spiritualism never died out completely in the United States, and every major city has its fair share of small churches, often in storefronts or private homes. It is impossible to know the extent to which rescue work is performed every day in these places of spiritual communion. It is also impossible to know who is benefiting from it.

CHAPTER **13**

THE SPIRITUAL SIDE
OF MULTIPLE PERSONALITY

"In the first case we got rid of four different demons," the conservative gentleman reported, "each representing a particular lie. After getting rid of these four, there only seemed to be two left, the demons of lust and hate. Those two were surprising to the team. The demons spoke in the third person. Whether that reflects something about demon's reality, I don't know, but it hid behind Jesus."

The speaker's audience was undoubtedly surprised by these candid remarks, since they weren't being offered by a priest, minister, self-styled exorcist, or even by a fundamentalist giving his personal "evidence" for Christianity. They were being offered by a respected psychiatrist who was talking about his work with two multiple personality cases. The psychiatrist was not speaking before a religious congregation, but to newspaper and media reporters meeting with him in Connecticut. His remarks were later incorporated into an interview published in the December 14, 1985 edition of the *Los Angeles Times*.

Dr. M. Scott Peck can be proud of his eminent career in conventional psychiatry. He received his education at Harvard University and served in the Army Medical Corps from 1963 to 1972, eventually becoming the assistant chief of psychiatry to the U.S. Army's Surgeon General. Since his resignation from the military, he has built and maintained a private practice in New Preston, Connecticut. Although Dr. Peck's background is primarily psychoanalytic, he does not share the

243

typical Freudian dislike of religion. He is actually fascinated by the possibilities of mankind's spiritual capacities.

The study of religion has led Dr. Peck through an intense spiritual odyssey, from practicing Eastern religion back to his original Christian faith. His interest in the spiritual side of life encouraged him to write his first book, *The Road Less Traveled*, in 1978, a best seller that concerned the spiritual side both of psychology and love. This volume was followed by an even more extraordinary book in 1983: *People of the Lie* concerns our capacity for psychological evil, a type of focused dysfunction more intricate than the simple unfeelingness and destructiveness of the common psychopath. The book also deals with spiritual evil, for Dr. Peck believes that he has confronted this force twice during the course of his career. In both cases the forces were focused on patients suffering from multiple personality, but their problems were spiritual rather than purely psychological. To put it more succinctly, Dr. Peck believes that some cases of multiple personality represent a form of demonic possession.

Because of his ethical concern for patient confidentiality, Dr. Peck doesn't offer his readers precise case studies. He talks about these two instances of spirit possession more generally but with enough detail for the reader to appreciate his extraordinary experiences.

These cases were exceptional in his career. He actually had to seek out examples of spiritual evil. "In fifteen years of busy psychiatric practice," he wrote in his book, "I had never seen anything faintly resembling a case." He was interested in the possible existence of such cases, though, and began asking his colleagues for referrals if they should encounter cases implicating spiritual evil in their own practices. He was soon receiving such referrals, but the first two patients he evaluated were false alarms, since they seemed to be suffering from conventional psychiatric disorders. But his third case and a fourth patient seemed to be the real thing—cases in which the presence of genuine evil was the spiritual root of the patients' problems.

The patients were very different people, explained the psychiatrist: the first was prone to bursts of mania and psychosis while the second suffered more from chronic depression. The first patient *knew* that he suffered from possession, although his previous psychiatrist refused to believe in the possibility. The gentleman had been referred to Dr. Peck when conventional psychotherapy and chemotherapy failed to work. The second patient wasn't so insightful, and it was his psychiatrist who first suspected demonic possession. "In both cases," reported the psychiatrist, "the major distinction in differential diagnosis was between possession and multiple personality disorders." But the cases didn't conform to the conventional clinical picture of such cases.

"In multiple personality disorder the 'core personality' is virtually always unaware of the existence of the secondary personalities," explained Dr. Peck in *People of the Lie*, "at least until close to the very end of prolonged, successful treatment. In other words, a true dissociation exists. In these two cases, however, both patients were either aware from the beginning or were readily made aware not only of the self-destructive part of them but also that this part had a distinct and *alien* personality. To the contrary, it quickly became clear that the secondary personality *desired* to confuse them. In many ways the secondary personality seemed like a personified resistance. The second differentiation is that while in multiple personality disorders the secondary personality may play the role of the 'whore' or 'aggressive one' or 'the independent one' or someone with other unacknowledged traits, it has never been reported to my knowledge as being frankly evil.* In both these cases before exorcism the secondary personality was revealed to be blatantly evil."

Both cases were finally diagnosed properly through a charismatic practice called "deliverance", which is part of a wider deliverance ministry currently popular among some Christian groups. Deliverance is a form of confrontational prayer challenge in which the participants (usually a minister and a prayer group) exhort a possibly possessed person to bring forth his demons. If the patient really is possessed, the entities controlling his body usually will emerge and reveal their identities by speaking through the victims. They usually don't give proper names but rather call themselves by the particular vice they sport. So according to charismatic Christianity, a person might be controlled by the demon of lust, or by the demon of slothfulness, or even by the demon of epilepsy.

What Dr. Peck feels were probably evil spirits presented themselves in both cases, though only after he and his colleagues engaged in prolonged work and exhortations with the patients. Even though he is openly critical of such procedures in most cases, he believes the revelations were justified in these particular instances. (Dr. Peck is critical

---

*This point could be debated since some secondary personalities can be genuinely psychopathic, bordering on evil. Henry Hawksworth, a California real estate salesman whose case is detailed in his book *The Five of Me*, had a secondary personality who went by the name of "Johnny." Even when Hawksworth was a child, this personality was prone to murderous inclinations and behavior.

of ministers who practice deliverance for keeping track neither of their failures nor of those patients who regress to their former problems. He also believes that the procedures can be harmful for some mental patients.)

Since conventional psychiatry wasn't working for either of these two patients, Dr. Peck decided to treat them with carefully planned exorcisms. These rites were not undertaken lightly, and he relied on groups of workers to administer them. The exact constitution of these exorcism teams is not explained in *People of the Lie*, but more details were offered by Dr. Peck in his 1985 newspaper interview. The first exorcism lasted for four days and the workers consisted of a bishop, a nun, a psychologist, a retired physician, and two additional lay persons. The second exorcism took place over a period of three days, with the ministrations of two psychologists, two psychiatrists, a minister, and three lay persons.

In order to properly appreciate what Dr. Peck witnessed, his own words should be cited.

> Once the exorcism was begun, with appropriate prayer and ritual, in both these cases silence seemed the most effective of the many means used for the final penetration of the Pretense. The team would speak either with the patient's healthy core personality or the demon(s) but would refuse to speak with some unclear mixture of the two. It took some time before the team in each case became adept at doing this. For the demon itself seemed to have a marked ability to draw the exorcist or team into confusing conversation that went nowhere. But as the team became more perceptive and steadfastly refused to be sucked in, both these patients began to alternate between a progressively more healthy-appearing core personality and a progressively more ugly secondary personality, until suddenly the secondary personality took on inhuman features and the Pretense was broken.
>
> As a hardheaded scientist—which I assume myself to be—I can explain 95 percent of what went on in these two cases by traditional psychiatric dynamics. For instance, the effectiveness of the aforementioned "silent treatment" required no demons for explanation. Perhaps particularly because they were lonely people, thirsting for relationships, the technique encouraged the appearance of separate selves (which could be related with) and hence the necessity to choose between those selves. In regard to the possession, I could talk in terms of "splitting" and "psychic introjects." And in regard to the exorcisms, I could talk in terms of brainwashing, deprogramming, reprogramming, catharsis, marathon group

therapy and identification. But I am left with a critical 5 percent I cannot explain in such ways. I am left with the supernatural—or better yet, subnatural. I am left with what [Malachi] Martin called the Presence.

When the demonic finally spoke clearly in one case, an expression appeared on the patient's face that could be described only as Satanic. It was an incredibly contemptuous grin of utter hostile malevolence. I have spent many hours before a mirror trying to imitate it without the slightest success. I have seen that expression only one other time in my life—for a few fleeting seconds on the face of the other patient, late in the evaluation period. Yet when the demonic finally revealed itself in the exorcism of this other patient, it was with a still more ghastly expression. The patient suddenly resembled a writhing snake of great strength, viciously attempting to bite the team members. More frightening than the writhing body, however, was the face. The eyes were hooded with lazy reptilian torpor—except when the reptile darted out in attack, at which moment the eyes would open wide with blazing hatred. Despite these frequent darting moments, what upset me the most was the extraordinary sense of a fifty-million-year-old heaviness I received from this serpentine being. It caused me to despair of the success of the exorcism. Almost all the team members at both exorcisms were convinced they were at these times in the presence of something absolutely alien and inhuman. The end of each exorcism proper was signaled by the departure of this Presence from the patient and the room.

Dr. Peck states, though, that an exorcism is not necessarily a complete cure for possession. Like his Kardecismo cousins to the south, the psychiatrist feels that repossession is a distinct possibility in such cases. He and his colleagues therefore had to watch the patients carefully for an extended period to make sure they would not be reinfected by the entities cast from their bodies.

"You really had to be there to see it," stated Dr. Peck during his interview. "It made me realize even further the inadequacy of words."

Dr. Peck does not believe that possession occurs casually but only by specific or perhaps unknowing design. "I very much doubt that somebody can go walking down the street one day," he writes, "and have a demon jump out from behind a bush and penetrate him."

In both of the cases he studied, Dr. Peck discovered specific psychological and spiritual causes for his patients' problems. Both were lonely people willing to accept the companionship of "imaginary" friends—somewhat like the imaginary playmates children like to create, which is certainly not pathological. But these imaginary companions (who resemble Elwood P. Dowd's invisible rabbit Harvey in the famous stage play and Hollywood film by that name) were evil entities in disguise. It seems that the first patient's "friend" came to him during a ouija board session, while the second patient underwent some sort of ghastly experiences while a small child. In each instance the patient's psychological shielding was faulty and contributed to his eventual possession. (The reader will recall that Dr. Titus Bull explained this process in more detail back in 1923.) Both patients had been undergoing multiple stresses before and after the possession, which probably exacerbated the situation.

So what are we to make of these claims and psychiatric evaluations?

When I first read Dr. Peck's book, I was impressed by the writer's psychiatric soundness and knowledge. It is clear from the volume that the psychiatrist is not in the least credulous, and the knowledge he displays of the world's religions is commendable. Even though he returned to the Christian faith in 1980, it is obvious that he is anything but a religious fanatic, and his writings carefully veer from the dissemination of any religious propaganda. It is also clear that despite his personal reservations about the charismatic deliverance ministry, Dr. Peck's encounters are similar to the possession cases seen during such services. So his personal experiences seem to be with some sort of fairly common syndrome often encountered by clergymen ministering to the spiritually unwell. So let's look at the deliverance ministry in greater detail.

For a fascinating inside look at the deliverance ministry, the reader should consult Rev. Don Basham's *Deliver Us from Evil*. Reverend Basham began his career as a conventional and theologically liberal minister of the Disciples of Christ but later began encountering cases of possession in his pastoral work. My feeling is that he eventually became *too* eager to find demons everywhere he looked, but his early experiences in Canada and Pennsylvania were very similar to Dr. Peck's encounters. Reverend Basham also feels that demonic possession could be lurking behind some cases of mental illness and that such incidents result from either physical or psychological trauma or from dabbling in Spiritualism. Several case studies are included in his short book.

Because of these intricate similarities, it is plain that Dr. Peck and Reverend Basham have eye-witnessed the same extraordinary syndrome—a syndrome that only seems to imitate psychological sickness but responds to a more spiritually insightful therapy. But is it really genuine possession, or is it only a bizarre form of multiple personality or other psychological problem? Both theories are genuine possibilities to my mind, and I don't think either psychiatry *or* religion has definitive words to say on the subject. It is certainly interesting that exorcism seemed to work with these cases, which points to their spiritistic nature. But there is also a phenomenon seen in clinical hypnotherapy that closely resembles the deliverance ministry but which is produced solely through psychological suggestion. Could this phenomenon be the clue to the cases seen by Dr. Peck and Reverend Basham?

This procedure was originally developed by John and Helen Watkins of the University of Montana, who call it "ego state therapy." The process is based on the premise that each person develops certain "ego states" during specific periods of life, usually beginning in childhood and subsequently during the next several years. These ego states either represent or become guided by specific emotions or emotional drives, which can sometimes momentarily take control of one's everyday thoughts and physical behavior. Such influences could cause a person who is normally conservative and reserved to suddenly become drunk and boisterous in public, for example. We tend to label this type of behavior with colorful expressions, such as "letting your hair down" or "overcoming your inhibitions," but the process might involve a deeper psychological process. Deep inside, believe the Watkinses, each person probably plays host to subsystems within the personality guided by these ego states, controlled by emotions normally inhibited by the conscious mind. They do, however, emerge briefly and very rarely.

This process is explained in some detail by M. Gerald Edelstein, a psychiatrist in San Francisco, in his book *Trauma, Trance, and Transformation*. Dr. Edelstein supports the concept of ego states and ego state therapy. He writes that "in effect, it is almost as though each of us were a multiple personality, but with one major difference. In the true multiple personality, the boundaries between the ego states are so impermeable that the actions of one ego state may occur without another ego state being aware of those actions."

In other words, each secondary personality represents a specific ego state of the patient. If we look back to the case of Doris Fischer, it is clear that "Sick Doris" represented the girl's psychological ego state of hurt, while "Margaret" was created from her ego state of hostility. Ego state therapy merely states that each of us maintains the germs of these personalities deep within our character.

Now it is possible through hypnosis and suggestion to evoke these ego states. The clinician merely places the patient in a dissociated state

(I don't like the word *trance*) and specifically asks to speak with such an inner entity. The clinician might say something such as "I wish to speak to that part of the patient that feels pain" . . . or hurt . . . or whatever. The patient will usually respond by bringing forth the appropriate part of his or her personality structure. The hypnotically created secondary personalities will then take on their own life.

"They can reveal when they first came into existence, what caused their formation, and what they are attempting to accomplish," explains Dr. Edelstein. "What they are attempting to accomplish is almost always a laudable goal, but their methods may leave much to be desired." For example, an ego state filled with self-hatred could cause a person to behave self-destructively in his or her personal life.

Now, these emerging ego states call themselves by generic names that they usually adopt from their guiding characteristics. These self-appointed ego states seem surprisingly similar (if not identical) to the "demons" called forth by deliverance ministers by their exorcisms. These secondary personalities, too, encapsulate such negative emotions as greed, avarice, slothfulness, and the other deadly sins. It seems likely to me that preachers practicing deliverance exorcism might be essentially practicing a form of psychotherapy . . . but taking a literal and simplistic stance toward their results. While they might be exorcizing a person's personal demons, these "demons" may not be genuinely evil beings from some dark Satanic realm.

But enough speculation for the time being. These issues will be discussed in more detail in Chapter 14. For now it is important to realize that Dr. Peck's psychiatric opinions are not unique. They have been repeated by other clinicians—especially by those working specifically with multiple personality patients.

Several years ago, very similar experiences were reported to me by a psychiatrist noted for his work with such clients. He even claimed that most psychiatrists working with these special patients regularly see cases of spirit possession in their practices—although they usually refrain from publicly reporting them as such! So let's look at the subject of multiple personality in more depth. First though, it will be necessary to repeat some of the information I offered briefly in Chapter 7.

The entire bizarre subject of multiple personality was foreign to most contemporary psychotherapists until 1957, when two Georgia psychiatrists published their block-busting *The Three Faces of Eve*. Dr. Corbett H. Thigpen and Dr. Hervey W. Cleckley were the therapists involved in the case, which concerned a client possessed by three totally different personalities. These personalities shared the same body but led separate lives. (There were actually several more personalities, but this fact was not disclosed in the book and only came to light in 1977 when Chris Sizemore—the real-life "Eve"—wrote her book *I'm Eve*.) The popularity of this book and its subsequent movie adaptation starring Joanne Woodward brought widespread psychiatric awareness to the syndrome for the first time in current decades.

Despite the brief popularity of the subject in the 1950s, though, the psychiatric community didn't take much notice of the phenomenon. Many psychiatrists were vocally skeptical of the case since the syndrome seemed so bizarre and rare. But the topic refused to die within psychiatry and has recently experienced a startling renaissance within the mental health professions. It now looks as if the syndrome is fairly common.

Psychiatrists also now realize that the syndrome usually develops in childhood, when the child is faced with a severe psychological or physical trauma that literally tears the personality into pieces. The specific role of sexual trauma and other forms of severe physical abuse in the development of the problem is especially becoming more apparent to today's clinicians. What results is often a sort of psychological split, in which the primary personality remains conservative and somewhat repressed while the secondary personality is carefree, daring, and devoted to pleasure-seeking behavior. The latter is also often ornery and psychopathic, and the two personalities take turns controlling the patient's body. The primary personality usually remains unaware of the split, however, and is burdened only by constant and inexplicable bouts of memory loss. Sometimes another personality will emerge from deep within the patient's unconscious. This personality is often fully knowledgeable about the other personalities and keeps track of them and keeps them in line!

This was certainly true of Chris Sizemore, whose case was a textbook example of the disorder. Sizemore's body played host to the following personalities:

The first face was Chris's repressed everyday self, "Eve White". She was a good but plain housewife, sometimes too inhibited for her own good.

The second face was the boisterous "Eve Black," a colorful and sexually flirtatious personality devoted primarily to pleasure. She disliked the other "Eve" and wanted complete control of the body.

The third of the *Three Faces of Eve* was called "Jane." She could take control of Chris Sizemore when trouble was brewing.

This is a rather oversimplified picture of what is an enormously complex syndrome, for the splitting process sometimes becomes continual for some patients. Each time the patient faces an unfamiliar set of psychological demands, a separate personality can emerge from the person's psyche to take care of it. Sybil Dorsett, the heroine of Flora Rheter Schreiber's book *Sybil*, eventually produced sixteen personalities. Most of them were unaware that they were sharing the body with other secondary personalities. Splits of even more personalities than that sometimes occur.

And some of these secondary personalities can be gifted with psychic powers, a condition that—as Dr. Peck believes—can lead to spirit possession.

That is also the opinion of Dr. Ralph Allison, who is a California psychiatrist currently living in Los Osos, a small but very pretty community near San Luis Obispo located just down the coast from the former residence of newspaper magnate William Randolph Hearst. (The estate is currently a popular tourist site.) Dr. Allison trained both at the UCLA School of Medicine and at the Stanford Medical Center, but he never suspected that he would become a recognized expert on the multiple personality syndrome. Since beginning his private psychiatric practice in the early 1960s, Dr. Allison has personally treated some thirty such cases. He has seen approximately sixty cases over the course of his clinical career, and he has delivered papers on the disorder to meetings of the American Psychiatric Association. In order to better acquaint the general public with his work, Dr. Allison wrote his controversial book *Minds in Many Pieces* in 1980. He has sparked considerable controversy since he is willing to openly discuss the psychic and spiritual sides to the disorder, probably because of his own religious background. Being that he is the son of a Protestant minister, Dr. Allison feels no embarrassment in believing in the existence of spirit possession—or in the possibility that it plays an important role in some cases of the disorder.

I was fascinated by the subject of multiple personality even before embarking on the present book, and I couldn't resist the temptation to meet with Dr. Allison when I first read his intriguing volume. Since he lived right up the coast from my own residence in Los Angeles, I made an appointment to see him during a convenient weekend in 1982. After sharing a few letters and phone calls, Dr. Allison agreed to let me interview him for *Fate* magazine, a publication on whose editorial staff I serve and that reports on parapsychology and other scientific controversies. I was probably actually too eager to see him, since I suffered the indignity of a speeding ticket on the way.

When I arrived in Los Osos, I discovered that Dr. Allison and his family were in the middle of changing residences. Since everything was a bit confused, Dr. Allison took me for a drive through the community and then to the office he shares with a fellow psychiatrist. There in his small office in the neighboring community of Morro Bay, we spoke about a side of multiple personality most therapists would never dream of openly discussing.

To initiate our conversation, I reminded Dr. Allison of a remark he makes on the fifth page of his book. "In my role as explorer," he states in *Minds in Many Pieces*, "I witnessed parapsychological phenomena for which there is, as yet, no satisfactory explanation." So I began by asking Dr. Allison just how commonly victims of multiple personality possess psychic abilities.

"Every one of them," he answered. "This is sort of a sine qua non that goes along with it. It may be the primary personality that has some ability to tell what's coming up in the future for her kids, or accidents they're going to get into. That happens quite frequently. They may not mention it unless you start asking. If the patient has a lot of personalities, there will be one who is very psychic, and the others will have average ability or no particular abilities."

These views didn't strike me as strange; they seemed to make a great deal of sense. Similar claims have been made by most recovered multiple personality patients in their retrospective books. Most people who suffer from this form of psychological dissociation report frequent psychic experiences. While studying the literature on the subject, this fact became evident to me. For example, look at the following three cases.

1. In her autobiographical book *I'm Eve*, Chris Sizemore talks casually about a period in her life when she was constantly making correct predictions. She was living in Roanoke, Virginia, during this phase of her mental illness. Her personality was still splitting since the cure previously effected by Drs. Thigpen and Cleckley was short-lived—a fact you won't read in their book on the case! The personality in charge of her during her Virginia phase often predicted family accidents and related personal crises. For example, she once begged her husband to play hookey from work because of a curious vision. She was sure he would be electrocuted if he went to work. Her husband stayed home to

humor his wife's whimsy, but sure enough, his replacement was accidentally electrocuted while working the same job. Later she became apprehensive when her daughter was scheduled to receive a polio vaccination. She didn't act on the impression, which was unfortunate for her daughter. The poor girl was injected from a spoiled batch of vaccine and nearly died from the complications.

Chris Sizemore had similar experiences even while a child, when the splitting process first started. When her sister was sick with pneumonia, she had a dream in which Jesus visited her room and explained that the true problem was diphtheria. The message proved to be correct, and the information saved the girl's life.

2. The bizarre case of Billy Milligan received wide public attention in 1977, when the young man was charged as the rapist terrorizing Ohio State University in Columbus. It was later discovered that he suffered from twenty-four alternating personalities! The rapes had been carried out by a self-perceived lesbian personality, much to the chagrin of several of Billy's male secondary personalities, who couldn't understand the situation. Despite his obvious psychological condition, Billy was found guilty of the charges and was sent to a state prison.

The fascinating story of Billy Milligan has been traced and recreated by Daniel Keyes, the famous author of the classic short story *Flowers for Algernon*. Keyes discovered that Billy could boast of a psychic side to his fragmented life. Even when he was still a child, the boy had had a penchant for knowing when his sister was in trouble, and a few such examples are included in the biography *The Minds of Billy Milligan*.

3. A very different story is told by Henry Hawksworth, a northern California real estate salesman whose multiple personalities sprang from his father's sadistic punishments. His repertoire of secondary personalities was rather limited since only five of them ever developed. Hawksworth tells his story in *The Five of Me*, which later served as the basis of a very fictionalized TV movie starring former *St. Elsewhere* star David Birney. Hawksworth's most delightful personality (indeed, likable secondary-personalities do exist) was "Peter," who still perceived himself to be a child. He was an innocent character gifted with clairvoyant powers. When Hawksworth would sometimes inexplicably find himself in Los Angeles with no money (usually flown there while controlled by the evil secondary personality "Johnny"), "Peter" would save the day by giving psychic readings for people visiting bars near Venice Beach, a base of the southland's counterculture.

Henry Hawksworth was thankfully cured by Dr. Allison. When I met with the psychiatrist, he explained that his former patient could also see people's "auras"—colored atmospheres that surround us and which psychics claim to perceive.

But the psychic world of multiple personality isn't always that benign and uncomplicated. Dr. Allison explained that in cases where the primary personality has undergone innumerable splits, the psychic abilities possessed by the secondary personalities can be utilized in destructive ways.

"You have a group of patients in which you have twenty, thirty, forty, even fifty personalities," he told me. "There's no stopping the splitting process. In these cases the primary personality is underneath them all and hasn't even shown up in therapy yet. All you see are the alternate personalities. Those are the ones where you will find the majority of the psychic ability. One, two, or three of the many, many personalities will have it. Others will have no ability at all. When you get into those patients with a multitude of personalities, there's a lot of pathology in the use of psychic abilities for dangerous activity."

Dr. Allison should know, for he has seen it work and has even been personally victimized by the force.

Before I drove to Los Osos to conduct my interview, the psychiatrist sent me a copy of a paper he had delivered at the American Psychiatric Association's 1976 annual meeting in Atlanta. The paper dealt with the dangers of treating patients with multiple personalities and the ways these people can use their psychic ability to sap people of their energy or to "zap" them physically.

Such a case of psychic sapping once occurred while Dr. Allison was treating a young woman named Gail. One day while visiting his office for therapy, she explained that she admired her psychiatrist's strength and wished she could draw upon it. The somewhat unassuming psychiatrist responded in kind. He told her that he'd gladly give her some of his vitality if he knew the proper procedures! He didn't realize that his chance would soon come.

The incident occurred one Saturday evening, while he was enjoying a party with his wife. They were socializing when Gail interrupted their evening with a frantic phone call. She was undergoing some sort of crisis, and since she tended to be self-destructive, Dr. Allison decided to drive to her residence immediately. He didn't want to deal with a suicide, but his worst fears were realized when he finally arrived at her home. He found her suffering from bloody gashes on her wrists. It seems that right after calling the therapist, Gail's destructive secondary personality took control of her body and forced her to slash her wrists. Dr. Allison immediately drove the woman to a local hospital, where he touched her gently while the emergency room physician stitched her wounds. Dr. Allison only returned to the party after the crisis was over; and that's when he realized that he was mysteriously drained of his energy.

"When I got back there my wife handed me a plate of food," he reported during his presentation to his colleagues at the American Psychiatric Association meeting. "I sat down but could barely lift the fork to my mouth. Emotionally, I felt normal, but I had barely enough energy to breathe. My wife told me I looked tired and suggested we go home immediately. I must have looked really terrible to her because this was a very special party for her and she liked to stay till the end."

It took him an entire day to recover from the episode.

Dr. Allison believes that he was psychically sapped by Gail, first when she grabbed him at her apartment and then during the stitching of her wounds.* He definitely doesn't believe that his weakness was a psychological reaction to the emergency.

Dr. Allison also feels that he has been telepathically attacked by some of his patients. He provided me with some very strange and shocking stories.

Dr. Allison was more than kind to me with his time that Saturday, and we spent considerable time discussing the use multiple personality patients can make of such powers. I eventually published my detailed interview with him in the July and August 1983 issues of *Fate* magazine.

During our talk, I found it very difficult to evaluate the incidents Dr. Allison was citing and reporting. His stories were certainly provocative, but it struck me that each of the incidents—taken separately—

---

* Parallels to Dr. Allison's claims can be found in the older literature on multiple personality. Mary J. (Mollie) Fancher was a bed-ridden multiple personality patient whose story was told in 1894 by Abram H. Dailey in *Mollie Fancher—the Brooklyn Enigma*. Not only was she psychic, but small pets left in her care invariably died. It seemed that she would draw energy from them, thereby causing them to expire within a few days. People could also feel the bizarre sapping process, which was a notable feature of the case.

could be explained on a purely psychological basis. Working with people with multiple personalities is a strenuous, draining, and sometimes totally unnerving experience. Every psychiatrist or psychologist who works with these people concedes this point. Because of this constant stress, it doesn't strike me that sudden episodes of exhaustion would be unusual for the therapist. Certainly losing your appetite after watching a patient being stitched up isn't inexplicable, especially for a psychiatrist with little contact with general surgical practices.

But despite my reservations, I found myself fascinated by Dr. Allison and his provocative experiences. His history of clinical success and his reputation in the field have proven his psychiatric skills with these particular patients, and it struck me that it would be arrogant to simply dismiss these stories and the interpretations Dr. Allison gives them.

During the course of that afternoon in 1982, Dr. Allison also discussed with me an even darker side of the multiple personality syndrome. He openly acknowledged in his *Minds in Many Pieces* that some cases of the disorder represent instances of spirit possession, a position later echoed by Dr. Peck in his *People of the Lie*. I was extremely interested in this possibility, since I was then still studying the work of James Hyslop and his successors. My chance to raise this important issue came when the psychiatrist began talking about his personal experiences investigating some local hauntings. Since Dr. Allison clearly believes in some sort of life beyond death (which I already knew from reading his book), I raised the issue of whether some cases of multiple personality could be spiritual rather than psychological disorders. I can't recall whether I was prepared for his uncensored and ready response to the point.

Dr. Allison explained that, in his opinion, spirit and/or demonic possession is an important part of the multiple personality syndrome in general. He further stated that in the course of his clinical work, sometimes a patient's secondary personalities don't seem to be the result of psychological dissociation. They appear instead to be some sort of invading entities independent of the patient's mind. It is common for patients suffering from innumerable secondary personalities to have a few who claim to be spirits or demons. Or they might be spiritual entities working behind the scenes with some of the patient's more hostile split-off personas. In these cases the spirit entities could be overshadowing the mental sickness while not actually appearing in the form of any of the patient's secondary personalities.

Dr. Allison believes he has encountered both forms of possession during his career.

"There was one man who wasn't my patient," he went on to say. "I saw him at a clinic for another therapist. He was an alcoholic who couldn't keep from going into bars. He'd go into bars even when he didn't want to."

The psychiatrist decided to explore the patient's problem by conducting some hypnotic sessions with him. Dr. Allison was a bit shaken by the results. "This voice came through and identified itself as a demonic spirit that kept leading this man into bars. It had no origin; there wasn't a psychic split in the man's personality or anything like that."

Dr. Allison specifically explored the patient's psychological background hoping to find a psychiatric basis for the personality, but failed.

"I had to make a quick decision because I was in as a consultant on the case," he said. "And I decided to go ahead and do an exorcism. I was in front of my boss, who was my supervisor. He was a liberal fellow, but I didn't need this sort of thing in a new clinic and with a new job. But there was the patient and, after once again checking everything out as quickly as I could, I had to come to a decision. I had to either let it sit or do something. I decided to go ahead with an exorcism in front of the therapist and the wife. I didn't want to proceed in front of a boss who didn't want to mix religion with county government. But I felt it was the right thing to do, and it worked. The man continued therapy and never showed any more signs of his difficulty. He stayed on the straight and narrow and did fine. It was a cure."

The only similar case the psychiatrist ever encountered came during his treatment of a workman's compensation referral in Santa Cruz. The man's injury had occurred while he was working on a ski lift in the vicinity of Lake Tahoe. He had previously undergone conventional medical treatment but failed to recover from his injuries and kept having seizures. He was eventually referred to Dr. Allison specifically for hypnotherapy to determine whether psychology could succeed where medicine had failed.

The psychiatrist was working with the patient under hypnosis when a strange voice suddenly issued from the patient's mouth. This unsuspected personality claimed to be a demonic presence who had begun possessing the patient years before in Japan, where the patient was stationed during a tour of duty with the military. The patient had been injured in a fire during his stay in the Orient, and the demon had entered him during his recovery in the hospital. The entity also claimed responsibility for the patient's current problem.

Dr. Allison's only recourse was to consult with a Catholic priest, whom he invited to work with the patient. When the priest also heard the demon speak, he made the proper arrangements for a formal exorcism. The ritual was apparently effective, though Dr. Allison wasn't able to determine whether the patient ever relapsed, since he left town shortly after undergoing the exorcism.

This kind of accidental possession also happens to people already suffering from multiple personalities, according to Dr. Allison. He once ran into this complication while working with a female patient suffering from a multitude of split-off personalities.

"Once this woman was missing from her apartment," he told me. "She called us about an hour later, saying that she was down by the Santa Cruz beach. She didn't know how she got there. We picked her up and brought her back home, and out came what claimed to be a spirit who had died in Myrtle Beach, where she had drowned while searching for her husband and son, who had walked out on her. They were down by the harbor, and she was looking for them but couldn't find them. She had walked into the ocean and drowned. She was still looking for them, but now she was on the other coast and she had allegedly possessed my patient."

Dr. Allison became very serious as he spoke. "Now I don't know where such a thing comes from," he continued. "It was not a personality, and it acted indeed like somebody who had gotten lost in the stage of death, life, and in between. It had no meaning therapeutically."

With no other resource at hand, the psychiatrist performed a brief exorcism by invoking the Trinity. He then ordered the spirit to go back to the dark recesses of the spirit realm. He never again confronted the entity while treating the patient, so the exorcism apparently banished this personality permanently.

While I was sitting in Dr. Allison's office, I felt as if I were taking a time trip into the past. It was fascinating to listen to a psychiatrist of today who has perhaps rediscovered what his predecessors had learned so many years before. His experiences and procedures reminded me forcefully of those of Dr. Carl Wickland, Dr. W. Franklin Prince, and Dr. Titus Bull and the ways they probably responded to the cases they confronted. Without realizing it, Dr. Allison was offering a contemporary chapter to a fascinating story that dates back some eighty years. Although it was difficult to evaluate each of the psychiatrist's cases, the sense of wonder Dr. Allison radiated gave me some insight into the impact that cases of possible possession probably made on the worldview of his long-departed colleagues-in-spirit.

So the next question I asked was predictable: "In what percentage of cases do you feel that one or more of the patient's personalities are really possessing entities?"

"I added this up once," replied the psychiatrist, "and I think it's twenty percent. These are primarily in the cases with many, many personalities."

Dr. Allison did not concur, however, with researchers such as Dr. Bull or Dr. Worcester who believed that most of these people are innocent victims of possession. His position is more like Dr. Peck's, who believes that such people usually psychologically cooperate in the process of possession. Dr. Allison finds this form of conspiracy especially common in multiple personality patients.

"These people are repressing their hatred massively," he explained to me. "They could be killers if they allowed themselves to act out. Some of them *are* killers, and I remember at least one patient who recalled killing at least three people. She was never discovered. The killings occurred because of her rage against these people, who she claimed had tried to kill her. But the alter-personalities would not have gone that far. They were joined by a whole number of evil spirits, who claimed that they had forced her to do the killings. These people are like magnets. The patient is full of hatred, and the personalities themselves call in the entities. They admit this. They literally call for help."

Dr. Allison proceeded to explain that most secondary personalities really serve as the patient's psychological protectors. They possess little capacity for physically harming the patient's enemies, since such strong emotions don't usually incorporate into their character structure. But sometimes this swelling hatred will reach the point where the patient's secondary personalities finally express their destructive urges. Dr. Allison believes that when the patient reaches this limit, a secondary personality will "call" or invoke a demonic or spirit entity to take charge of the situation. If a disembodied entity happens to be in the patient's physical or psychological vicinity, the presence will usually undertake the job—by taking physical possession of the invoker!

It was obvious to me that Dr. Allison was speaking from personal experience, since he originally received this information directly from some of his patients. He cited an example during his presentation to the American Psychiatric Association. The incident began when his duodenal ulcer began bleeding profusely. It was very puzzling, since his intestinal problems had never previously been so seriously and potentially dangerous. He later learned that the cause was due to a specific client under his care. She liked to dabble in the occult and she suffered both from multiple personality and from possible possession, and the demonic entity occasionally controlling her body claimed responsibility for creating the problem. The entity was avenging himself upon Dr. Allison, who was trying to oust the intruder from his patient.

The upshot to the story revealed an even greater evil. Dr. Allison believed it best to withdraw from further involvement in the patient's treatment. Gradually she became more immersed in the world of the supernatural. Her boyfriend finally tried to perform a makeshift exorcism, but the impact of the ritual was too much for his weakened psyche. He became a religious fanatic and returned to his home in Florida, where he killed a possible convert while proselytizing on the street. He beat the man to death after he failed to convert him.

"Such can be the fate of some who are too close to multiples and don't have their psychic shields about them," Dr. Allison warned his psychiatric colleagues.

Fortunately, some cases can be resolved more successfully. Dr. Allison chronicled his most bizarre but successfully treated multiple personality-cum-possession case in his *Minds in Many Pieces*. The patient's name was given as Elise.

The psychiatrist first met the patient when she was twenty-four years old. She had already developed sixteen personalities, and several more were uncovered or emerged during her therapy. Even a relatively minor problem or set of circumstances in her life would encourage further splits within her psyche. Dr. Allison began suspecting Elise was also possessed while he was conducting a hypnotic session with her at a California hospital. He was exploring her reaction to her grandmother's death when an unfamiliar entity, who called himself "Dennis," suddenly popped forth. He stated that he was possessing Elise because of his sexual attraction toward "Shannon," an important secondary personality of the patient's! Dr. Allison worked with "Dennis," but despite his psychiatric expertise he couldn't find a psychological basis for him. "Shannon" on the other hand, had been created by Elise when she was twenty-two. She had been pregnant when she emerged. This secondary personality formed completely when Elise lost the baby. "Shannon" controlled Elise every October through March, which was the anniversary of the baby's illness and death. The inexplicable appearance of "Dennis" considerably confused Dr. Allison, since he had never heard of one secondary personality falling in love with another.

The only way to handle the situation therapeutically was to reason with "Dennis." So the therapist asked "Dennis" just how he expected to consummate his love for Shannon. "Dennis's" response was convoluted, to say the least! He replied that he could possess anyone Elise dated. "Shannon" was called forth at this point in the session, and she corroborated "Dennis's" story.

"I knew something was wrong," writes the psychiatrist. "The idea that one alter-personality could leave the body at will is nonsense. There is sound reason for the creation of an alter-personality. Either the stories I heard about Dennis were not accurate or he simply was not an alter-personality."

Dr. Allison finally decided to contact some wiser personalities deep within the patient's unconscious. They confirmed that "Dennis" was a spirit being and couldn't be eradicated therapeutically.

This situation left the baffled psychiatrist to work directly with "Dennis." He began by tracing the entity's life history. He wanted to know when "Dennis" had first encountered "Shannon," other people he had possibly possessed, and his attitude toward Elise's several secondary personalities. "Dennis" assured his interrogator that his only real attachment was to "Shannon." He also explained that in his earthly life he had been a pawnbroker in Louisiana before the turn of the century. He had died from a gunshot wound he received when his store was robbed. But then the psychiatrist pressed for more information, "Dennis" suddenly became defensive.

Even with all this data in his grasp, Dr. Allison only took action to remove "Dennis" after consulting with one of Elise's inner-self helpers (ISHs). * This element of her unconscious mind told the psychiatrist that the possessing entity could be exorcised the next day but that it would be a dangerous undertaking. Dr. Allison, it seems, would have to be careful not to become possessed himself. The ISH also explained that "Dennis" had taken control of Elise because of her experiments with witchcraft, which had opened her to the evil.

By way of some hypnotic probing the next day, Dr. Allison confirmed this story and regressed his patient back to the time she first began experimenting with witchcraft. Later he made Elise listen to the tape of the session in order to convince her that her problem was a repercussion from her experiments. This session seemed to be proceed-

---

* The "inner-self helper" is a wise part of the patient's mind usually contactable by way of hypnosis. Dr. Allison routinely contacts the IHS of each of his patients in order to help them progress in therapy. "Sleeping Margaret" may have been this sort of inner-self helper for Doris Fischer.

ing pretty well, but then the amazed psychiatrist was suddenly confronted by yet another surprise. A *second* possessing entity now emerged from Elise's psyche, and this entity wouldn't leave without a fight! The stress of the treatment was becoming obvious, and Elise's fragile mind reacted violently to the situation. By the time night fell, Elise was so traumatized that her several secondary personalities were alternating control of her body every thirty seconds.

It was fortunate for Elise that the hospital duty nurse knew of Dr. Allison's crisis intervention methods, so while waiting for the psychiatrist to arrive, she quickly contacted two of the patient's ISHs. They told the nurse that the time had finally come to rid the patient of "Dennis" and the other possessor. Dr. Allison, in the meantime, rushed to the hospital and took the patient outside to the hospital grounds. While she kicked and screamed in what seemed like violent paroxysms, Elise—under the psychiatrist's direction—exorcized *herself* by demanding that the psychic invaders leave her body. She then lost consciousness.*

The patient awoke moments later, but she wasn't the same Elise who had originally entered the hospital. She was now being controlled by a personality repressed a year before—who promptly became hysterical. Then another personality took immediate control of the body. This personality called herself "Sandi" and told Dr. Allison that the patient's possessors had fled.

Of course, the critical reader or student of psychical research may remain unimpressed by these reports. The skeptic could choose to believe that the spirit entities confronted by Dr. Allison were merely transitory creations produced by people already prone to psychological fragmentation.

There is, in fact, a rich historical tradition that relates similar forms of mental illness to possession claims. Back in the 1880s, for instance, the famous French psychologist Pierre Janet discovered that people suffering from hysteria—a form of dissociation caused by unconscious guilt—often believe themselves to be possessed and even create demonic secondary personalities in order to fulfill their delusions. In his *L'Automatism Psychologique*, Janet cited irrefutable evidence that these demons were merely creations of the unconscious minds of the hysterics themselves. Since the multiple personality syndrome is related to this form of psychological dissociation, perhaps there is a common link be-

---

*The possibility that people suffering from possession can exorcise themselves is not only Dr. Allison's view. It plays a role in the Christian deliverance ministry and is described, for example, by Rev. Don Basham in his *Deliver Us from Evil*.

tween hysteria, dissociation, and possession delusions. It also strikes me that the entities Dr. Allison has seen in therapy behave suspiciously like the spirits contacted by amateur ouija board operators. These personalities, too, are prone to telling fanciful stories about themselves; they claim to be spirits and demons but are really repressed aspects of the operator's psyche. Most ouija board entities are also notorious for evading any questions regarding their earthly lives, especially if this information can be checked. Dr. Allison has confronted this same problem time and time again with the "spirits" he's contacted. So just because an entity claims to be a spirit, it doesn't necessarily mean that the claim is true.

Dr. Allison is, of course, concerned about these important issues. He told me that some stories told by possession spirits are total and deliberate fabrications.

"I've been fooled," he admitted candidly. "You can never be sure."

He proceeded to cite an interesting example for me. He was treating a young woman for multiple personality at his office when the spirit of a deceased girlfriend suddenly spoke through her. The patient and her friend had been in a car accident in which the latter was killed. The spirit explained that the patient's child—who had been taken from her years before—had been recently killed in a similar car accident. When the patient's own personality took charge of the body later during the session, she was told of the sad news. The patient went into throes of remorse. Dr. Allison was intrigued by this unexpected development, since this was a case in which the information offered by a spirit could be checked. What he eventually uncovered came as a big disappointment.

He subsequently learned that no accident had befallen the child, who was still alive and well. He later learned from his patient's ISH that the message had been a deliberate fabrication orchestrated for the young woman's own psychological good. It seems that the patient had never properly grieved for the loss of her daughter, who was born when the patient was too young to handle motherhood's many responsibilities. She was still repressing her reaction to the loss, and these feelings were blocking her progress in therapy. The ISH produced the spiritlike incident to force the young woman to confront and work out her emotions thoroughly.

Not every case of apparent spirit contact ends so disappointingly, though. Dr. Allison once confronted a spirit entity capable of communicating a range of evidence even the worst skeptic would be impressed by. The incident occurred while he was working with another female patient.

He was treating the patient in his office when the woman suddenly produced a secondary personality who claimed to be the deceased son of her employer. Although the patient consciously knew that this young man was dead, she had never met him even socially. He had been only nineteen-years-old when he died from a rare disease. She had felt so sorry for her employer during the boy's fateful illness that on one occasion she actually prayed to die in his place. The entity had returned from the beyond, he told the bewildered psychiatrist, to help the patient and repay her past kindness. Dr. Allison was especially interested in exploring whether this personality could prove his earthly existence, so he requested that the entity write out his name, address, and a personal message—a message meaningful only to himself and to his father—on a piece of paper. The entity obliged and wrote some words that his father had once scribbled on a Christmas card to him.

The patient, too, was eager to discover the root of the matter, so she showed the entity's father the note. He was impressed by it and willingly conceded that the message and information were correct; but there was an important catch to the incident. Even though the entity's message was factually correct, he had incorrectly given his middle name! Dr. Allison pressed the entity about the error when they next interacted, and the entity explained that the patient had to trust him if she wanted his help. Giving the incorrect middle name, he explained, had been meant as a specific test of her trust.

Explanation or subterfuge? It's hard to say. This is just one of the many maddening experiences Dr. Allison has confronted while trying to establish the genuinely spiritual nature of "spirit" entities.

In the long run, though, does it really matter? During our conversation Dr. Allison constantly emphasized that he is neither an experimenter nor a parapsychologist but a clinician. His primary job is to cure his patients, not to conduct research with them. For this reason, he explained, he has neither the time nor the inclination to research the many strange stories these entities are prone to tell.

He sums up his position concisely in his *Minds in Many Pieces*, where he explains why he has entertained and used the concepts of spirit guides, obsessors, demons, and exorcism in his practice. "I can only reiterate my own belief . . . that an effective doctor must use whatever methods benefit the patient most," he writes. "In my own cases this has often entailed the utilization of techniques that are bizarre, unorthodox, and even religious in nature. But these methods have successfully cured many patients, and the patient's welfare must be the only concern.

James Hyslop, Dr. Titus Bull, and Dr. Carl Wickland would have undoubtedly agreed.

Before I concluded my meeting with him, Dr. Allison offered me a curious warning and prediction. He told me that most researchers working with such patients can cite similar experiences. Most of them secretly believe in spirit possession and its possibility, he confided to me. This was a claim I couldn't evaluate in 1982, since the study of multiple personality was simply not popular back then. Today, however, an increasing number of psychologists and psychiatrists are specializing in the study and treatment of the disorder. So I started asking some of these therapists whether they had ever encountered cases of spirit possession in their practices. Most of them were openly critical and skeptical of Dr. Allison's views. Although they all acknowledged his expertise as a clinician and admired him personally, they were doubtful that possession cases really exist.

What these clinicians did know was that multiple personality patients are extremely suggestible. It therefore seems to me that, should such a patient realize that his or her therapist believes in possession, this knowledge could serve as an implicit suggestion to unconsciously manufacture such personalities. Perhaps this is why Dr. Allison has seen so many possession cases in his practice.

Or perhaps he has simply been in the right place at the right time to encounter something even more extraordinary than multiple personality.

CHAPTER **14**

OBSESSION AND
THE CASE FOR SURVIVAL

At the beginning of this volume I stated that this book could be read in several different ways. It could be read as a unique chapter in the history of psychiatry, as interesting footnotes to the study of psychic phenomena, or as a serious study of the evidence for life after death. Little more need be said regarding the first two readings. The cases and anecdotes included in the book speak for themselves, no matter what interpretation the reader prefers to apply to them. But as this book comes to a close, some further comments should be addressed to the third crucial issue: Do the cases surveyed in the previous chapters point to the literal reality of spirit possession? Can this syndome sometimes masquerade in the form of common mental illnesses? Do we ultimately survive death, and can we subsequently reach back and contact the living?

Parapsychologists, philosophers, and theologians have been debating these important problems for decades upon decades. The debate has never been resolved, probably because no evidence for survival after death can ever be ironclad or perfect. Parapsychologists realized this many years ago when they were intensively studying the phenomenon of trance mediumship. The founders of both the Society for Psychical Research in England and its counterpart in the United States found several gifted Spiritualist channels between 1880 and 1930, but they could never determine if these psychics were contacting the dead or merely using phenomenal powers of extrasensory perception to collect information pertaining to their clients' deceased relatives. This latter possibility became known as the super-ESP or super-psi theory, and it soon became a hungry shark forever ready to gobble up the evidence for survival. The super-ESP hypothesis caused a hopeless impasse which caused the field to eventually abandon survival research in the 1930s and enter the psychology laboratory.

It would be impossible to use the evidence for spirit possession/obsession either to prove or to disprove the survival theory. Greater minds than mine have tried to resolve this great enigma, and I can hope to do little better. So in this concluding chapter I prefer to examine what theory for the evidence makes the best sense, even if this evaluation falls short of offering formal proof either of survival or any other hypothesis.

To give the reader a feel for the complexities of the survival question, let's retrace the case studies included in this book beginning with the Thompson/Gifford case. This complicated case is certainly the most striking evidence for personal survival that James Hyslop or his successors ever collected. Despite the impact of this unforgettable case, though, there are three mutually exclusive theories by which it can be explained.

The first theory posits that we simply take the case at face value: that Frederic Thompson's mind and body were being influenced by the deceased painter R. Swain Gifford, who coerced him to paint pictures in his own earthly style.

The second theory is that Frederic Thompson was a powerful psychic who for some reason formed a close psychological bond with the painter during the latter's lifetime. After Gifford died in 1905, Thompson began to personally and perhaps pathologically identify with him. He not only developed several characteristics reflecting the painter's personality, but used his psychic powers to reinforce his delusions. What resulted was simply a semblance of spirit possession that emerged from a breakdown within his personality.

The third theory is rather more mundane and banal: that Thompson faked the entire case in order to promote his second-rate pictures.

Now let's see which of these theories works best when we apply to the specific features of the case:

The Fraud Hypothesis

Finding a motive for Frederic Thompson's possible fraud wouldn't be too difficult. We could suggest that the craftsman, a second-rate Sunday painter at best, wanted to leave the jewelry business to become an artist, even though his talents were limited. Realizing that he needed a gimmick, he began to claim that he was possessed by the spirit of R. Swain Gifford to impress James Hyslop. Seeing that the professor was eager to promote the case publicly, Thompson used the publicity to commercialize his burgeoning painting career.

Suggestions of this sort have been put forward by the skeptics ever since the Thompson case was first reported in 1909. Despite these suggestions, though, I know of no detailed charge of fraud in parapsychology's published historical literature ever presented against the case. But these suggestions do get resurrected periodically, even though most of the specific charges turn out to be baseless. One of the psychiatrists who examined Frederic Thompson told Hyslop that his client was probably making up the story, but the professor considered this opinion the result more of personal bias than proper psychiatric judgment. Some years after Hyslop's death, however, charges were leveled (and privately confirmed by Dr. W. Franklin Prince) that Thompson's paintings had been touched up before being published by the professor. This claim may have been true, but it was usual in the early 1900s to slightly refurbish paintings before reproducing them in books and/or magazines. Paintings didn't reproduce very well unless their highlights were exaggerated for the camera. That the paintings reproduced by Hyslop in his reports were retouched suggests no wrongdoing on his part or any one else's.

Recently, a more serious charge was made against the Thompson case by an employee of the American Society for Psychical Research. During a discussion we shared in Boston in the summer of 1985, I was told that Frederic Thompson often secretly and illegally camped on the Elizabeth Islands. My informant believed the painter journeyed to the islands to paint scenes from the local landscapes for Hyslop to later find during his own romps. She had made this discovery while reviewing Hyslop's files on the case, which are still preserved in New York. She apparently found some incriminating correspondence between the professor and the owner of Naushon Island that (my informant claimed) Hyslop had unethically covered up in his report.

My heart sank when I heard this revelation, but luckily, I found that the charge was completely unfounded! The employee was confused by the correspondence because—by her own admission—she had never bothered to read Hyslop's lengthy report on the case. The professor had actually published the correspondence openly; it confirmed a single incident in which Thompson was found camping on the land. But this incident only occurred after the craftsman placed his original sketches in Hyslop's hands. He had apparently never been to the island prior to that time, and it is obvious that this encounter took place while he was trying to locate the scenes of his psychic visions. (See Chapter 2.)

If fraud is to be charged in the case, we would also have to posit that Gifford's wife had collaborated with Thompson. She was the only person familiar with R. Swain Gifford's unfinished paintings, which were so uncannily finished by the New Bedford craftsman. But for what purpose? R. Swain Gifford was a famous and successful painter and it seems clear from Hyslop's report that Mrs. Gifford gained nothing from the publicity resulting from the case. We would also need to explain Minnie Soule's stunning successes in bringing through R. Swain Gifford during Hyslop's sittings, successes later repeated when Mrs. Cleaveland came to New York from her home in Virginia.

Of course, these psychics could have been reading the minds of both Frederic Thompson and Hyslop. But remember that some of the information communicated during these sittings was corroborated only through Mrs. Gifford or her daughter.

Because of my own desire to cast new light on the fraud hypothesis, during the summer of 1986 I began tracing the remainder of Frederic Thompson's career. I was curious to know exactly what became of him following the publication of Hyslop's report in 1909. Did he, for example, continue to claim that the deceased R. Swain Gifford was influencing him? Finding this information was no easy matter, and I initially uncovered some evidence that seemed to indicate fraud on Thompson's part while reading through popular art directories from the 1910s and 20s. (I had been hoping to find listings for the inspired painter.) My research continued to be a resounding failure until I chanced upon *Mantle Fielding's Dictionary of American Painters, Sculptors and Engravers*, originally issued in 1926. There on page 365 was a brief entry for Frederic Thompson, complete with some rather surprising information. The entry stated that Thompson had been born in Chilmark, Massachussets. That struck me as strange, since Chilmark is a small community on Martha's Vineyard just across a narrow channel from the Elizabeth Islands. He was also listed as a former pupil of George H. McCord, who was a noted painter during the 1890s. The entry also stated that our painter was a member of the exclusive Salmagundi Club. This club was a private fraternity founded in New York in 1871, and membership was originally by election by an artist's peers. It wasn't the sort of club that elected nobodies or untrained second-raters!

This information was surprising since it contradicted what was originally published by James Hyslop. Prof. Hyslop stated that Thompson was born in Middleborough, Massachusetts, and possessed no previous artistic training. Could Thompson have misled Hyslop in order to capitalize on the professor's promotion of his paintings? Could the entire case have been a carefully orchestrated publicity stunt by Frederic Thompson?

The only way to resolve this possibility was to determine whether or not Fielding's information was correct. I was initially pessimistic, since most entries in directories of this sort were (and still are) usually written by the contributors themselves. To make matters worse, Mantle Fielding offered preciously little data on the sources he relied upon while compiling his encyclopoedia. So I assumed that he obtained the entry from Thompson himself because the painter's business address is listed along with the short biography.

My assumption turned out to be incorrect. Checks undertaken for me both in Chilmark and in Middleborough proved that the *Dictionary* was wrong about Frederic Thompson's place of birth. He *was* born in Middleborough, to a Lewis H. Thompson and Mary W. Holmes on November 5, 1868, precisely as Hyslop's report stated. His birth was duly recorded at the city's town hall. It was many years later, sometime during the 1920s, that Thompson resided briefly on Martha's Vineyard. Perhaps this residency confused Mantle Fielding, who mistakenly believed that he had been born there and printed this information without further checking. I also subsequently learned that by the turn of the century the Salmagundi Club had opened its doors to general membership.

But what about Frederic Thompson's possible prior training in landscape painting? This issue will probably never be conclusively resolved. It would not necessarily indicate fraud on his part if he had studied painting *after* working with Hyslop, but since Fielding's information was incorrect about Thompson's place of birth, whether the painter really studied with George H. McCord is likewise suspect. The only information I could collect concerning McCord's career is also minimal. He was a prominent landscape artist in New York, but he died in 1909 when Thompson's career began. This date is close to the time Hyslop's work with Thompson ended, so it doesn't seem likely that the jeweler subsequently studied with him. We do know, however, that Frederic Thompson never denied his previous psychic story and during the 1920s still claimed spiritual contact with R. Swain Gifford.

So what can we conclude on the basis of this information? It seems to me that despite certain suspicions, the Thompson/Gifford case refuses to bow before skeptical scrutiny. While suggestions of deliberate fraud by either Thompson or Prof. Hyslop still continue to be voiced, there remains neither solid nor even inferential evidence to indict the case. Every criticism of the case I've heard or collected can be readily dismissed.

Spirits vs. Telepathy: The Issue Revisited

"Spirits vs. telepathy" was the way Prof. Hyslop titled psychical research's survival controversy. The debate is probably no better named today, though contemporary parapsychologists extend the argument: We now speak in terms of super-ESP and no longer simply worry about telepathy! To place this issue more within the current context, was Frederic Thompson possessed by the surviving soul of R. Swain Gifford? Or did he clairvoyantly tap into the memories and personality of the deceased painter? Did this extrasensory contact lead to a pathological identification with the deceased artist—so strong that Thompson believed himself possessed by Gifford's soul?

The standard reply to this theory is to point to Thompson's skill as a painter. Although he didn't possess much personal talent, he certainly began developing the requisite skills when the spirit, soul, or whatever of R. Swain Gifford began influencing him. Some researchers believe that while information can be transferred by extrasensory perception, such could not be true for skills. Skills are learned faculties that develop over extended periods of time through practice. The instantaneous transferrence of a skill by extrasensory perception has never been reported by parapsychologists. Some researchers reject the super-ESP theory as an explanation for the Thompson/Gifford case for this reason.

But this is hardly the final word on the subject. A fascinating psychoanalytical and non-survivalistic explanation of the case was offered to me in 1970 by Dr. Jule Eisenbud, a psychoanalyst and psychiatrist practicing in Denver, Colorado, whose theory is primarily based on the super-ESP hypothesis. It has never before been published, since it was sent directly to me in response to an early draft of this book. So I would like to take this opportunity to present it to a larger readership.

Dr. Eisenbud begins his exploration of the case by seeking some motivation behind Frederic Thompson's close identification with R. Swain Gifford. Why did this psychological and psychic bonding begin in the first place? What Dr. Eisenbud calls "slender threads" toward answering this question were some unintentional slights the jeweler suffered while talking with the famous painter. The first probably occurred when Gifford refused to encourage Thompson's painting career, and in Dr. Eisenbud's own words, "in effect telling him to stick to his metal working." It is clear that Thompson respected and probably even idolized R. Swain Gifford. But when the craftsman visited the celebrated painter's studio in New Bedford, Gifford didn't even recognize him. It was another psychological slap in the face for the aspiring painter!

It is at this point that Dr. Eisenbud draws upon his psychiatric background. He suggested that,

These slights may appear to be meager enough data upon which to base a serious supposition concerning the underlying dynamics of the Thompson-Gifford case. However, psychiatrists regularly see the far-reaching and sometimes quite astonishing effects of what might superficially seem to be slight enough rejections. If in fact Gifford had become a kind of admired ideal image for the youthful Thompson, a target for unconscious identification—and we are certainly not postulating in this anything at all uncommon between a young man aspiring to a vocation and an older one with considerable gifts along the lines aspired to—such treatment could be crushing. On one hand it might well have resulted in what might superficially appear to have been a complete withdrawal of interest on Thompson's part in Gifford's subsequent life and work. (There is some ambiguity on this point, but there were several years during which Thompson is alleged neither to have sought nor to have had any further contact with Gifford, not even learning of his death until almost two years after it had occurred.) But it could at the same time have resulted in a compensatory strengthening of the unconscious bonds of identification with Gifford. This would have amounted to an unconscious attempt to capture and hold the rejecting ideal figure through a kind of psychic incorporation, which psychiatrists commonly see in similar situations. And this could well have led ultimately to a delusion on Thompson's part that Gifford's spirit had actually invaded and informed his own by way of singling him out to be the vehicle for continuing his work.

This type of feeling-idea is consistent with a wide range of phenomena commonly seen when people feel rejected or abandoned by someone whose love and appreciation they desire. It is perhaps most often—in fact classically—seen in the subtle kinds of identifications which develop during and after mourning for a love object lost through death or other type of desertion.

I think this theory can best be exemplified with an example taken from a related field of study. My original training (apart from parapsychology) was for a career in music. Like most young and enthusiastic oboists in the 1960s and 1970s, I studied with a former student of the great Marcel Tabuteau, who served as the first chair player of the Philadelphia Symphony for several years. He was a greatly respected teacher and player, but he was personally a harsh and rejecting taskmaster who sometimes destroyed his students psychologically. Despite these unpleasant characteristics, some of his students developed curious fixations with the man. My own teacher explained that one player he knew (himself a phenomenally gifted musician) began to identify with his mentor to a pathological degree. He started walking like the man, put on a French accent while speaking, and even mimicked several of his personal habits—such as smoking a cigarette through a piece of bamboo cane. In such a case, it is difficult to know where psychological identification ends and pathology begins.

This is the sort of emulation and identification that Dr. Eisenbud believes could have influenced Frederic Thompson, probably orchestrated by his subconscious fixation on painting. But the psychiatrist doesn't stop there, for he is a good enough parapsychologist to realize that some sort of paranormal factor complicated the case. Frederic Thompson may have been psychic to begin with, he suggests. So when this process of identification began (perhaps when Gifford died), Thompson may have used his clairvoyance to "connect" with scenes from the painter's beloved Elizabeth Islands. Perhaps his sixth sense even led him to envision Gifford's unfinished paintings. Dr. Eisenbud believes that such an explanation is more expedient psychologically than believing in spirit return and possession.

> From a purely motivational standpoint, it would appear somehow easier to envision what had occurred as a natural, if psi-mediated, projection of Thompson's unconscious fantasy than as some kind of emanation from someone who in life seems to have found Thompson uninteresting both as a person and as an aspiring painter. Indeed nothing, under the circumstances, ought less to be taken at face value than the statement of a medium consulted by Hyslop that a communicator, assumed to be Gifford, looked "elated over his power to return and finish his work." It is not likely that the real Gifford, who held classes at an art school, would have had little trouble in finding among his former students any number of channels for this power more promising than Thompson's.

It is here where I think Dr. Eisenbud's logic stumbles badly, and I can easily think of a rejoinder to this point: Perhaps the surviving spirit of R. Swain Gifford couldn't find anyone psychic enough to incorporate with. In other words, perhaps he was drawn to Thompson precisely because the jeweler was both psychically and psychologically bonded to him.

But what of the skills he displayed? Dr. Eisenbud believes that Thompson probably possessed some undeveloped talent to begin with that simply blossomed further when his identification with the deceased painter began. Is this likely?

Indications can be found in Hyslop's report that Thompson's skills didn't blossom instantaneously, but grew steadily under the Gifford influence. The professor stated that the original sketches and paintings placed in his possession (which represented some of Thompson's first artistic endeavors) were not very good. Of course, it is difficult to know whether Hyslop was a good judge of sketches and oil paintings. But this artistic judgment was recently confirmed by the only person I know who ever saw these early works. The files and archives of the American Society for Psychical Research were sorted through during the late 1960s, when the organization moved to new quarters. An employee of the society came upon what were probably the critical pictures. She didn't initially recognize them, and since they were so inferior in content and style, she condemned them to the trash bin.* While the destruction of these works is a real loss, there is good evidence that Thompson later developed pretty fair skills and continued working successfully as a painter well into the 1920s. He sold several of his paintings to clients who knew nothing of the story behind their production. I have recently learned, too, that many gifted painters show little promise during their early careers and only develop with time and when their skills become more advanced.

The problem with Dr. Eisenbud's line of psychodynamic thinking, though, is that it can't be empirically falsified. There is simply no way of disproving the concepts and reasoning the psychiatrist puts forth. So whether the reader believes in spirits or in psychoanalysis is simply a matter of personal predilection. It really comes down to whether each reader considers the prospects for survival of death likely.

I personally feel that considerable evidence does point to psychic

---

* Several of the original sketches by Thompson surfaced in the ASPR files in 1986. Whatever paintings were also originally placed in the files were probably accidentally destroyed.

survival. This evidence comes to us through the study of purported post-mortem contact, through psychological research on near-death experiences, through the reality of out-of-body experiences, and through the existence of several other forms of paranormal phenomena. (Some of this research is summarized and evaluated in my previous books *The Welcoming Silence* [1973] and, more recently, in my *Life after Death*.) So I don't think that the evidence for spirit possession can be evaluated apart from the larger context of this related research. To posit a psychodynamic explanation for cases of spirit possession, we would have to posit similar explanations for all the evidence for survival. This is where many critics of the survival theory fail. By trying to explain each case of possible spirit return piecemeal, they ignore the fact that the collected evidence for survival constitutes an intricate interconnected mosaic. Extracting a tile from this mosaic doesn't destroy the larger picture, and the little piece makes no identifiable sense unless placed back within it.

Researchers who support the super-ESP theory also refuse to contend with the fact that extrasensory perception seems in general to be a relatively weak capacity. While parapsychologists continue to collect impressive evidence pointing toward survival, evidence for the existence of super-ESP is practically nonexistent. So the skeptic must resort to explaining away the empirical evidence for survival by constructing a hypothetical capacity!

This isn't to say that Dr. Eisenbud's explanatory model is wrong, by any means. He is certainly aware of the problems to which such rampant speculation is prone, and Dr. Eisenbud has even tried to uncover specific evidence for the super-ESP hypothesis by studying the evidence for spirit possession. (We'll be examining this evidence momentarily when we reconsider the Doris Fischer case.) But for the present, it strikes me that the survival theory explains the Thompson/Gifford case more simply, directly, and cogently than any other. There is no single aspect of the case that doesn't directly fit the explanation that R. Swain Gifford's surviving personality was somehow controlling Frederic Thompson.

I think we can say the same thing about the De Camp/Stockton and the Rogers/Abbot cases. I explained my reasons for favoring survivalistic interpretations of these cases in Chapters 5 and 6, so I will only briefly review them here.

The evidence for survival displayed in these two cases differs significantly from that displayed in the Thompson case. It rests not on the experiences of the protagonists but on the sittings Hyslop had with Minnie Soule. It is easy to believe that Etta De Camp had literary ability buried within her subconscious. She worked in the literary field, and when she published her Stockton stories in 1913, she wrote an epilogue entitled "Why I Know Frank Stockton Writes Through Me." This brief essay runs little more than four pages, but it shows that Miss De Camp was capable of putting together a sentence or two. Although her prose is straightforward and colorless, the reader is left wondering what literary skills she really possessed. Similar sentiments could be applied to the career of Miss Ida Rogers, since many singers of that era blossomed with little or no formal musical training. But although these cases do not present strong evidence for survival, the experiments Hyslop undertook with Minnie Soule certainly did!

In both these instances Mrs. Soule brought through spirit entities directly in keeping with the possession/survival theory. Convincing representations of both Frank Stockton and Emma Abbott communicated through her, and the personas offered considerable information then unknown either to the sitters or to Hyslop. Even more impressive is that each of these communicators seemed to be totally separate entities. They possessed their own personalities, their own reasons for contacting the living, and their own idiosyncratic methods of communicating.

One specific incident reported from the Stockton sittings points even more directly to spirit return. During their first sittings, Hyslop and Miss De Camp encountered problems establishing contact with the Stockton personality. But the evening after the second sitting, the Stockton personality came to Miss De Camp at her hotel and offered a strange explanation for the difficulty. She was simply sitting too close behind the psychic. Hyslop and Miss De Camp followed the presence's recommendation and the sittings immediately improved—and continued to improve steadily for the rest of the series. Now, where did this important information come from if not from the personality trying to reach Hyslop through Minnie Soule in the first place?

The messages Mrs. Soule delivered from the late and great Emma Abbott were filled with similarly impressive details. The scenario she and the other communicators offered for Ida Rogers's musical development was completely inconsistent with Hyslop's expectations. So if this complex "plot" didn't come either from the sitters or from the psychic, whence did it come?

In other words, the communicators who controlled Mrs. Soule didn't seem to be shadowy or monodimensional split-offs from the psychic's own mind. They appeared to be real people eagerly seeking to complete their earthly missions by contacting the living. In light of such complexities as these, in fact, the survival theory becomes more and more enticing and probable.

So far then, it appears that the survival theory can best explain the cases of spirit obsession James Hyslop investigated between 1907 and 1920. But if the reader expects me to completely endorse the survival theory, he or she will be disappointed. For even though I think the survival theory works best for the Thompson, De Camp, and Rogers cases, I am equally reluctant to explain the related Doris Fischer case the same way. This case is actually an embarrassment to the survival theory on several counts, not the least of which is the dubious revelations offered by Mrs. Soule's controls and communicators—the same sort of communicators whose evidence is so impressive in the prior cases. While the Doris case looks today like a textbook example of multiple personality, Mrs. Soule's communicators were hopelessly befuddled by their sitter. Even though her controls successfully brought through some impressive messages from Doris's deceased mother, they offered equally implausible information concerning the girl's psychological problems.

It seems that only James Hyslop was oblivious to these problems with the sittings. After he published his report on the experiments in 1917, other researchers were left shaking their heads. Perhaps the most pertinent comments came from Prof. F.C.S. Schiller, a philosopher well-known in his day who was a president of the Society for Psychical Research. He reviewed the report that same year for the *Proceedings of the Society for Psychical Research*. The sentiments he expressed in 1917 were similar to my own reaction to the case today.

Professor Schiller wrote that "Dr. Hyslop not unnaturally prefers to believe in his medium's 'controls,' but he hardly appears to recognize what a monstrous tale they have induced him to tell." Mrs. Soule's controls didn't suggest merely that Doris was possessed but that "a titanic struggle between the powers of good and evil was going on for years over, and in, the soul of Doris Fischer."

This purported struggle, the reader will recall, was being masterminded by the surviving spirit of the infamous Giuseppe Balsamo (alias "Count Cagliostro") in collaboration with several other discarnates. Some of these spiritual beings were working behind the scenes with Doris's secondary personalities. But as the British philosopher stated so cogently, Soule's controls "think that the struggle is still on, and are unaware that Doris has been cured, and is now as sane and normal as anyone. . . . If such are the ignorance and sense of values that prevail among the good influences on the spiritual plane, it is no wonder that the devils have things pretty much their own way on the earthly."

By the end of his interesting commentary Schiller pretty much supported telepathy over the spirits. He suggested that Mrs. Soule was merely reading Hyslop's mind and presenting evidence—some of it collected clairvoyantly—consistent with his expectations.

This nonsurvivalistic approach to the case does make considerable sense. It's possible that Doris was extremely sensitive to the spirit realms. But there is little evidence that such influences played any role in her mental illness. The possibility that she suffered from possession was often implicitly and explicitly suggested to her—first by Dr. Prince through his informal exorcisms, and then by James Hyslop by taking her to Minnie Soule. These psychological suggestions probably contributed to the possession delusions that incapacitated Doris after her father died in 1934. These delusions were more a complication of her prior problems than integral to them.

But although it is easy to dismiss Minnie Soule's revelations about Doris Fischer, neither Professor Schiller nor anyone else ever explained the psychological dynamics that led her psyche to concoct such a wild story. From whose mind or expectations did the *soi-distant* "Count Cagliostro" emerge to play such an important role in the sittings? For some possible insight into this problem, we will refer again to the writings of Dr. Jule Eisenbud, who has spent considerable time researching the Doris case. His findings were not published until 1983, when he included a chapter on the Fischer/Soule sittings in his *Parapsychology and the Unconscious*.

If you recall from Chapter 8, there were three primary communicators during these sittings. Included among them were the purported spirit of Doris's beloved mother (who shed considerable light on the girl's past); a childish Indian spirit who claimed responsibility for some of Doris's early escapades; and the ultimately nefarious "Count Cagliostro." His purported role in Doris's sickness was as an organizer for several discarnate entities wishing to control Doris. It was this scenario that led Professor Schiller to criticize the survivalistic elements in the Doris sittings. He considered this entity to be merely a creation from Minnie Soule's mind, while Prof. Hyslop was more prone to accept the personality's bona fides. Or at least the notion that the communicator was some sort of earthbound entity, perhaps making fanciful claims about himself. It wasn't until Dr. Eisenbud delved into the "Cagliostro" communications, though, that new light was shed on the Soule sittings. The evidence he uncovered indicates that perhaps both Schiller and Hyslop were only partially correct.

Dr. Eisenbud was primarily interested in two aspects of the "Cagliostro" personality when he undertook his research: the stories the entity told of his earthly life and the social philosophy he presented in his communications.

The Cagliostro personality first appeared to Mrs. Soule during the subliminal stage of her trance. She saw him simply dressed in a long cloak with a hood falling back from his head, and she was immediately repulsed by the figure. She was specifically frightened by his piercing eyes, a characteristic for which the Count had been famous in life. When this communicator first interrupted the Doris sittings, his initial speech was a scathing indictment of several social conventions. Hyslop's only reply—which Dr. Eisenbud feels is significant and revealing—was to ask the entity whether he was a womanizer and a seducer. The communicator responded with a burst of enmity, severely criticizing a society that would condemn a woman for her lost virtue. The professor immediately took issue with the entity and responded with some moralistic chatter, but the communicator countered that "freedom without fear" was society's only goal.

This same communicator appeared two days later and once again interrupted the Doris sittings. This time the communicator offered a rousing condemnation of religion, especially Christianity. "I tell you there is more falsity under the cloak of religion," the entity related, "than in the life of a libertine, who is true to the instincts of his nature." He then told Hyslop (without mincing words) where to go.

"Now the remarkable thing about this material," writes Dr. Eisenbud in his book, "is not just the appearance out of the blue of a communicator who gives a lively representation of a character with ideas about sexual morality and religion completely out of tune with his time, but the fact that, as it developed, it was almost sixty years before anything came along publicly to support such a characterization."

By scouring books about the life of Cagliostro published prior to the Soule sittings, Dr. Eisenbud learned that the famous romancer was known to be a liar, swindler, and fake miracle-worker. But no indications existed that he was ever either a critic of Christianity or a social reformer and philosopher. New light on the life of this fascinating personality was published only in 1974, when Roberto Gervaso's book *Cagliostro* was translated from the original 1972 Italian edition. This biography included several details about Cagliostro's trial by the Holy Inquisition in Rome in 1789, where the Count was charged with heresy and for being a Freemason. It is clear from this recently revealed information that the opinions expressed by Mrs. Soule's "Cagliostro" matched some of the (then) unpublished charges brought by the court. During this trial the self-ordained Count lashed out at the Church and expressed his belief in sexual emancipation. Some of these speeches closely match the diatribes he later made through Mrs. Soule. Even some of the entity's specific wordings echoed speeches delivered by Cagliostro to the Inquisition. Roberto Gervaso had collected his material from an unpublished Italian manuscript stored in a Rome library. This manuscript was based on a more complete document still held by the Vatican but never publicly released, so it is ludicrious to think that Minnie Soule ever had access to the information.

Even the skeptical Dr. Eisenbud concedes that only two explanations can account completely for Minnie Soule's "Cagliostro" communications. Either the real Count Cagliostro was communicating during the Doris sittings, or Mrs. Soule was displaying some sort of super-ESP power while fashioning the personality from within her own mind.

Dr. Eisenbud finally does opt for the super-ESP theory, but he promotes this explanation by way of a detailed psychological analysis of the Doris sittings. He begins by explaining why he feels the "Cagliostro" personality is ultimately unconvincing and flat. Cagliostro probably died, explains the psychiatrist, a broken man in solitary confinement, but the entity brought forth by Mrs. Soule seemed to be an embodiment of the earlier Cagliostro—the defiant egoist whose career was ultimately destroyed by the Church he so despised. It is the broken Cagliostro who should have communicated through Mrs. Soule and not the defiant romancer, or the previously defiant Count made wiser by his suffering in prison.

Even though the psychiatrist rejects the spiritistic claims of Mrs. Soule's "Cagliostro," Dr. Eisenbud realizes that his presence at the Doris sittings can't be dismissed so easily. The communicator was a drop-in communicator par excellence and had certainly never been expected either by Doris or by Hyslop. Being that he is a psychoanalyst by training, Dr. Eisenbud properly realizes that there must have been a psychological reason for his existence.

The Denver psychiatrist found the first clue to this mystery in Hyslop's strong reaction to the personality's presence and outspoken views. Although Hyslop clearly disliked both the entity and everything for which he stood, Mrs. Soule's "Cagliostro" seemed similar to the many other obsessing personalities the professor contacted with the help of the Boston psychic. It would even seem, writes Dr. Eisenbud, that Hyslop was locked into "some sort of Manichean struggle against the forces of evil." Based on this curious fact, he notes "that there could be an internal dynamic connection between the spiritually inclined professor and the low, sensuous characters who kept turning up at the séances he attended was not yet widely appreciated as a psychological possibility."

The same psychological factors may have been true of Doris Fischer, who from all contemporary accounts was something of a prude. In fact, she was continually castigated by sexual imagery when she finally lost her reason.

So what Dr. Eisenbud is saying is relatively simple. James Hyslop's moral rigidity and Doris Fischer's prudery may have been reactions to their strong but unconscious libidinous desires. Now most people adopt just these defenses in order to deal with uncomfortable desires, and this phenomenon is called "reaction-formation" in psychology. So communicators such as the self-proclaimed "Count Cagliostro" could simply be repressed aspects of the sitters' own selves. Mrs. Soule was probably drawing upon some hidden dimension within her sitters' minds when she created her "Cagliostro." The bogus communicator then served as a means to express a social and sexual philosophy that Doris and Hyslop consciously rejected but secretly favored.

Dr. Eisenbud's analysis of the Doris sittings doesn't end at this point. He finds considerable evidence supporting his solution to the case in Minnie Soule's own responses to "Cagliostro." Even though she initially feared him, she later began to cry hysterically after Hyslop banished him from the séances. She wanted him back! She, too, was most likely secretly attracted to the inconoclastic and sexually rebellious persona.

Dr. Eisenbud also cites reasonable confirmation that Mrs. Soule's "Cagliostro" was responding to feelings secretly entertained by Doris's mother, which she presumably transferred to Doris during their life together. Remember that Mrs. Fischer eloped when she was sixteen and later suffered the psychological loss of her parents, who condemned her in the name of their religion. (They were strict Methodists who disowned their daughter for her rebelliousness, even after she begged for a reconciliation.) Mrs. Fischer must have been an unruly girl, and some of her sexual and religious rebelliousness was probably instilled in Doris.

Of course, we see these same dislikes for religion and sexual restriction in "Cagliostro's" speeches.

"So we have more than ever reason to suspect that Cagliostro may not have been the unwelcomed intruder he seemed at first," concludes Dr. Eisenbud. "He could very well have been, as suggested earlier, some sort of dream figure omnibus for the unconscious hankerings of all the principals in the sittings, including now the medium herself who may, deep down in her own femininity, have shared the hidden yearnings of Doris and her mother—and yes of Hyslop himself—for the uninhibited life of the senses."

I have not been citing Dr. Eisenbud's writings on the Doris sittings because they represent the final word about them. My intention has been to show that the Soule/Fischer sittings can be provisionally explained without recourse to the survival hypothesis. The confusion that Schiller found in the sittings can be possibly explained by taking a psychodynamic perspective on the case.

But is Dr. Eisenbud's interpretation of the Doris sittings the correct one? I personally don't believe that the psychiatrist's analysis can withstand serious critical scrutiny. For one thing, there is no reason to believe that James Hyslop, Doris Fischer, or Minnie Soule were particularly socially or sexually repressed. Most people living in those post-Victorian decades—even in the rough and rugged United States—bowed before rigid codes of personal and sexual behavior. They reflected a culture that was generally rigid, unenlightened, and repressed. So why didn't similar entities appear during Hyslop's sittings with Frederic Thompson, Ida Rogers, or Etta De Camp? The communicators at their sittings were sometimes somber, sometimes pugnacious, sometimes helpful, and sometimes confused. But they were never unpleasant or particularly licentious!

The real crux of Dr. Eisenbud's theory is that Mrs. Soule's "Cagliostro" couldn't have been the historical seducer. But his view is based on the psychiatrist's arbitrary opinions about the state of Cagliostro's mind when he died in prison. It strikes me that if the historical Cagliostro were truly rebellious, his prison term would have fired his scorn for the Church and simultaneously entrenched his conviction in moral and social freedom. I personally couldn't fault the out-and-out Spiritualist for believing Mrs. Soule's "Cagliostro" to be a bona fide spirit.

So does the Doris case and her sittings with Mrs. Soule constitute evidence *for* survival? I really don't think so, even taking into consideration the caveats outlined in the previous paragraph. For there is simply nothing in the phenomenology of Doris's multiple personalities that directly suggests spirit possession. Although it is true that informal exorcisms seemed to momentarily relieve her problems, Doris (or her secondary personalities) was probably responding to strong implicit and explicit suggestions from her foster father. The virtue of Dr. Eisenbud's critique is that it perhaps offers certain possibilities towards some future solution to the case. For the present, though, just what psychological and parapsychological dynamics were taking place during the sittings remain enshrouded in confusion. But it is doubtful if the spirits intervened very much during them.

This ultimate interpretation of the Doris case and sittings brings us to the next phase of our discussion. If the Doris case doesn't point to the reality of spirit possession, what can we say about other similar cases? What about Dr. Allison's claim that some patients suffering from multiple personality can become genuinely possessed? Or Dr. Peck's clinical experiences with possession and exorcism? Or the claims of such researchers as Dr. Titus Bull and his present-day Kardecismo colleagues who believe they can successfully treat these special patients with spiritistic therapy?

My personal opinion is that relatively little of the evidence points directly to survival or to the reality of spirit possession. But before discussing this position further, I'd like to explore some recently completed research into this strange disorder. By reviewing this fascinating chapter in contemporary psychiatry, I think we can understand why the early researchers were so often baffled by their experiences.

Despite the historical research we've been covering in this book, the existence of multiple personality wasn't officially recognized by the psychiatric community until 1980. Several criteria for properly diagnosing the disorder were included at that time in psychiatry's official *Diagnostic and Statistical Manual*. This breakthrough was followed by the founding of the International Society for the Study of Multiple Personality in 1982. The first international conference on the subject convened two years later in Chicago. The upshot of the conference was that four psychology and psychiatric journals devoted entire special issues to the subject. Each year a similar conference on the subject is sponsored in Chicago by the society in collaboration with Rush-Presbyterian-St. Luke's Medical Center. Several experts believe that the problem of multiple personality should be of growing concern to psychiatry, since one out of every twenty thousand people could be suffering from the disorder.

Dr. Bennett Braun is a leading researcher in the field of multiple personality. Not only has he been a president of the International Society for the Study of Multiple Personality, but some of his pioneering work promises to open new chapters in the study of this disorder. While it has long been known that the various personalities that make up a case are psychologically independent and distinct, Dr. Braun and other researchers recently discovered that each of these personalities *may also be biologically distinct*.

Dr. Braun first documented this discovery in 1983, when he reported on brain-wave tracings he had taken from two of his patients. The first subject was a middle-aged woman named Jane, whose original complaint was her problem with weight control. The psychiatrist only gradually learned that she also suffered from competing multiple personalities. The patient became extremely depressed when she realized the extent of her problems, and she had to be hospitalized, during which time several of her secondary personalities emerged to the amazement of her therapist. They were a colorful group of characters that included a teenaged girl, a sexually manipulative personality, a self-debasing entity who was totally preoccupied with her physical appearance, an infant, and several others. The patient was treated by way of hypnosis, and Dr. Braun successfully fused most of the secondary personalities into his patient's primary self.

One particularly strange feature of the case was that the patient was originally color-blind. This fact was formally proved through an isochromatic color-blindness test. But when the secondary personalities fused, the newly integrated Jane wasn't!

But this was hardly the most amazing aspect of the case. During the course of the patient's therapy, Dr. Braun decided to explore what was occurring within his patient's brain, especially when her secondary personalities were controlling the body. To implement this project, Dr. Braun took Jane to the National Institute of Mental Health in Bethesda, Maryland, where the patient underwent brain-wave (electroencephalograph or EEG) monitoring while staring into a flashing light. This is a test for what is called the visual evoked response. The procedure momentarily increases electrical activity within the brain, which thereby gives the clinician a look inside his patient's neurological functions. EEG tracings are taken of the brain's electrical activity as it responds to the light, which a computer then translates into a topographical map. This mapping process shows those locations in the brain that tend to be either active or electrically calm, since the active parts will be darker. Such topographical maps were taken from four of Jane's conflicting personalities, and to everyone's surprise each revealed separate electrical patterns. When these personalities were successfully fused, the resulting personality produced its own individually patterned topographical map.

Dr. Braun later replicated this work with a second female patient. She was a skilled worker in the medical field who was reasonably self-sufficient—except for the several competing personalities who constantly battled for control of her body. Oddly enough, while the patient was clinically diabetic, each of her secondary personalities required *different* insulin doses. One of the personalities even suffered from lead poisoning, which was (apparently) not suffered by the others! Dr. Braun was able to obtain topographical maps from the patient's brain while she was being controlled by each of the competing personalities. The use of the visual evoked response was the basis for the mapping procedure. These displays seemed to be different for each personality but not to the remarkable extent noted in Dr. Braun's earlier case.

What does all this mean? The visual evoked response helps a psychologist or physician see the way a patient's brain responds to and processes information. Dr. Braun's innovative and exciting research is telling us that the secondary personalities who comprise cases of multiple personality tend to be biologically independent of each other. They are not merely distinct psychologically.*

Although the use of topographical brain mapping is a breakthrough in the study of multiple personality, it has merely confirmed what many clinicians have suspected for years. Psychiatrists researching this disorder collected similar data in the 1950s and 1970s. That EEG tracings change between the patient's personalities was first uncovered by an Italian psychiatrist in 1953. These findings were later substantiated by some research undertaken at the University of Kentucky by Dr.

---

*There is, however, one problem with this interpretation of Dr. Braun's research. In order to carry out his EEG studies, the psychiatrist had to place his two subjects under hypnosis and then "evoke" their split-off personalities. This procedure was necessary so that the patients could be studied under uniform conditions. Could his results have been a product of hypnotic suggestion, and not the result of the patient's true brain changes? Dr. Braun considered this a possibility in his report, but he pointed out that, according to some extensive experimental evidence he surveyed, hypnosis doesn't significantly influence the evoked response.

Arnold Ludwig in the early 1970s. He and his colleagues eventually published their research in 1972 in the *Archives of General Psychiatry*.

The patient was a twenty-eight-year-old black man who originally came to the hospital because of chronic headaches. He was also experiencing problems in his private life, since he was suffering emotional reactions to his legal separation from his wife and daughter. It didn't help when his psychiatrist discovered that his real problem was multiple personality. He had been suffering from the syndrome since childhood. The different personalities controlled his body for periods up to several days. The birth of these personalities seemed to date from a traumatic experience early in his life, when he saw his mother assault his father with a knife. The incident had been frightening enough to put the boy in the hospital. During the course of the patient's treatment, an additional personality began to emerge. Each of these secondary personalities served specific functions in the patient's life. One of them (who called himself "Sammy") took control when the patient was in legal difficulties. Sexual gratification was the primary interest of another secondary personality, while the resources of a third "self" were relied upon for the patient's self-defense. Only the cool, calm, and collected "Sammy" was aware of the existence of the other personalities, who often fought for control for the patient's body like a bunch of squabbling children.

The results of several psychological tests revealed that these personalities were interrelated in many complex ways. They shared *some* psychological features with each other, such as similar capacities for rote learning. But neurological testing provided the psychiatrists with a different clinical picture. EEGs, taken from each of the secondary personalities showed definite physiological differences in brain function among them. These findings certainly corroborate Dr. Braun's later topographical studies. Dr. Ludwig later collaborated on a similar study which focused on a female patient. Similar findings with regard to the evoked response were obtained at that time.

These studies must be kept in perspective, however, since such changes are not inevitable components of the multiple personality disorder. When the case reported in *The Three Faces of Eve* first came to light, for example, no EEG differences could be found between the young woman's personalities. So EEG changes cannot be considered a predictable element of the disorder. There is also the curious fact that EEG changes can be produced by a trained clinician *simulating* multiple personality, according to a study published in 1982 by Dr. Philip Coons of the Indiana University School of Medicine.

Despite the promise and problems associated with this and related research on multiple personality, clinicians treating the disorder have long known that each component personality will exhibit individual physiological quirks. Some of these stories recently came to the notice of Dr. Daniel Goleman while he was researching a story on multiple personality for *The New York Times*. What especially piqued his interest was the evidence that different secondary personalities sometimes suffer individual visual problems, and will differ in their tolerance to general anesthesia. One psychiatrist even claimed that some people with multiple personalities like to carry several pairs of eyeglasses, never knowing which personality might take over at any given time!

The way patients with competing personalities respond to anesthesia is even stranger. But for information on this subject, let's switch locations to California. For it is there that a group of mental health professionals have been studying multiple personality—totally out of the limelight—for eight years and have documented this strange discovery.

The founder and current leader of the group is Dr. Donald Schafer, who was a faculty member at the University of California, Irvine, when he began his work. The UCI Multiple Personality Group was originally organized when a young therapist approached him with a problem. She had found herself grappling with a case of multiple personality but didn't know the first thing about treating it. This wasn't strange, since few mental health workers ever receive instruction on the clinical handling of such cases. Dr. Schafer was just as baffled, but through trial and error, the two clinicians gradually uncovered the best way to treat the disorder. They realized that other clinicians might be coming upon similar cases and could use their professional guidance. So a small group of psychologists and psychiatrists united together and joined forces in the study of multiple personality.

Since the UCI group is primarily concerned with the treatment of the disorder, they have collected some fascinating stories and case studies. They, too, have learned that a patient's secondary personalities can be biologically independent from each other. During the group's early studies, for instance, they learned that one of their patients needed surgery. They didn't expect any complications to result from her mental problems, but they had underestimated the disorder.

"The anesthesia worked on a few, but not on the majority of the personalities," Dr. Schafer told an interviewer from the *Los Angeles Times*. When the surgery was completed, several of the personalities came forth and openly complained of the pain. This wasn't play-acting, either, for they were able to describe the surgical procedures employed by the physician. The patient later required a second operation, so her therapist had to contact her several component personalities and explain the problem to them. The personalities had to choose a specific member of their group to accept the anesthesia for their collective selves.

I found this story so strange that I phoned Dr. Schafer in June 1985 to confirm it. I tracked him down at his office in Orange County, introduced myself, and asked him about this particular report. Not only did he confirm the story, but even told me that it was a fairly common phenomenon. He further explained that his group had studied two such cases. The upshot of our talk was that Dr. Schafer invited me to visit the next meeting of his study group, which was scheduled for the following week.

This meeting was held at the University of California, Irvine Medical Center, located a mile or two down the road from Disneyland (probably the city of Anaheim's only claim to international fame). The meeting was certainly enlightening and approximately a dozen therapists were present. Each of them was actively treating (or had recently treated) patients with multiple personality. The meeting confirmed the emerging view that this disorder is more common than most psychiatrists believe. It was also interesting to learn of the disruptions these cases can cause for mental health workers, who often find themselves treating a dozen or more "patients" for the price of one! No wonder, I thought as the meeting progressed, these clinicians found it necessary to join together into a mutual support network. Dr. Schafer geared this particular meeting more toward administrative matters than clinical issues, since he was trying to affiliate his group with the larger Chicago-based group. Despite the important matters on the schedule, he took time to introduce me to the group members. This courtesy provided me with the time to explain my interest in the biological and physiological features of the disorder.

I pursued this subject further with some for the therapists after the meeting adjourned. These conversations enabled me to gather more information about their extraordinary patients. I wasn't provided with particular case studies, since the group members were understandably concerned with the ethical issue of patient-therapist confidentiality. But they were willing to discuss the purely physiological features of their cases if I was willing to conceal their names and any specific identifying features of the cases. I willingly agreed to these stipulations.

After the atmosphere was cleared of the confidentiality issue, the therapists collectively agreed that three major physiological variables were typical of the syndrome.

The first of these is right-vs.-left-handedness. In cases where a patient exhibits several secondary personalities, it is common to find that reliance on either the right or left hand is distributed between them. This struck me as a particularly revealing finding, since such preference is programmed within the organization of the brain.

The second physiological variable is the patient's response to allergic substances. Some patients suffer extreme allergic responses to specific substances, but their secondary personalities are sometimes totally immune to the same items. Sometimes a rival secondary personality will even expose the patient to such a substance, relinquish control, and leave the primary personality to suffer the consequences!

Eyesight and related visual problems is a final commonly complicated physiological variable in multiple personality. One of the psychiatrists I spoke with had treated just such a case. The patient was forced to wear glasses *over* her contacts whenever her secondary personality was in control.

When I delved further into the literature on multiple personality, it became clear that the experiences reported by this group of therapists were not rare. Dr. Bennett Braun had previously collected several similar reports, and he published a paper on the subject in 1983 in the *American Journal of Clinical Hypnosis*. The following, for example, is taken from some data Dr. Braun collected with regard to a patient who was allergic to citrus juice.

The problem was suffered by each of the patient's personalities with one single important exception. "If this personality ate an orange," explained Dr. Braun, "and remained in control of the body for a sufficient period of time to digest and metabolize the orange, no ill effects would be experienced by the system. Conversely, if he switched executive control too soon, a rash which itched and blistered would often be the result. If the personality that was *not* allergic to citrus resumed control, the itching would cease . . . 'as if I had taken an antihistamine.' If this personality remained in executive control for a significant period of time, the blisters would reabsorb much more quickly than if other personalities had control of the body. However, since the physiologic damage was done, only a more rapid healing would take place, not a miraculous, instantaneous recovery."

Dr. Braun also reports a similar case in which the patient "had a personality who was deathly allergic to cats. She would have runny eyes, a runny nose, wheezed and developed an itching rash when exposed directly to a cat. In another personality, she could sit and play with a cat for considerable periods of time, even be scratched and licked by the cat, without any apparent allergic response."

Competing personalities who exhibit idiosyncratic skin problems crop up again and again in the literature on multiple personality. Dr. Braun even found a case where one personality was severely epileptic, while the secondary personalities were immune to seizure behavior. It was later learned, in fact, that the competing personalities were *sending* the patient into convulsions in order to make him relinquish control of the body.

Similar cases could be cited from Dr. Braun's report, but more important is the light they shed on the enigma of multiple personality in general. While conducting his research on the physiology of the multiple personality patient, Dr. Braun came to one inescapable conclusion: The kinds of reactions most commonly reported match those bodily functions most easily manipulated by hypnosis. This is especially true of skin maladies, while hypnotic suggestion has also been used to inhibit allergic reactions and even seizures. Dr. Braun has even suggested that "a form of hypnosis/autohypnosis may be a common denominator" linking the diverse physiological phenomena exhibited by these extraordinary patients. Does it therefore follow that multiple personality itself is a form of self-hypnosis, or perhaps a form of self-hypnosis rampantly out of control?

This is the theory many experts currently favor. They believe that some sort of splitting process is programmed into the patient when he or she is a young child. I pointed out earlier that this process is usually a response to physical and/or sexual abuse. The child reacts to the conflict by spontaneously entering into some kind of trance, thereby creating a secondary personality to handle the ordeal. It is no secret that multiple personality patients are usually excellent hypnotic subjects. For this reason hypnosis and suggestion serve as the best form of therapy for them. It is therefore the most likely basis of the disorder in the first place.

Now, what does any of this contribute to the study of possession?

It seems to me that sometimes we oversimplify the phenomenon of multiple personality. We typically believe that these patients possess a primary personality that is being persecuted by several inferior split-off or fragmented selves. Our choice of terminology betrays this stark but

dubious conceptual model. We even call these split-offs by such con-
descending names as subpersonalities or secondary personalities. We
usually see them as psychologically subordinate to the patient's basic
personality, forgetting that some flaw within this original personality first
caused it to fragment. But a patient's separate personalities may each be
completely realized individuals. They probably constitute separate people coupled together within a common body, much to their (perhaps
understandable) disdain. Each of them possesses the capacity for love,
anger, hate, fulfillment, and a congeries of other emotions. They even
control the body's physiological functions in each of their personalized
and unique ways.

Because a patient's personalities can be so independent and psychologically separate, I think we can understand why some clinicians
come to believe in spirit possession. Some of these personalities may
appear so independent that they seem both physically and psychologically separate from the patient's primary personality. I tend to think that
some clinicians sometimes underestimate the way these secondary personalities function and thereby become seduced by the sheer complexity
of the disorder. Further evidence currently exists that patients suffering
from both multiple personality and temporal lobe abnormalities specifically develop possession delusions. No wonder some psychiatrists are
confused by these people!

The fact that multiple personality is a form of self-hypnosis also
explains why exorcism sometimes cures such patients. These people must
be exceptionally sensitive to psychological suggestion. So just as suggestion causes them to dissociate, it is likely that it can be used to cure the
condition. In fact, I am sorely tempted to think that John—the sexually
confused youth we discussed in Chapter 1—may have suffered from
some form of dissociative behavior. Maybe his feminine identity was
some sort of incipient secondary personality that gradually usurped control of the boy's psyche. The youth's primary personality was perhaps
only partially repressed, leaving him with strong and confusing feminine
feelings. John's extreme gender dysphoria did not seem to be a constitutional (genetic or biological) problem. Every indication exists that his
mother encouraged and rewarded his transsexual tendencies. The shock
of the exorcism and the later prayer service could have fused these di-
vergent aspects of John's mind, thereby resulting in the reinstatement
or reintegration of his original masculine personality.

In order to test this informal theory, I started reading extensively
into the clinical literature on gender dysphoria. I was hoping to find

clues by which we could explain John's bizarre cure. I didn't find anything enlightening until I read *The Spirit and the Flesh* by Walter L. Williams, a book devoted to the subject of sexual diversity in our indigenous Indian cultures. The book primarily concerns those tribes that recognize and institutionalize the *berdache* role. These people—the *berdaches*—consider themselves neither male nor female and represent a cross between what we call transsexuals and transvestites. (Neither designation is perfect, since no exact cultural equivalent exists in Western society.) These young Indians usually take on partially feminine sexual and social roles within the tribe, including female dress. They do not receive the condemnation of their culture, but Dr. Williams did find a peculiar case in which a *berdache*—like John—was "cured." This came by way of a strong supernatural experience, and the *berdache* reverted to dressing and behaving like a regular (male) member of the tribe in response.

Psychologists know, in fact, that conditioning and learning can be erased by a powerful physical or emotional shock. This fact was discovered first by I. P. Pavlov, the great Russian scientist who pioneered the study of classical conditioning. He is best remembered for his work with dogs, whom he conditioned to salivate at the sound of a bell that had been previously associated with food. Pavlov's laboratory suffered from a severe flood in 1924 which trapped several of the dogs, who were forced to swim frantically in their cages to keep from drowning. When they were mercifully saved by the researcher's assistant, the dogs fell into a state of collapse which constituted a delayed response to the crisis. Later it was discovered that the dogs' recently conditioned reflexes were gone—erased and destroyed by the watery ordeal and their subsequent collapse. Psychologists later developed intense forms of psychotherapy by inducing similar forms of stress and collapse, using it predominantly for the treatment of phobias and battle fatigue.*

The use of emotional stress coupled with powerful suggestion could be the reason exorcism and depossession often work with some patients. John underwent this sort of collapse upon being exorcised by his fundamentalist doctor, and psychological suggestion can also explain the embarrassing cultural differences that seem to mark the possession syndrome. To summarize from the material we covered in the previous chapters:

---

*For a popular history of this form of psychotherapy, see *The Mind Possessed* by Dr. William Sargant.

- The possessors contacted and exorcised by Dr. Carl Wickland, Dr. Titus Bull, and other Spiritualist clinicians always claimed to be spirits of the dead. Dr. Wickland's contacts specifically denied the existence of reincarnation.
- The possessors contacted and exorcised by Kardecismo practitioners claim to be either discarnate entities or the patient's previous incarnations.
- The possessors exorcised by deliverance ministers never claim to be spirits of the dead but evil agencies from the Satanic realms.

So does this information suggest that spirit possession is, in the final run, merely a bizarre psychological phenomenon?

This is certainly not the conclusion I wish to leave the reader with. What I am trying to say is that the psyche is enormously complex. Before pronouncing on the existence or nonexistence of spirit possession, we must keep these complexities continually in mind. Many of the psychologists, parapsychologists, psychiatrists, and clergymen discussed in this book believed that much spirit possession and obsession looks like mental illness. Perhaps it would be wiser to say that much mental illness looks like spirit possession! Most of the case studies reported in the previous chapters probably represent the far reaches of psychological pathology and involve the psyche's innate power to dissociate in response to implicit or explicit suggestions.

But in making this claim, I am certainly not saying that we can dismiss the considerable evidence Hyslop and his successors collected. We still have to respect people such as Dr. M. Scott Peck and Dr. Ralph Allison, who firmly believe in the existence of spirit and/or demonic possession. These men are skilled psychiatrists equipped with enormous clinical experience. We should respect their opinion that they occasionally see rare psychiatric cases resembling nothing they've experienced before. I was particularly impressed by Dr. Peck's comment that the cases of possession he exorcised only superficially resembled cases of multiple personality. The more he studied these patients, the clearer their pathology seemed to differ from the classic clinical picture.

Even if we dismiss Dr. Peck's and Dr. Allison's specific interpretations—and perhaps the skeptic has every right to—there still remains the parapsychological evidence for spirit possession to contend with. I pointed out before that psychological and/or super-ESP theories fail to explain some of James Hyslop's original cases. I can see no other explanation than spirit possession to account for the Thompson/Gifford case. Other cases also remain that seem to defy conventional psychological explanations. I personally remain impressed by the possessed morphine addict whom Dr. Worcester cured, by the spirit presence that sprang out of Dr. Allison's workman's compensation patient, and by some of the cures Dr. Bull implemented with the help of Carolyn Duke. These cases extend far beyond conventional psychiatry's wisdom and dogmas. What I don't believe is that psychopathology is commonly produced by such spiritual invasion, which is the belief of most Kardecismo practitioners and today's deliverance ministers. Cases of genuine spirit possession probably really do exist, but it is most likely an extraordinarily rare phenomenon. I can say little more for now.

The infinite boundary is that invisible border forever separating the living from the dead. But while infinite and unfathomable, the boundary may not be completely impermeable. In this book, I hope some light has been shed on the extent and complexity of this psychic frontier. It will be the responsibility of future researchers, clergymen, and psychiatrists to explore its perimeters further. So until that time comes, perhaps we should end by expressing our thanks to James Hyslop and his successors for pointing the way. They have shed important light on a phenomenon that psychiatrists are only today beginning to reevaluate and openly consider. This book is both a homage to their memory and a call for future research.

EPILOGUE

Pvt. George G. Ritchie "died" sometime during the early morning of December 19, 1943. He was stationed at Camp Barkeley, Texas, and the cause was severe bacterial pneumonia. When his body finally succumbed to the infection, some aspect of his self—maybe it was the soul itself—left its fleshy encasement. Private Ritchie was amazed by his sudden freedom, and while perfectly invisible to everybody in the infirmary, he began exploring the base and countryside while out-of-body. His experiences weren't all pleasant, though. He often saw spirits of the dead trying to influence the living. They were unaware that they were dead and could be neither heard nor felt. Later the young soldier found his way to a dingy bar where sailors were getting drunk. Spirits of the dead hovered close by the drinkers. Private Ritchie could tell the difference, since a bright aureole surrounded each of the sailors.

"Then I noticed a striking thing," wrote the former private. "A number of the men standing at the bar seemed unable to lift their drinks to their lips. Over and over I watched them clutch at their shot glasses, hands passing through the solid tumblers, through the heavy wooden counter top, through the very arms and bodies of the drinkers around them.

"And these men, every one of them, lacked the aureole of light that surrounded the others."

These were unpleasant earthbound spirits trying to enjoy the liquor being drunk by the sailors.

"It was obvious," continued Ritchie, "that these living people, the light-surrounded ones actually drinking, talking and jostling each other could neither see the desperately thirsty disembodied beings among them, nor feel their frantic pushing to get at those glasses."

Then Private Ritchie saw what happened when the drinking went beyond control.

> I thought I had seen heavy drinking at fraternity parties in Richmond. But the way civilians and servicemen at this bar were going at it beat everything. I watched one young sailor rise unsteadily from a stool, take two or three steps, and sag heavily to the floor. Two of his buddies stooped down and started dragging him away from the crush.
>
> But that was not what I was looking at. I was staring in amazement as the bright cocoon around the unconscious sailor simply opened up. It parted at the very crown of his head and began peeling away from his head, his shoulders. Instantly, quicker than I'd ever seen anyone move, one of the insubstantial beings who had been standing near him at the bar was on top of him. He had been hovering like a thirsty shadow at the sailor's side, greedily following every swallow the young man made. Now he seemed to spring at him like a beast of prey.
>
> In the next instant, to my utter mystification, the springing figure had vanished. It all happened even before the two men had dragged their unconscious load from under the feet of those at the bar. One minute I'd distinctly seen two individuals; by the time they propped the sailor against the wall, there was only one.
>
> Twice more, as I stared, stupefied, the identical scene was repeated. A man passed out, a crack swiftly opened in the aureole round him, one of the non-solid people vanished as he hurled himself at that opening, almost as if he had scrambled inside the other man.

Private Ritchie seemed to intuitively understand what was happening. "Was that covering of light some kind of shield then?" he asked. "Was it a protection against . . . against disembodied beings like myself?"

Private Ritchie luckily survived his ordeal. After enjoying several more adventures while traveling light, the base physician finally revived him. It took an adrenalin injection directly into the heart to start it beating, and Private Ritchie required three days to recover. He subsequently went to medical school, became a psychiatrist in Virginia, and in 1978 wrote his *Return from Tomorrow*. The book tells the story of his near-death experience and the way it influenced his life.

But I am left wondering about this protracted experience. Was this episode merely a vision, or perhaps an hallucination? Or did Private Ritchie actually witness the precise process of spirit possession? Did he directly observe the same process suggested by Dr. Titus Bull, Dr. Carl Wickland, Dr. M. Scott Peck, and others on the basis of their clinical experiences?

Did Private Ritchie tread the infinite boundary to make these extraordinary observations?

REFERENCES

Chapter 1

Barlow, David H., and Gene G. Abel. "Gender identity change in a transsexual: an exorcism." *Archives of Sexual Behavior* 6 (1977): 387–95.

Barlow, David H., J. Reynolds, and W. S. Agias. "Gender identity change in a transsexual." *Archives of General Psychiatry* 28 (1973): 569–76.

Gross, Martin. *The Psychological Society.* (New York: Random House, 1978).

Torrey, E. Fuller. *The Mind Game.* (New York: Emerson, 1972).

Chapter 2

Hyslop, James H. "A case of veridical hallucinations." *Proceedings of the American Society for Psychical Research* 3 (1909): 1–469.

Chapter 3

Anderson, Rodger I. "The life and work of James H. Hyslop." *Journal of the American Society for Psychical Research* 79 (1985): 167–204.

Berger, Arthur. "The early history of the A.S.P.R.: origins to 1907." *Journal of the American Society for Psychical Research* 79 (1985): 39–60.

Berger, Arthur. "Problems of the A.S.P.R. under J. H. Hyslop." *Journal of the American Society for Psychical Research* 79 (1985): 205–20.

Hyslop, James H. "A case of veridical hallucinations," op. cit.

Hyslop, James H. *Contact with the Other World.* (New York: Century, 1919).

Hyslop, James H. "Observations on the mediumistic records in the Thompson case." *Proceedings of the American Society for Psychical Research* 3 (1909): 593–613.

Hyslop, James H. "Preliminary report on the trance phenomena of Mrs. Smead." *Proceedings of the American Society for Psychical Research* 1 (1908): 525–722.

Hyslop, James H. *Psychical Research and the Resurrection.* (New York: Small, Maynard & Co., 1908).

Hyslop, James H. "The Smead case." *Proceedings of the American Society for Psychical Research* 12 (1918): 11–667.

Hyslop, James H. "The Thompson case." *Journal of the American Society for Psychical Research* 3 (1909): 309–45.

Chapter 4

Fox, Oliver. *Astral Projection.* Reprint. (New Hyde Park, N.Y.: University Books, 1963).

Hufford, David J. *The Terror that Comes in the Night.* (Philadelphia: University of Pennsylvania Press, 1982).

Hyslop, James H. "A case of incipient obsession." *Proceedings of the American Society for Psychical Research* 13 (1919): 478–528.

Katz, Richard. *Boiling Energy.* (Cambridge, Mass.: Harvard University Press, 1982).

Katz, Richard. "Education for transcendence: lessons from the !Kung Zhu/Twasi." *Journal of Transpersonal Psychology* 5 (1973): 136–55.

Sannella, Lee. *Kundalini—psychosis or transcendence?* (San Francisco: H. S. Dakin, 1976).

White, John. *Kundalini, Evolution and Enlightenment.* (Garden City, N.Y.: Anchor/Doubleday, 1979).

Chapter 5

de Camp, Etta. *The Return of Frank R. Stockton.* (London: Rider, 1913).

Hamilton, W. H., J. S. Smyth, and James H. Hyslop. "A case of hysteria." *Proceedings of the American Society for Psychical Research* 5 (1911): 1–656.

Hyslop, James, H. "A complicated group of experiences and experiments." *Proceedings of the American Society for Psychical Research* 6 (1912): 181–265.

Hyslop, James H. *Contact with the Other World.* (New York: Century 1919).

[Hyslop, James H.] "Mediumistic experiments." *Journal of the American Society for Psychical Research* 3 (1909): 176–90.

[Hyslop, James H.] "Personal and experimental incidents." *Journal of the American Society for Psychical Research* 2 (1908): 492–503.

Hyslop, James H. "President G. Stanley Hall's and Dr. Amy E. Tanner's studies in spiritualism." *Journal of the American Society for Psychical Research* 5 (1911): 1–98.

Hyslop, James H. "Summary of experiments since the death of Professor James: I. Professor William James." *Journal of the American Society for Psychical Research* 6 (1912): 29–126.

Chapter 6

Hyslop, James H. *Borderland of Psychical Research.* (Boston: Small, Maynard, 1906).

Hyslop, James H. "A case of musical control." *Proceedings of the American Society for Psychical Research* 7 (1913): 429–569.

Chapter 7

Hyslop, James H. *Contact with the Other World.* (New York: Century, 1919).

Hyslop, James H. "The Doris Fischer case of multiple personality." *Proceedings of the American Society for Psychical Research* 11 (1917): 5–866.

Prince, W. Franklin. "The Doris case of multiple personality." *Proceedings of the American Society for Psychical Research* 9 (1915): 1–700; 10 (1916): 934–1419.

Prince, W. Franklin. *The Psychic in the House.* (Boston: Boston Society for Psychic Research, 1926).

Prince, W. Franklin. "The mother of Doris." *Proceedings of the American Society for Psychical Research* 17 (1923): 1–216.

Smith, Alson J. "Walter Franklin Prince: cleric, therapist, researcher." Reprinted in *Exorcism: Fact not Fiction*, edited by Martin Ebon. (New York: New American Library, 1974).

Tietze, Thomas. "Ursa Major: an impressionistic appreciation of Walter Franklin Prince." *Journal of the American Society for Psychical Research* 70 (1976): 1–34.

Tietze, Thomas. "Who was the 'Real Doris'?" In *Exorcism: Fact not Fiction*, edited by Martin Ebon, op. cit.

Chapter 8

Hyslop, James H. *Contact with the Other World*. (New York: Century, 1919).

Hyslop, James H. "The Doris case of multiple personality, Part III." *Proceedings of the American Society for Psychical Research* 11 (1917): 1–866.

Hyslop, James H. *Life after Death*. (New York: Dutton, 1918).

Prince, W. Franklin. *The Psychic in the House*. (Boston: Boston Society for Psychic Research, 1926).

Chapter 9

Bull, Titus. *Analysis of Unusual Experiences in Healing Relative to Diseased Minds*. (New York: James H. Hyslop Foundation, 1932).

Bull, Titus. *The Imperative Conquest*. (New York: James H. Hyslop Foundation, 1936).

Bull, Titus. *Nature, Man and Destiny*. (New York: James H. Hyslop Foundation, 1936).

Bull, Titus. "Report of the president to the James H. Hyslop Foundation." (New York: James H. Hyslop Foundation, Oct. 1, 1929).

Burns, Geoffrey C. H. "A case of apparent obsession." *Journal of the American Society for Psychical Research* 22 (1927): 319–334, 389–401, 439–52.

Howard E. Lee. *My Adventure into Spiritualism*. (New York: Macmillan, 1935).

Irion, Clyde. *The Profit and Loss of Dying*. (Los Angeles: DeVorss & Co., 1969).

Lambert, Helen. "The case of Mr. C. E., an obsession case treated by Titus Bull, M.D." *Psychic Science* 7 (1928) 197–214.

Leonard, Maurice. *Battling Bertha—the biography of Bertha Harris*. (London: Regency Press, 1975).

Prince, W. Franklin. "Review of 'A case of apparent obsession'." *Proceedings of the Society for Psychical Research* 38 (1928): 388–99.

Weldon, Warren. *A Happy Medium—the life of Caroline Randolph Chapman*. (Englewood Cliffs, N.J.: Prentice-Hall, 1970).

Wickland, Carl A. *Thirty Years Among the Dead*. (Los Angeles: National Psychological Laboratory, 1924).

Wickland, Carl A. *The Gateway of Understanding.* (Los Angeles: National Psychological Laboratory, 1934).

Chapter 10

Prince, W. Franklin. "Two cures of 'paranoia' by experimental appeals to purported obsessing spirits." *Bulletin of the Boston Society for Psychic Research* 6 (1927): 36–66.

Chapter 11

Bruce, H. Addington. "In Memorium—Elwood Worcester." *Journal of the American Society for Psychical Research* 35 (1941): 144–62.

Hyslop, James H. "Theoretical problems of mental healing." *Journal of the American Society for Psychical Research* 5 (1911): 341–68.

White, Sarah Parker. "Elwood Worcester and the case for survival." *Journal of the American Society for Psychical Research* 43 (1949): 98–107.

Worcester, Elwood. *Life's Adventure.* (New York: Charles Scribner's Sons, 1932).

Worcester, Elwood. "Recent development in the Doris case of multiple personality." In *Walter Franklin Prince: a tribute to his memory.* (Boston: Boston Society for Psychic Research, 1935).

Worcester, Elwood, and Samuel McComb. *Body, Mind, and Spirit.* (New York: Charles Scribner's Sons, 1932).

Chapter 12

Dooley, Ann. *Every Wall a Door.* (London: Abelard-Schuman, 1973).

Krippner, Stanley. "Cross-cultural approaches to multiple personality disorder: therapeutic practices in Brazilian Spiritism." Paper delivered at the Second International Conference on Multiple Personality/Dissociative States, Chicago, October 25–27, 1985.

Playfair, Guy Lyon. *The Unknown Power.* (New York: Pocket Books, 1975).

Playfair, Guy Lyon. *The Indefinite Boundary.* (New York: St. Martin's Press, 1976).

St. Clair, David. *Drum and Candle.* (Garden City, New York: Doubleday, 1972).

Chapter 13

Allison, Ralph, with Ted Schwartz. *Minds in Many Pieces.* (New York: Rawson Wade, 1980).

Bartlett, Kay. "Exorcisms defended by psychiatrist-author," *Los Angeles Times*, December 14, 1985.

Basham, Don. *Deliver Us From Evil.* (New York: Bantam Books, 1977).

Dailey, Abram. *Mollie Fancher, the Brooklyn Enigma.* (Brooklyn, N.Y.: privately printed, 1894).

Edelstein, M. Gerald. *Trance, Trauma, and Transformation.* (New York: Brunner/Mazel, 1981).

Hawksworth, Henry, with Ted Schwartz. *The Five of Me.* (Chicago: Henry Regnery, 1977).

Keyes, Daniel. *The Minds of Billy Milligan.* (New York: Random House, 1981).

Peck, M. Scott. *People of the Lie.* (New York: Simon & Schuster, 1983).

Schreiber, Flora Rheta. *Sybil.* (Chicago: Henry Regnery, 1973).

Sizemore, Chris Costner, and Ellen Sain Pittillo. *I'm Eve.* (Garden City, N.Y.: Doubleday, 1977).

Thigpen, Corbett H., and Hervey M. Cleckley. *The Three Faces of Eve.* (New York: McGraw Hill, 1957).

Chapter 14

Braun, Bennett. "Neurophysiologic changes in multiple personality due to integration: a preliminary report." *American Journal of Clinical Hypnosis* 26 (1983): 84–92.

Braun, Bennett. "Psychophysiologic phenomena in multiple personality and hypnosis." *American Journal of Clinical Hypnosis* 26 (1983): 124–37.

de Camp, Etta. *The Return of Frank R. Stockton.* (London: Rider, 1913).

Coons, Philip, Victor Milstein, and Carma Marley. "EEG studies of two multiple personalities and a control." *Archives of General Psychiatry* 39 (1982): 823–25.

Eisenbud, Jule. "Comments on the Thompson/Gifford case." Unpublished communication to the author, c. 1970.

Eisenbud, Jule. *Parapsychology and the Unconscious.* (Berkeley: North Atlantic Books, 1983).

Goleman, Daniel. "New focus on multiple personality." *The New York Times*, May 21, 1985.

Larmore, Kim, Arnold Ludwig, and Rolene Cain. "Multiple personality—an objective case study." *British Journal of Psychiatry* 131 (1977): 35–40.

Ludwig, Arnold M., et. al. "The objective study of a multiple personality." *Archives of General Psychiatry* 26 (1972): 298–310.

Mesulam, Mansel. "Dissociative states with abnormal temporal lobe EEG." *Archives of Neurology* 36 (1981): 176–81.

Rogo, D. Scott. *The Welcoming Silence*. (Secaucus, N.J.: University Books, 1973).

Rogo, D. Scott. *Life after Death*. (Wellingsborough: Aquarian Press, 1986).

Sargant, William. *The Mind Possessed*. (Philadelphia: Lippincott, 1974).

Schiller, F. C. S. "Review: The Doris Fischer case of multiple personality." *Proceedings of the Society for Psychical Research* 29 (1917): 386–403.

Shelley, Walter B. "Dermatitis artefacta induced in a patient by one of her multiple personalities." *British Journal of Dermatology* 105 (1981): 587–89.

Williams, Walter L. *The Spirit and the Flesh*. (Boston: Beacon, 1987).

About the Author

D. Scott Rogo is well-known as a researcher, educator, and writer in the field of parapsychology. He currently serves on the graduate faculty of John F. Kennedy University in Orinda, California. His previous positions have included visiting posts at the former division of parapsychology and psychophysics at Maimonides Medical Center in Brooklyn and the Psychical Research Foundation, formerly in Durham, North Carolina. He is the author of over twenty-five books in the field and was a columnist for *Human Behavior* magazine. Currently the consulting editor for *Fate* magazine, his work has also appeared in such publications as *Omni* and *McCall's*. Mr. Rogo makes his permanent home in Los Angeles, where he shares his house with his library and two golden retrievers.

INDEX

Abbott, Emma, 98, 100, 276, 277
  apparition of, 100, 110-111, 142
  return of, 101-115
Abel, Gene, 2, 5-7
allergic reactions, 290-291
Allison, Ralph, xiv, 252-266, 284, 294, 295
  views on multiple personality, 253, 255-56
  views on possession, 257-58, 260
  work with possession cases, 257-66
All Saints Episcopal Church, 120-121, 130
American Art Galleries, 17
American Art News, 37
American Institute for Scientific Research, 13, 18, 35, 40, 150, 152
American Journal of Clinical Hypnosis, 290
American Psychiatric Association, 252, 260
American Society for Psychical Research, 13, 18, 22, 32, 35, 36, 39, 46, 63, 72, 122-23, 139-140, 155, 164, 181, 185, 186, 192, 194, 194n, 196, 210-211, 231, 269, 275, 275n
Analysis of Some Unusual Experiences in Healing, (Bull), 179
Anderson Galleries, 50
Anderson, Rodger, 31n
Andrade, Hernani G. 230-31, 231
Annals of Psychical Science, 47
apparitions, 32, 33, 96, 100, 110-111, 131, 135, 152-53, 191-92
Archives of General Psychiatry, 287
Archives of Sexual Behavior, 8

art, 37-39, 167-68
Atlantic Monthly, The, 47
Atwood, Charles C., 39-40
aura, 162, 255
automatic painting, 17, 174, 187-88, 194, 205
automatic writing, 19, 57-58, 76-80, 80-81, 82, 90n, 98-99, 110, 126-27, 185-86, 197

Balsamo, Giussepe, 148n (see also Cagliostro, Count)
Barlow, David, 2, 5-7
Basham, Don, 248-49, 263n
Baylor, Courtney, 204n
Beauchamp, Christine, 134n, 146
Beckwith, J. Carroll, 38, 39, 39n
behavior identification, 2
Bellevue Medical College, 163
Bennet Divorce Case, 132
berdaches, 293
Bessinet, Ada, 72-73, 73n
Birney, David, 254
Boiling energy (Katz), 66
Borderland of Psychical Research (Hyslop), 96
Boston Society for Psychic Research, 155, 199, 210-211
Bourne, Ansel, 33, 72
brain tumors, 240
Braun, Bennet, 285-86, 290-91
Brazil, obsession research in, 219-32

311

Brazilian Institute for Psychobiophysical Research, 230
breathing techniques, 66
Brewin, Charles P., 72
Broadway magazine, 75
Bronson, Matthew, 234-40
Bull, Louis, 181
Bull, Titus, xiv, 39, 163-81, 183, 204, 205, 209, 209-210, 215, 231, 240, 248, 259, 260, 266, 294, 295, 299
    death of, 181
    discovery of Mrs. Duke, 165-66
    early investigations, 164
    founding of the James H. Hyslop Foundation, 175-76
    later work with psychics, 176-77
    life of, 163-64
    procedures for research, 166-67
    success rate of cures, 177-79
    views on obsession, 179-80
    work with obsession cases, 167-75
Burns, Geoffrey, 180-81
Burton, Mrs. (see Bessinet, Ada)

Cagliostro (Gervaso), 280-81
Cagliostro, Count, 143, 148, 278-84
California State University, Sonoma, 233
Callaway, Hugh, 59-60
Cambridge University, 31
cancer, 237, 241
Candomblé, 220
catalepsy, 57n
C.E., Mr. (case of), 167-71
channeling, 233-34, 235-36
Chapman, Caroline Randolph, 165-66
chemotherapy, 178
Chenowith, Mrs. (see Soule, Minnie)
Chicago Daily Tribune, 161
clairvoyance, 41, 108, 131, 132, 164, 173, 175, 254-55, 279
Clark University, 73
Cleaveland, Mrs. Willis M., 46-50, 74, 87-88, 99, 108, 270
Cleaveland, Willis, 47
Cleckley, Hervey, 250-52, 253
Columbia University, 31-33, 35, 37, 202
color blindness, 293
Common Cause, The, 88
computer technology, 84-85
congenital adrenal hyperplasm, 3
Conklin, Mrs., 176-77

Contact with the Other World (Hyslop), 50, 73n, 139, 140
Coons, Philip, 287
Craigie Foundation, 204
Cristiani, Léon, 224n.
Crookall, Robert, 60
cross references, 43
culture and possession, 231, 293-94
Cuttyhunk, 22, 24

Daily, Abram, 256n
De Camp, Etta (case of), 74-94, 95, 96, 99, 100-101, 107, 115, 137, 140, 141, 142, 149, 154, 276, 277, 283
De Praestigiis Daemonum (Weyer), 138
Deliver Us from Evil (Basham), 248, 263n
deliverance ministry, 245-46, 248, 294
dementia, 167
deobsession, (see rescue work)
derealization, 87
Diagnostic and Statistical Manual, 284
dissociative behavior, 84, 96, 118, 185, 263-64
Dooley, Ann, 224-25
Dorsett, Sybil, 252
Dow, Arthur, 37-38
Drew Seminary, 122
drop-in communicators, 143, 143n
drug addiction, 206-209
Duke, Carolyn C., 165-66, 169, 169-71, 171-73, 173-75, 177, 180, 181, 185, 295
Duke University, 215
Durham Medical College, 160
Duysters, George F., 76, 79, 80, 86, 90

Edelstein, M. Gerald, 249, 250
Edwards, Frederick, 211
EEG monitoring, 285-87, 286n
ego-state therapy, 249-50
Eisenbud, Jule, 272-76, 279-84
electroconvulsive shock therapy (ECT), 178, 223
Elements of Ethics (Hyslop), 31
Elements of Logic (Hyslop), 31
Elise (case of), 261-63
Elizabeth Islands, 22, 23-24, 25, 29, 44, 49, 50, 269, 270, 274
Emmanuel Church, 201, 203, 204n, 205
Emmanuel Movement, xiv, 203-204
epilepsy, 226
Esalen Institute, 67

Evidence of Satan in the Modern World (Cristiani), 224n
exorcism, 6-7, 8, 123-24, 125, 126, 139, 148, 189-91, 194, 196, 196n, 246-47, 258-59, 265, 279, 293
extrasensory perception, 211, 167, (see also: telepathy, clairvoyance)

faith healing, 7
Fancher, Mollie, 256n
Fate magazine, 252, 256
Faust (Gounod), 112n
Fechner, Gustav, 140, 202
Ferrari, Conrado, 224-25
Ferreira, Inacio, 225, 230, 231
Fischer, Doris, 117-35, 137-55, 183, 211-15, 228, 249, 278-84
  cause of problems, 118
  communications from mother, 144-45
  emergence of Real Doris, 127
  emergence of secondary personalities, 118-19, 119-20
  exorcism of, 125-26
  history of case, 130
  life with the Princes, 129-35
  interpretations of sittings with Mrs. Soule, 278-84
  meeting with the Princes, 121
  psychic experiences of, 131-35
  possible contacts with the dead, 150-54
  sitting with Mrs. Soule, 141-45
  subsequent life and insanity, 211-15
  therapy with Prince, 124-25
Five of Me, The (Hawksworth), 245n, 254
fluid (psychic), 64-65, 66
Foster, Ben, 38, 39, 39n
Foundations of Abnormal Psychology (London), 194
Fowler, Clara (see Beauchamp, Christine L.)
Fox, Oliver (see Callaway, Hugh)
Freud, Sigmund, 1, 164
Fritschle, Brittia L. (see Fischer, Doris)
Funk, Isaac K., 160-61

Gail (case of), 255-56
Gateway of Understanding, The (Wickland), 162
Gaule, Margaret, 24, 25, 45, 276
Gause, Grace, 176-77
gender dysphoria, 2-8, 292-93

General Survey of Psychic Phenomena (Lambert), 170
General Theological Seminary, 203
Gervaso, Roberto, 280-81
ghosts, 32 (see also, apparitions)
Ghosts I Have Talked with (McComas), 169
Gifford, Robert Swain, 14-27, 29-51, 71, 72, 74, 79, 88, 94, 101, 118, 138, 139, 164, 268, 270, 271, 272, 273-75, 294
  biography of, 14
  return of, 14
Goleman, Daniel, 288
Gounod, Charles, 112n
Grof, Stanislov, 67
Gross, Martin L., 2
group ritual therapy, 228
Gurney, Edmund, 31

Hall, G. Stanley, 31, 73
Happy Medium, A (Weldon), 166
Harper's magazine, 79-80
Harris, Bertha, 163
Harvard University, 32, 243
Harvey, E. Margaret, 164, 164n
hauntings, 154
Hearst, William Randolph, 252
Henry, S. (case of), 54-69, 71
Hiawatha (Longfellow), 146
higher selves, 128
Hodgson, Richard, 32, 33, 34, 35, 72, 134n, 143, 146
Holmes, Mary C., 271
Holy Inquisition, 281
Homer, Winslow, 38
Howard, E. Lee, 161-62
Hudson River School, 14
Hufford, David J., 57n
Hypnagogic images, 57n, 97
hypnosis, 126, 165, 207, 249-50, 286, 292
Hyslop, James H. xiii-xiv, 130, 135, 150, 155-56, 159, 160, 161, 163, 164, 183, 201, 202, 204, 205-206, 210, 215, 266, 268, 269, 270, 271, 272, 274, 276-77, 278-80, 280-84, 294
  background in psychology, 140
  controversy over Mrs. Piper, 73-74
  death of, 156
  investigation of Ada Bessinet, 72
  investigation of Brewin case, 72
  sittings with Mrs. Piper, 33-35

Hyslop, James H. (*continued*)
   views on obsession, 71-74, 95-97, 136-
      41, 159-60
   work with De Camp/Stockton case, 81-
      96
   work with Doris case, 141-50
   work with Henry case, 53-69
   work with Mrs. Cleaveland, 47, 47-50
   work with psychics, 71-73
   work with schizophrenic girl, 140
   work with Thompson/Gifford case, 13-
      17, 29-51
Hyslop, Winifred, 73, 155
hysteria, 263-64

I'm Eve (Sizemore), 251, 253-54
imaginary playmates, 247-48
Imperative Conquest, The (Bull), 179
incipient obsession, 54-69
incorporation with spirits, 235-36, 238-39
Indefinite Boundary, The (Playfair), 230n
Indiana University School of Medicine, 287
inner-self helpers, 262, 262n, 264
invalidism, 164n, 240
Irion, Clyde, 176

James H. Hyslop Foundation, 175-76
James, Henry, 50
James, William, 32-33, 87, 98-99, 138,
      184
Janet, Pierre, 196n, 263
J.D. (case of), 173-75
John (case of) 3-7, 293
Johns Hopkins Hospital, 4, 31, 73, 169
*Journal of the American Society for Psych-
      ical Research*, 174, 181, 204
Journal of Transpersonal Psychology, 66

Kalahari bushmen, 66
Kardec, Allan (see Rivail, Hyppolyte)
Kardecismo spiritism, 220, 221, 222, 224,
      225, 230, 231, 236, 240-41, 247, 284,
      294, 295
Katz, Richard, 66
Keyes, Daniel, 254
K.L. Mrs. (case of), 171-73
Krieger, Dolores, 223
Krippner, Stanley, 226, 228, 229, 230
kundalini, 62-63, 65-67
Kundalini—psychosis or transcendence?
      (Sannella), 67
!Kung bushmen, 66

Lake Forrest University, 30
Lambert, Helen, 166, 167-69, 177
Latimer, Phyllis (case of), 187, 196, 197
"Laughing Water", 146-47
laying-on-of-hands, 165, 171
Lehigh University, 202
Life after Death (Hyslop), 147
Life after Death (Rogo), 276
Life's Adventure (Worcester), 204
Livre des Ésprits, Le (Rivail), 220
Lohengrin (Wagner), 112n
London, Perry, 194-95
Longfellow, Henry W., 146
Los Angeles Times, 243, 288
Low Art Tile Co., 15
Lowell, Percival, 46-47
Ludwig, Arnold, 287

Maine Wesleyan Seminary, 122
*Mantle Fielding's Dictionary of American
      Painters, Sculptors and Engravers*,
      270, 271
manic depression, 171
Martha's Vineyard, 50, 270
McComas, Henry, 169
McComb, Samuel, 204, 205
McCord, George H., 270, 271
McDougall, William, 210-211
Meader, John, 88-89
Melville, Herman, 13
Mendes, Eliezer, 225, 226-30, 230, 231
mental illness, 1, 9, 39-40, 58, 63-64, 67-
      68, 84, 87, 95, 96, 137-39, 140-41,
      167-69, 170-71, 171, 173-75, 177-78,
      185-99, 204-205, 205-206, 212-14,
      223, 224-25, 244, 267, 294
mesmeric passes, 223
Milligan, Billy, 254
Mind, Body and Science (Worcester and
      McComb), 204, 209
Mind Game, The (Torrey), 9
Mind Possessed, The (Sargant), 293
Minds of Billy Milligan, The (Keyes), 254
Minds in Many Pieces (Allison), 253, 257,
      261, 265
Mitchell, S. Weir, 202-203
Moby Dick (Melville), 13
Mollie Fancher—the Brooklyn Enigma
      (Daily), 256n
moral diseases, 203
morphine hallucinations, 207
Muehler, Karl (see Muller, Karl)

Muller, Karl, 104, 105-106, 110
multiple personality, 33, 72, 88, 96, 116, 117, 117-21, 124-35, 146, 248-49, 250-66, 278, 284-92
My Adventure in Spiritualism (Howard), 161
Myers, F.W.H., 31

Nashawena, 24
Nation, The, 33
National Academy of Design, 14
National Institute of Mental Health, 285
National Psychological Institute, 160
National Psychopathic Institute, 160
Nature, Man and Destiny (Bull), 179n
Naushon Island, 22-23, 23-24, 26, 38, 269
neurology, 164
New Bedford, xiii, 13-14, 15, 17, 21, 45
New York Times, The, 50, 72, 288
Newcomb, Simon, 32
Nonquitt, 24, 25, 45
Nordica, Lillian, 98, 102
n/um, 66

Occult Review, 59
Ohio State University, 254
One Thing I Know (Storr), 164n
Ousler, Fulton, 123n
out-of-body experiences, 58-59, 59-61, 67, 68, 297-99
organic psychosis, 174
ouija boards, 84, 118
overshadowing, 148

Pairpont Manufacturing Co., 15
paralysis, 240
paranoia, 40, 137, 139, 140-41, 178, 188, 189, 195-96, 204-205, 205-206, 209
paranoid schizophrenica (see schizophrenia)
Parapsychological Association, 232-33
Pavlov, I.V:, 293
Peck, M. Scott, 243-48, 249, 250, 252, 257, 260, 284, 294, 299
People of the Lie (Peck), 244, 245, 246-47, 257
Philadelphia Post, 78
physical mediumship, 72
physiology, 285-91
pineal doorway, 59
Piper, Leonore, 32-35, 47, 73-74
Pittham, Oscar, 222
planchette, 84

Playfair, Guy, 230n
poltergeists, 183 (see also, raps)
Porto Allegre, 214-15
possession, 8, 58, 62, 117, 123-25, 138, 243-48, 257, 258-59, 264 (see also, spirit obsession)
Prayer, 126, 202, 203, 206, 207
precognition, 131, 253
Prince, Lelia, 121, 122, 130, 132-33, 151, 154
Prince, Morton, 124, 134n, 146, 153-54
Prince, W. Franklin, xiv, 141, 142, 149, 183-99, 201, 209, 210-212, 215, 228, 231, 259, 265
  biography of, 122-23
  death of, 211-212
  description of, 123n
  move to Boston, 154-55, 210
  problems with depression, 184-85
  work with Doris case, 121-35, 150-55
  work with possession cases, 185-99
Problems of Philosophy, (Hyslop), 35
Proceedings of the Society for Psychical Research, 278
Profit and Loss of Dying, The, (Irion) 176
Psellus, Michael, 8
psychic attack, 260-61
psychic healing, 236, 240
Psychic in the House, The, 154
psychic music, 22-23
psychic odors, 80
psychic photography, 183
Psychic Science, 170
psychic zapping, 255-56
psychical research, history of, 31-35, 210-211, 215
Psychical Research and the Resurrection (Hyslop), 47
Psychical Research Foundation, 61
psychoanalysis, 1, 196
psychokinesis, 55-56, 61, 63, 82, 85, 100, 150-51, 152-54, 155, 207
psychological bonding, 272-75
Psychological Society, The, (Gross) 2
psychology, 2, 140
Psychological Synthesis in Clinical Para psychology (Mendes), 226
psychopathology (see mental illness)
psychotherapy, 178, 195, 196, 293, 293n

raps, 55-56, 61, 100, 102, 102-103n, 150-51, 152, 155, 207

Rathbun, Mrs. (see Gaule, Margaret)
Ranger, Henry, 38, 39, 39n
reaction formation, 282
reincarnation, 220, 221, 221-22, 229, 231, 259, 294
REM sleep, 57n
remote viewing, 131
repossession, 230, 247
rescue work, 138, 161-62, 226-28, 230, 234, 236-41 (see also Wickland, spirit obsession, channeling, spiritualism)
Return of Frank R. Stockton, The, (de Camp), 77-78, 94
Rhine, J.B., 165, 215, 232
right vs. left handedness, 290
Ritchie, George Jr., 297-99
Ritchie, Ida (see Rogers, Ida Marie)
Rivail, Hyppolyte, 220-21
Road Less Traveled, The (Peck), 244
Roberts, Jane, 233
Roche, Mrs. William W. (see Bessinet, Ada)
Rochester University, 201
Rogers, Ida Marie (case of), 97-116, 136, 140, 142, 149, 276, 277, 278, 283
Roman Catholic Church, 224n
Roth, Kathy, 221-22
Rush-Presbyterian-St. Luke's Medical Center, 284
Russell, Benjamin, 14

Salmagundi Club, 50, 51, 270
Sannella, Lee, 67
Sargant, William, 293
Saybrook Institute, 226
Schafer, Donald, 288-89
Schiller, F.C.S., 278, 279
schizophrenia, 140-41, 167, 168, 171, 174, 194-95, 224, 226
Science and a Future Life (Hyslop), 54
Schreiber, Flora Rheta, 252
Scribner's Monthly, 122, 202
self-hypnosis, 292
self-suggestion, 183-84
Selleny, Josef, 167-68
"Seth", 230
shamanism, 8-9
Sidgwick, Henry, 31
Sizemore, Chris, 251-52, 253-54
slate writing, 183
sleep, 57n, 61
skills (as evidence for survival) 30, 272

Smead, Mrs. (see Cleaveland, Mrs. Willis M.)
Smith College, 31, 40
Snider, Mrs. Milton (see De Camp, Etta)
Society for Psychical Research, 18, 31-32, 33, 35, 231, 267, 278
Sonia (case of), 228-29, 231
Soule, Minnie, 20-21, 25, 29, 40-46, 73, 74, 88, 89-94, 95, 97, 99, 101-115, 130, 137, 139, 141-50, 155, 163, 201, 206, 276-77, 277-78, 278-84
spirit hospitals, 222-24
spirit obsession, 13-18, 36, 53, 71-72, 74, 82, 95-97, 99, 115-116, 137-39, 140-41, 141-42, 147-49, 155-56, 159-81, 185-91, 204-209, 212-13, 221-22, 223, 224-25, 228, 236-41, 257-66, 293-95, 297-99
spirit vs. telepathy controversy, 29, 272-84
Spiritism, 219-220 (see also, Kardecismo, Umbanda, Condomblé)
Spiritual Emergence Network, 67
Spiritualism, 31, 72, 75-76, 97-98, 137-38, 159-60, 162, 194, 219, 226, 267 (see also, Spiritism)
Spirit and the Flesh, The (Williams), 293
St. Anne's Church, 122, 202
St. Elizabeth's Hospital, 9
St. Mark's Church, 150, 183, 188
St. Stephen's Church, 202-203
static electricity, 162
Stead, W.T., 75-76
super-ESP hypothesis, 268, 276
Stockton, Frank R., 77-78, 78-94, 95, 96, 101, 112, 142, 276, 277
  automatic scripts from, 79-81
  biography of, 78
  messages from, 89-94
Storr, Ella Mabel, 226
Studies in Spiritism (Tanner), 73
survival issue, 267-81, 276-77, (see also, spirit vs. telepathy controversy)
Sybil (Schreiber), 252

table-tilting, 82-83, 86-87
Tabuteau, Marcel, 274
Tanner, Amy, 73-74
Teachers College, 37
telepathy, 29-30, 31, 108, 132-33, 134, 254
telepathic dreams, 132-33, 134
Temple of Light, 74, 160

temporal lobe seizures, 54, 54n, 60
Terror that Comes in the Night, The (Hufford), 47
therapeutic touch, 223
Thigpen, Corbett H., 250-51, 253
Thirty Years Among the Dead (Wickland), 161, 163, 240
Three Faces of Eve, The (Thigpen and Cleckley), 250, 287
Thompson, Carrie, 17, 46
Thompson, Frederic, xiii, 13-27, 29-51, 71, 72, 79, 88, 94, 99, 100, 107, 115, 118, 137, 138, 141, 149, 164, 268, 268-75, 278, 283, 294
  artistic talents and skills, 36-39
  interpretation of case, 272-76
  later life, 50-51
  mental evaluation, 39-40
  possibility of fraud, 269-72
Thompson, Lewis H., 271
thought transference (see telepathy)
Tiffany Glass Co., 15
Torrey, E. Fuller, 9
Townsend, James B., 36-37
trance mediumship, 20-21, 32-33, 33-35, 40-43, 43-51, 72, 73-74, 87-88, 89-94, 101-110, 111, 115, 142-49, 169-70, 172-73, 208-209, 276-78, 278-84
transpersonal psychology, 66-67
transsexualism (see gender dysphoria)
Trauma, Trance and Transformation (Edelstein), 249
traveling clairvoyance, 131
Traviata, La (Verdi), 231
Tubby, Gertrude, O., 210
Turn of the Screw, The (James), 50
Tyrrell, Leonard (case of) 185-87, 196-98

U.C.L.A. School of Medicine, 252
Umbanda, 220, 234-36, 238
University of California, Irvine Medical Center, 289
University of Kentucky, 286-87
University of Leipzig, 30, 202
University of Tennessee Medical School, 4
Unknown Power, The, (Playfair), 230n
Unseen Doctor, The (Storr), 164n

visual evoked response, 285-86, 286n

W., Mr. (case of), 96-97
Wagner, Richard, 112n
waking suggestion, 126, 165, 202, 206, 240
Walker, W.K., 126
Watkins, Helen and John, 249
Welcoming Silence, The (Rogo), 276
Weldon, Warren, 166
Weyer, Johann, 138
White, Eve (case of) 250-52, 287, (see also, Sizemore, Chris)
Wickland, Anna, 162, 163, 166
Wickland, Carl, xiv, 160-63, 223, 240, 259, 266, 294, 299
Williams, Walter L., 293
Wooster College, 30
Worcester, Elwood, xiv, 201-215, 231, 260, 295
  biography of, 201-204
  death of, 215
  work with possession cases, 204-209
Wundt, Wilhelm, 140, 202

Yale University, 122
yoga, 66